VOYAGE OF THE
"AGE UNLIMITED"

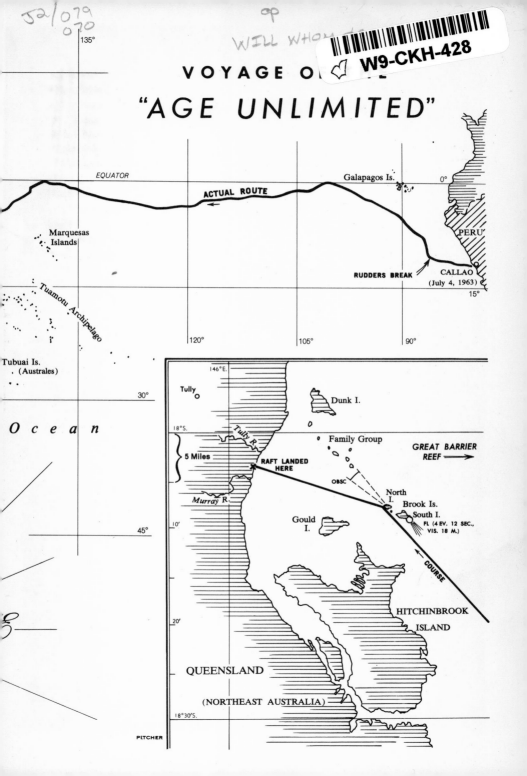

EQUATOR

ACTUAL ROUTE

Galapagos Is.

0°

Marquesas
Islands

PERU

Tuamotu Archipelago

RUDDERS BREAK

CALLAO
(July 4, 1963)

15°

Tubuai Is.
(Australes)

120°

105°

90°

30°

Ocean

146°E.

Tully

Dunk I.

18°S.

Tully R.

Family Group

GREAT BARRIER
REEF ➡

5 Miles

RAFT LANDED
HERE

Murray R.

OBSC

North
I.

Brook Is.

South I.
FL (4 EV. 12 SEC.,
VIS. 18 M.)

45°

10'

Gould
I.

COURSE

20'

HITCHINBROOK

ISLAND

QUEENSLAND

(NORTHEAST AUSTRALIA)

18°30'S.

PITCHER

Whom the Sea Has Taken

Books by WILLIAM WILLIS

THE GODS WERE KIND
DAMNED AND DAMNED AGAIN
HELL, HAIL AND HURRICANES
WHOM THE SEA HAS TAKEN

Burton Turner
Aug 1969

Whom the Sea Has Taken

by WILLIAM WILLIS

MEREDITH PRESS
New York

Library of Congress Catalog Card Number: 67-11029

MANUFACTURED IN THE UNITED STATES OF AMERICA FOR MEREDITH PRESS

VAN REES PRESS • NEW YORK

*To Teddy, who made this voyage
possible, and to all the other
toilers and dreamers of the sea*

Acknowledgments

The author gratefully acknowledges the help of the following persons and organizations:

United States Lines, New York; Grace Line, New York; Farrell Lines, New York; Moran Towing & Transportation Co., New York; United States Rubber Co., Providence, R.I.; Weyerhaeuser Lumber Co., New York; Nopco Chemical Co., Newark, N.J.; American Smelting & Refining Co., New York; Columbian Rope Co., New York; Paulsen-Webber Cordage Corp., New York; Atlas Rigging Co., Kearney, N.J.; H. J. Heinz Company, Pittsburgh, Pa.; The Quaker Oats Co. (Puss 'N' Boots), Chicago, Ill.; Pet Milk Co., St. Louis, Mo.; Pik-Nik Sales Co. (Theodore H. Eggers), San Francisco, Calif.; Harold J. Robson, Marine Equipment, City Island, N.Y.; Ford Yachting Agency, City Island, N.Y.; G. W. Vallentine & Son, Sailmakers, City Island, N.Y.; Paul Coble, Marine Architect, City Island, N.Y.; Mineford Yachting Yard, City Island, N.Y.; Frank O. Braynard, Moran Towing Co., New York; Werner Woehlk, Milford, Conn.; Manhattan Marine Co., New York; New York Nautical Instrument Corp., New York; Chas. F. Guyon, Inc., Harrison, N.J.; Dr. Bernard J. Schuman, New York; The Marconi International Marine Co. Ltd., London, England.

Officers and Men of Peruvian Navy Base, Callao, Peru; U.S. Naval Mission, Callao, Peru; Australian Trade Commission, Lima, Peru; Agua Mineral Litimada San Mateo, Lima, Peru; International Petroleum Co. (Esso), Lima, Peru; Cia. Nacional de Fosforos "La Llama," Lima, Peru; Bahco-Primus, S.A., Lima, Peru; Lima Rubber Co. (B. F. Goodrich Co.), Lima, Peru; Goodyear Del Peru, Lima, Peru; Carlos Caravedo Arca, Lima, Peru.

Union Steamship Co., Apia, Western Samoa; Public Works of Apia, Western Samoa; Merchants of Apia, Western Samoa.

Australian National Lines, Melbourne, Australia; John Buesst, Bingil Bay, N.Q.L., Australia.

Illustrations

Documents

The following is a list of documents I have pertaining to the voyage:

All clearance papers.

Doctors' certificates from Apia and New York (for hernia and back injury).

Clippings from Samoan newspapers explaining why I left in the middle of the night, also my letter to the Prime Minister and the names of my friends who had assisted me.

Letter by the New Zealand Air Force in the Fijis stating when they picked up my "All's Well" messages.

Notice of the Australian Government to all shipping to keep look-out for raft.

Radio reports of the S.S. Whakatane and S.S. Baron Jedburgh.

Report by Doctor of fractured spine.

Letter (Document) signed by Rear Admiral G. I. Dufek, U.S.N. Ret., Director of The Mariners Museum, Newport News, Virginia, of acceptance of raft for the Museum.

And others.

William Willis

Whom the Sea Has Taken

1

I WAS a tot of four when, having disregarded my mother's warning one day to stay near the house and not run off, I stood on the waterfront of Hamburg, the city I was born in, and gazed upon the gray flow of the Elbe and saw my first ships. After this first glimpse, my little feet took me back regularly and seemingly without will of my own. We were living then in a dark and dingy little flat not far from the waterfront in the oldest part of the city. Our family fortunes were at low ebb, and my mother besides my father had to go to work every day, and so there was no place to put me except on the street.

Every morning, after I had been washed and fed, I was turned loose with a key to our flat in my pocket, a final anxious kiss from my mother, and a warning to stay near the house and play with other children. Otherwise, I was told, all kinds of terrible things would happen to me, such as being run over and trampled under the hooves of the big draft horses or falling into one of the canals. As soon as my mother was gone, I forgot every word she had said and trundled off on my own, invariably toward the waterfront.

The age-old streets through which I made my way were narrow, crooked, and paved with cobblestones, and high-gabled houses, standing close together as if for support, lined each side. Doors and windows were tiny, and each floor jutted out a bit above the last, so that on top, high above the street, they almost came together and, like bonneted old women in worn garments sticking their heads together, seemed to be talking of the centuries gone by. Each house had a cellar in which people lived, sometimes running a little store where vegetables, coal, and firewood were sold. During the big storm tides which came up the Elbe from the sea, the cellars were often flooded, so that the people in them had to flee.

Beyond this warren of crooked streets were broad thoroughfares fronting the canals and waterfront for the traffic to and from the ships. London, Antwerp, Hamburg, and Hong Kong were at this time the leading ports of the Europe-Asian continent. The canals were lined with the same kind of high-gabled houses, used as warehouses, and men could be seen toiling on hand winches on the different floors, hoisting sling loads of sacks and bales out of lighters and barges lying beneath. Warehouses also lined the streets, and great wagons were backed against the doors and goods loaded or stored, while the big draft horses stamped their iron-shod feet or stood quietly with a nosebag tied to their heads chewing their oats. Other wagons went by in never-ending stream, drawn by the, to me, gigantic-appearing horses with their proud manes and tails and bushy fetlocks, while the drivers, high on their seats, shouted to each other or jauntily cracked their whips. Sometimes they bawled at me when I barely cleared the horses, darting in front of them. How I admired the horses in their brass-studded harness, their straining haunches stretched and muscles turned to iron, pounding frantically for a footing when starting the wagons on wet cobblestones or in snow and ice.

After crossing the last street, I stood on the stone quay of the waterfront, on the bank of the Elbe. The river lay before me—miles of steamers and each funnel belching smoke or steam, billowing up white and black and mingling with the gray sky, to the incessant tooting and shrieking of tugboats pulling strings of barges and churning up the river, and the measured, booming drone of the big ships moving in and out of their berths. Walking on, I could see the tall masts and yards of a different type of ship crowded together in a space of their own. These, I learned in time, were sailing ships. Here I stood longest. Perhaps something stirred within me at their aloof height, standing apart and mysterious where the sky was clear of smoke.

All the scents of the earth flowed into me, walking along the quay, and filled me with wonder and longing and often hunger. There were steamers with whole cargoes of oranges from Spain and Italy, ships from Madeira and the West Indies with bananas and pineapple, fruits far beyond the means of our frugal household, as well as coffee from Brazil unloaded at riverside factories to be roasted and packed, sending its aroma over the river. Other ships brought dried fish from Scandinavia and Canada, hides from Argentina, and stumpy logs of teak, ironwood, and mahogany. Most alluring to me was the pine timber and lumber from Finland and Russia smelling of northern woods and often with thick bark still on them, of which I always broke off a piece to take with me. Then I imagined myself in the pine forests my mother had told me about. Her grandfather had been a forester in Bohemia, in some mysterious forest alive with deer and bear and wolves, which during cold winters came out and attacked the peasants in their wagons and even went into the snow-covered villages.

I came to know the men whose muscles moved the great traffic of the harbor—brawny, rough men with powerful chests, swinging arms, and weather-beaten faces, loud of speech and often shouting. I watched them in all their labors, sweating and straining and staggering under loads, and also through the open doors of saloons, glass in hand and faces mellow, standing in the smoke-laden semidarkness amid the hum and roar of voices. I liked them. Warm and friendly they were to my eyes. I liked their very movements and voices and, above all, their fitness and strength. Sometimes they tossed a kindly or gruff word at the little boy who got in their way or gazed at them, standing transfixed as if he wanted to look right through them

5

in an unknown search. I heard all their curses, without knowing what they meant. To my ears they were a necessary part of their brawny life. I knew their language, having learned it from other urchins on the street. It was Low German, spoken on the waterfront and on ships and by the dwellers along the North Sea Coast, and in essence is the language of the Dutch today and closely related to Scandinavian, especially Danish and Norwegian. Neither my father nor mother could speak Low German. My father understood a little, but my mother never learned a single word. She was full-blooded Czech, born in the heart of Bohemia, and had learned German only at the age of fifteen. When sometimes, unthinkingly, I said something in Low German, she looked at me as if I had suddenly turned into a little Chinese. Like my father, who came from Hanover and so was of Saxon blood, she had never seen the sea, though Hamburg lies only about sixty miles from Cuxhaven where the Elbe empties into the North Sea.

On the waterfront, roaring with the voices and shouts of all the world, I spent my early childhood, trudging through summer's heat and snow and ice of the winters, as often as not in water-soaked shoes and with frozen fingers and toes, forgetting all about going home for shelter till evening. There was no hunger, at least no pain that had to be stilled, for I was raised on a very meager diet and used to it, and besides came from stock inured to hardships without complaining. I do not remember that I ever sat down when I was tired.

I went farther and farther in my wanderings along the river, as my strength and my imagination grew, and one day climbed into one of the rowboats tied up along the quay and used by harbormen. I untied the rope and drifted down the river, helpless after losing one of the oars. A police launch came alongside, notified by people ashore, and I was taken to the police station. Since I did not know the name of our street, they kept me. In the evening my mother came rushing in. "My son is lost," she cried, fearing I had drowned or something else had happened to me. The bearded sergeant growled,

"He is here. He was halfway over to America. Better keep him tied up."

Perhaps my mother realized that I had inherited my wanderlust from her. From the village in Bohemia to Vienna and then to Hamburg, where she had met my father, had been her trail. I remember sitting on her knee while she told me stories of her childhood and of Imperial Vienna and of the beauty she had seen in things. And always there had been a longing in her face and voice, straining toward something faraway. We were in complete harmony at such times—the oracle and seer and the little worshipper. My mother was of small and slender build, gentle and seemingly even submissive, but with an indomitable will in important matters and could be fierce when aroused. She was tireless physically and possessed great nervous energy and intensity. Her movements were quick and graceful.

A little distance from where we lived was the Museum of Art. I was six years old when my mother took me there one Sunday afternoon to see the paintings, for I had shown great interest in drawing. Near the entrance was a hall with the white marbles of Greek antiquity. I became so enthralled by the beautiful figures that my mother finally had to pull me away. They had made a lasting impression on me, which became deeper as the years went by, coupled with the desire to possess a similar body. I often went to the museum for a quick look and with my heart full of joy went out again.

At the age of six I was sent to public school. We had then just moved away from the old neighborhood to a section at the farther end of the city, miles away, and so my wanderings on the waterfront came to an end. I also had little time to myself now, for school was six days a week with long hours and homework and the strictest discipline. We only had young male teachers, and tough kids were given a hiding with a cane. A few times I got a taste of it. I didn't mind it much, for I was used to an occasional caning from my father and knew how to handle myself, having worked out a technique of straightening up the very split second the cane came down on my backside as I stood bent over. My father once said disgustedly to

7

my mother that the only way I could be hurt was to tie me down. A proper caning was quite effective and left thick welts which stayed for weeks.

During my first year at school, I began to draw regularly, copying at home and also going to the Museum of Natural History and drawing animals. Sometimes I copied a painting in the Museum of Art. I only used a pencil having no interest in colors. Afterwards my interest turned to human bodies and faces with a turn towards the heroic and even more for caricature.

When first going to school, I had to wear glasses, for I was nearsighted. I was born with some sort of eye condition, some infection which had been treated almost since birth. One day while I was still a babe, my mother, smiling into my face, noticed that there was no response in my eyes, no sign of recognition. She became alarmed and, after a few other futile attempts to get me to react, realized that something was wrong, snatched me up, and rushed out of the house crying to her neighbors that her baby was blind. At the hospital it was found that my eyes were in bad shape. It seemed that the medicine which had been used was destroying my sight. The treatment now became different, but considerable damage had been done, and my eyes remained the weak spot in an otherwise healthy body.

I submitted to wearing glasses for about a year; then, since they prevented me from fighting other boys and playing the rough games that I enjoyed, I discarded them and still managed to get along in my classwork. My mother did not find out for a long time, for I didn't tell her. In her eyes, glasses made me look more scholarly, something which she always dreamed I should be, and also made me look more dignified and genteel.

At the age of nine, after a burst of intellectual awakening which amazed my teachers, I received a scholarship to a private Jewish school of high scholastic standards. It was situated near my old waterfront haunts, far from where we lived now at the outskirts of

the city, close to open fields. I could get to it by streetcar, trans-
ferring from one to another, or by taking—part of the way at least
—one of the small passenger boats running on the Alster, a great lake
surrounded by villas, mansions, and parks in the heart of Hamburg
and originally created by damming up a stream.

Money was scarce as ever in our household, and the best that
could be done for me was a ride part of the way by streetcar or
lake steamer, leaving me an hour or so to walk. Coming back from
school, it was foot work all the way—two hours with my stack of
books. I had never had money in my hand before, but now every
morning when leaving for school, I was given a sandwich of buttered
bread and fare for a steamer or streetcar. When there was no money,
I had to get up earlier and walk.

My life now consisted of the school and the long trek back and
forth. There was little time for anything else. The requirements of
the school were high, and I was ambitious; I wanted to learn and
liked to study. It was six days a week again and the hours longer,
and there was more homework. We also had more subjects. All our
teachers were professors with long gray beards, bespectacled and
serious.

I loved the long walks. In the morning it meant rushing through
the crowded streets after getting off the streetcar or little steam-
boat, often running when I was late, and in the afternoon walking
along the great lake where it was beautiful with green lawns and
trees. My eyes were mainly on the great expanse of the lake, blue
and shining in the sun and in winter full of ice floes, broken and
forced edge-up by the wind, so that it looked like great fields of
tombstones. Often the weather was stormy and the sky gray with
low drifting clouds and the water covered with foam and spray, so
that one couldn't see across. Then I had the banks all to myself. Once
a week I came home late at night, after attending a special drawing
class in my school given by my art teacher, Professor Schwartz, to
selected students from throughout the city. He was a handsome man

with a red face and snow-white beard who took great interest in me and taught me the rudiments of drawing. At school I was taught, besides German, English and French and other subjects of advanced schools. I liked history best and throughout my school years was at the top of the class.

The first book I had ever read, with painful slowness and tears streaming from my eyes and occasional help from my mother, was the story of Robinson Crusoe. Then came Cooper's *Deerslayer* and *The Last of the Mohicans*. Gradually I went through all the lists of adventure stories, with special liking for those of the sea. Captain Marryat was one of my favorites. *The Three Musketeers* were later devoured in breathless suspense besides books of travel and discovery. I passed a public library on my way and generally stopped to pick up or return a book. Dime novels fell prey to my hunger also, and, passing a pushcart in one of the side streets near the school, I generally managed to get a used copy or exchange one I had. When I came to the banks of the Alster, with no traffic and street crossings to stop me, I read while walking till the story was finished. Most of them were of Buffalo Bill, Texas Jack, and other Indian fighters, all heroes who had an uncanny capacity for getting into hair-raising adventures and escaping death.

My interest in physical development, which was born in me, came more and more to the fore as I grew up. I not only wanted strength, speed, and flexibility but also the ability to endure hunger, thirst, and pain and all manner of hardships. I admired the ancient Spartans and the Indians of North America for their hardihood, stoicism, and the pain and severe tests to which they were put in their youth.

At fourteen I became acquainted with a seventeen-year-old boy in our neighborhood who was working in a factory and practiced weight lifting and wrestling. Since I had always been interested in wrestling, he offered to teach me. We practiced on the hard floor in a room, or on Sundays, when the weather was fine, went out to the woods and worked out on some convenient grassy spot, coming home in the evening with bruised knees, elbows, and shoulders, and now and then a black eye. Once a little tournament was arranged in which I won a book of essays on health. One of the articles stressed the importance of deep breathing. This I at once considered of greatest importance and began to practice on my walks back from school, till it became automatic.

A catastrophe now began to develop in our home, which threatened to break up the family. It was six months before my final examinations, but things looked so bad that I was ready to quit school and go to work somewhere. My mother wouldn't hear of it. "Without the examination you have no future," she said. "Finish your school and graduate; then you can do what you want." It had been decided already that I should study art and become a caricaturist. At this time I was still in number three place in my class, never having gone below it. I could read English, both prose and poetry, fairly accurately, and in French Voltaire's *Charles XII* caused me no difficulty.

According to my mother's wish, I stayed at school and passed the examinations, then enrolled at the Art School of Hamburg. My drawing teacher, Professor Schwartz, an important figure in Hamburg art circles—who was very enthusiastic about my future and even predicted my early recognition as a caricaturist—had procured a scholarship for me. I was the youngest student in the great institute, the others being nearer twenty.

Then the final crash came, inevitable for years—my mother and father separated. There was no money, and I had two little brothers of two and three. I stayed away from art school and walked about the streets, wondering what to do. My future as an artist was shattered, I saw plainly, for I couldn't let the burden of supporting me be on my mother, and there was no way of working my way through. I had sent in drawings on and off to the large comic magazines, like *Simplicissimus,* in order to earn money, but they had been returned. My mother, always of indomitable courage, maintained that there would be a way for me to continue, but I remained in a state of utter dejection. The dream of years had been concentrated on becoming an artist, and now everything was shattered. And more important than my own future was the fate of my mother and little brothers. Everything had fallen into ruin. If there had only been something I could do to earn money at once. As an apprentice in some trade, even if a place could have been found, it would take years.

My feet took me to the ancient part of the city where we once lived, and I trudged through the streets, as if there I could find the peace of my childhood again. Everything seemed unchanged in outline but hard, bare, and matter-of-fact and in as hopeless a state as I. I walked along the riverfront, and my eyes saw the steamers and tugboats, and my ears heard the roar of the traffic, but I was aware only of my shattered dreams, our broken-up home. What was the way out?

I passed a house that had a sign over the cellar which read "Shipping Master." I looked down the narrow steep steps, grimy and worn and littered with paper. I had read of shipping masters in novels. Was this one of the places where they shanghaied sailors? A thought flashed through my mind: Go down those stone steps and ask for a job as deck boy on some ship.

Hesitatingly and frightened, I went down, my heart beating. My hand stopped after touching the heavy knob of the door; then I opened it slowly. Again I paused.

"Come in, come in—what's the matter?" a harsh voice shouted from the interior.

I went into the low room and saw a man sitting in a chair. He had gray hair and a big bony face I didn't like. "Could I perhaps get a job as a deck boy on a ship?" I asked in a low voice.

He looked hard at me, then said, "I have nothing for you. I get my deck boys from orphan asylums and put them on barges going up the river and through the canals. I don't handle regular ships." Then he turned his back on me.

I was on the street again and walking in the sun, feeling as if I had just escaped a terrible fate. To be on a barge and pulled by a smoke-belching tug through canals and waterways and tie up at warehouses and grimy factories... My mind went back to books and poetry, to drawings and the easels in art school, the teachers and the students, men and women, many of them already supporting themselves. To go on a barge to live—that was falling too low. I had seen those barges—some with the captain's wife on board and the washing hanging from a line and even children. I would perhaps have to do the washing and watch over the children so they wouldn't fall overboard. Rather be an errand boy in some store, riding a tricycle with a big box on top for taking goods to the customers. One had to have powerful legs for that—in rain, snow, and ice, and through all the traffic. I had known a boy who was seventeen and as big and strong as a man who had done this sort of work. That's what my father wanted me to be; he had even told my mother of a store which would take me on his recommendation.

I passed a café with tables on the sidewalk. A young sailor wearing a visored cap and pea jacket sat at one of the tables, a glass of beer before him. His seabag was beside his chair. He looked as if he had just come from a ship, for his face was red and deeply tanned. I stopped and watched him as if he had something of importance for me. He seemed utterly happy and looked, smiling contentedly, at the busy scene of the waterfront. A feeling stole over me that I had known him for a long time. I wanted to go to him and talk and hear something about the ship he came from and about the open sea. I felt certain that he came from one of the big square-riggers in port, which sailed around the world to strange ports. But I didn't have the courage to address him. I was only fifteen and not used to speaking to grown persons I didn't know. I had not only lived a sheltered and disciplined life but was also naive and shy by nature, and only at art school had begun to expand a little. With heavy heart I went on.

That evening after my little brothers had been put to bed, I told

13

my mother that I had decided to go to sea and that nothing would stop me. I told her about the shipping master in the cellar and everything I had been thinking of during the day. There was no other way out, I said, unless she wanted me to become an errand boy. I told her I would work hard on a ship, which of course had to be a square-rigger, and would soon work my way up to become a mate and earn good money. The father of one of my classmates at school had been a mate, and he was always well dressed and could afford to pay the stiff tuition, I said. We talked for a long time, and finally my mother agreed to let me go and promised to try everything to get me on a big sailing ship.

A week later she told me I could get a position with the firm of Schmidt & Company, owners of large square-riggers, if I could pass the doctor.

"No difficulty about that," I said. "I have never been sick."

"You have to have good eyesight, that's the main thing," my mother replied and gave me two slips, one for the eye doctor and one for a general examination.

My eyes had never been strong and, after years of schoolwork, the cramming for the final examinations, and later the drawing at art school, often in bad light, were quite run-down.

I walked past the building in which the eye doctor was located a few times before mustering courage and going up the stairs. I rang the bell. If I failed to pass, there would be nothing left except to become an errand boy.

A nurse opened the door, let me in, and told me to take a seat in the waiting room. Then she disappeared in the back. A man was sitting in one of the chairs awaiting his turn. I sat down but after a while got up and began to walk nervously up and down. An open door led from the waiting room to another, seemingly used by the doctor for I saw medical equipment inside. I went closer and looked in. On the wall straight across from the door was a chart with letters. It had a number of rows, each one with smaller letters. I could read the first row from the door but none of the others. Then it flashed through my mind that this was a chart used for testing the eyesight. With a shock that almost stopped my heartbeat, I realized I would fail if asked to read it. I stepped into the room and, trembling with apprehension that the nurse or doctor might appear at any time, learned the letters by heart. I devoured them. My mind was used to memorizing from years of schoolwork, and I had no difficulty. Then I stepped back and remained at the door, repeating what I had learned and checking over and over again.

"You're so excited," the man in the chair said, watching me. I merely glanced at him, for to speak would have meant to let go of my letters for a moment.

A little later the nurse came and called the man in. He came out shortly, and then it was my turn. I felt my heart beating right in my eyes, but the light with which the doctor probed them somehow didn't show it. "Ever have any trouble with your eyes?" he asked.

"No," I said.

"They're a little red, you know."

"I've been studying hard at school and done a lot of drawing."

"All right, let's go to the letters," he said. I read off the letters without making an error but purposely not too rapidly, and he wrote out the certificate that I had passed the test.

I jumped as high as a deer that has struggled out of a trap when I was on the street, and leaped and ran to the nearby doctor who was to give me the general check-up. "Never have been sick, Doctor," I said in my exuberant mood, "never even had a cold."

"Measles?" he asked.

"I don't remember, Doctor." He laughed.

How my mother managed to get the necessary clothes required by ship owners for deck boys on a first voyage on a square-rigger was at first a mystery to me. Then I found out that she made several trips to the pawnshops with a few cherished household articles like linen sheets still left from better days. A featherbed or two went also, the filling plucked years ago in Bohemia from the softest breast

15

feathers of geese, as warm and light as sunbeams and equal to the finest eiderdown. At last the only thing left to get was the sea chest, also a requisite. After considerable searching, we located one in a secondhand store on the waterfront.

"That will be your seat on a ship," the storekeeper said, after dragging out the chest where we could look at it, "for there are no chairs on a windjammer, you may be sure. It's been around a bit and just a while ago made a trip around the Horn. It's a real good one. They don't make them that solid these days."

"It's so old," my mother said, trying to bring down the price.

"Old it is, but I'm letting it go cheap," the shopkeeper replied. "I paid almost as much for it, but it takes up a lot of room in my little shop, and that's why I want to get rid of it."

"It's so battered-looking."

"Look inside—as good as new. Something solid for him to sit on when the ship rolls. Sure it's a bit battered-looking. If your boy knocks around forecastles as long as this chest has, he'll look battered too. Slap a coat of paint on it, and it'll look like a new chest. Why buy a new one when your boy may jump ship in the first port? He can't take a sea chest with him, you know, when he slides down a rope in the middle of the night."

"My son wouldn't jump ship," my mother said quickly.

"Don't be too sure of that," the old man remarked, grinning slyly. "You can't tell what he'll do once he gets away from you. You take that chest now, my good woman, and he's got something that'll last him till he's a captain. He'll be one for sure some day—I can tell by his eyes. And I'll throw in that old seabag there—see, it's got a patch or two, but that makes no difference. A seabag comes handy. He can put his gear inside and drop it to the pier from the rail when he runs away some dark night, and nobody can hear it."

"I told you he wouldn't run away," my mother said and fished out the money to pay for the chest.

Then came the biggest hurdle—the legal consent permitting me to go to sea. My father was against it, for he wanted me to become an errand boy and earn money at once. He had wanted this long before the breakup of our home. His word was still law, for the divorce decree had not yet become final. My mother got busy again, and reluctantly my father finally signed the paper. "And now I wash my hands of him," he declared bitterly. "He will never amount to anything—that I can tell you."

2

THE four-masted bark *Henriette*, a three-thousand-ton ship, lay among other square-riggers and was due to sail for Santa Rosalia in the Gulf of California—around the Horn and halfway around the world. I had signed on as deck boy at a wage of five marks a month ($1.20) and for a period of three years.

My father came around once and told my mother what he had heard of the *Henriette* on the waterfront. She was known to sailors as a hellship, he said, and it had been hard for her to get a crew. On the last voyage the captain, a brutal driver, had died of blood poisoning while rounding the Horn. He had lain unattended and helpless in his cabin for days and then been thrown overboard without proper burial. Then the mate had taken over and, rigged out in the old captain's gala uniforms, had strutted about the deck. He became insane and drove the crew aloft with a six-shooter and shot at them on the yards, till they mutinied and barricaded themselves under the forecastlehead. With most of the sails hanging in tatters in the rigging, they had finally cleared the Horn and crept into Iquique, Chile, where the mate was taken off. For this voyage the owners had picked the toughest captain and mate they could get to prevent anything of the sort from happening again. My father had also been on board and talked to the mate about me, and this had my mother worried.

The day after signing on, I hired a pushcart and with a neighborhood boy to help me put my sea chest on it. Then we started out for the waterfront, miles away through the city's traffic. Sailors carried the chest on board, and shortly afterwards I was changing my school clothes for dungarees and jumper and went to work. The mate was a heavy square-built man with a big head, bushy beard, and light gray eyes. He looked hard, cruel, and brutal to me.

Coming out of the forecastle, I stood on deck amid mountains of rope and cables, amid chains and sails and blocks lying on deck or hanging down from aloft in such masses that it was impossible to take a step without touching them. And laboring in this strange world, this seemingly inextricable confusion, were herculean men on deck and aloft, shouting to each other and emitting animal-like grunts in unison when hauling on the ropes. All were young fellows. When we stopped work in the evening and were standing naked under the forecastlehead washing ourselves in wooden buckets, I thought, looking at the torsos and limbs around me, that the Greek statues of the museum had come to life.

The *Henriette* had shipped a whole new crew with the exception of an ordinary seaman, a Dane who was the ship's night watchman while it lay in port. He was in the same forecastle with me, and after the sailors had gone ashore for a final fling, he told me of some of the happenings of the last voyage. He repeated, though with more dramatic details, what I had heard already. He even showed me the marks of some of the bullets that the gun of the insane mate had left. Walking up and down beside the rigging with him, I asked whether I would be allowed to go aloft, for I seemed to have dreamed of it since I had first put eyes on square-riggers.

"It's up to the mate when," the ordinary said. "But don't worry—you'll get more of it than you'll want. Wait till you get in bad weather—she wouldn't lie as steady as now, tied up to the pier." He laughed.

"Can I go up now and try it?"

He shook his head. "Not now—it's still daylight and somebody aft might see you," he replied. "And if you should fall and break your neck, I'll get the blame."

"Perhaps you could call me during the night sometime when everybody's asleep?" I pleaded.

"You want to go aloft at night?" He looked at me and grinned slyly, no doubt thinking that I wouldn't go through with it. "All right, I'll give you a call."

We walked yet a while, and then I lay down in the narrow, coffinlike bunk and fell asleep at once. Someone shook me by the shoulder, and, opening my eyes, I saw that I lay in total darkness. I heard the snoring of men. Then a low voice said in my ear, "It's one o'clock—if you want to go aloft." It was the ordinary seaman. I heard him close the door of the forecastle as he went out.

I crawled out of my bunk, a lower one, groped for my pants lying on my sea chest and put them on, then my shoes and jumper, and went out into the night. The air was fresh, and I saw stars overhead amid the rigging. Glorious life, it flashed through my mind. The ordinary was standing nearby. "Going up?" he asked.

"Yes," I said and went to the rail.

"Hang on," he warned. "Don't trust the ratlines—the ropes for your feet. The last crew didn't do any work in the rigging on the way back, and everything is rotten."

I swung myself to the top of the rail and made my way up. Higher and higher I climbed through the maze of ropes hanging down from the heights, always making sure that I had something solid to hang on to and never trusting the ratlines as the ordinary had warned me. I passed yard after yard. The air became freer, the outlook farther, and there were fewer ropes and stays. At last I stood on the royal yard, the topmost one. The night lay big around me. The ship, deep below, had disappeared in the darkness and the mass of rigging through which I had made my way. My eyes went to the section where we lived—where my mother and little brothers lay asleep. Perhaps my mother was dreaming about me. Well, I knew I would move heaven and earth to get somewhere and help. I stood there for a few minutes and was ready to go down again when I looked up at the masthead a few yards above my head. I would master that too, the highest point on the ship, and hugging the mast climbed up and patted the knob on top a few times.

The next day was our last in port, and my mother came on board to say farewell. It was in the afternoon and in the middle of the summer. I was working forward in the deckhouse, trimming the coal coming on board for the galley. It was tough work, lying on my back and filling every inch of space between the deck beams. "Somebody wants to see you," the third mate bawled into the deck-house. I crawled out. My hands were covered with blisters from shoveling and my knuckles bleeding from hitting the deck beams, and I was coal black from head to feet and drenched with sweat.

My mother was standing near the gang plank and didn't recognize me coming along the deck. "Mother," I said, standing before her. Her eyes filled with tears. After half an hour we parted, and I watched her go down the gangplank. On the wharf, she turned around and waved. Then I went back forward.

The next morning early a towboat came alongside, the hawsers holding us to the pilings were let go, and the tow down the river began. In the afternoon, after passing Cuxhaven, the sails were dropped from the yards and began to fill with wind. The tug let go. We were on our way.

I was sweeping the deck when the burly mate came up to me and said in a matter-of-fact, cold voice, "Remember this, if you don't like it on board, there is the rail—you can jump overboard."

I was wondering what had caused him to say such a thing without apparently the slightest reason. Then I remembered that my father had spoken to him about me. What had he said? Realizing that I was in bondage to him and the ship for three full years, I felt like a captive; then my eyes saw beyond the high bulwarks encasing the deck the wide and endless sea with all my dreams. But I was sorry I was on the mate's watch and not on the second mate's—a blond giant not much taller than I but broad and with the muscles of a draft horse and the innocent stare of a blue-eyed boy when looking at a man. But he was as explosive and swift as a tiger, and had hurled an iron belaying pin at the blacksmith or donkeyman who had climbed down into a launch the last night against orders to go ashore, only missing him by a few inches.

Through the Atlantic from northeast to the south we sailed, and then battled to get to the westward around the Horn and into the Pacific. We lay down in our bunks only for short snatches, fully clad in oilskins and heavy leather seaboots and with our sou'westers tied to our heads, ready to dash on deck should we strike an iceberg, perhaps to live only long enough to see the shattered ship go down before we ourselves sank in the freezing seas. For six weeks we were lost in the titanic vortex of never-ending gales, struggling amid the icebergs against relentless head winds, driving through the gloom, through sleet, hail, and fog as into the very annihilation of the world.

After 168 days we dropped our anchor in the roads of Santa Rosalia, a little Mexican port in Baja California. The next day we went 'longside the single pier and began to unload our cargo of coke, destined for the smelter of a large copper mine. Almost twenty square-riggers lay in the roads, having discharged, waiting for orders or trying to pick up enough sailors to sail. Every morning at six o'clock, I went down into the hatch and shoveled coal beside a sailor, filling the large basket which held three fourths of a ton. A whip snatched the loaded basket up and swung it to a hopper on the pier where a Mexican tipped it. The next moment the basket was back in the hold. From six in the morning to six o'clock at night and six days a week we worked. After almost two months the cargo was out and ballast taken in.

On the last night at the dock, I packed my clothes into the old, patched seabag, tossed in as a gift by the storekeeper in Hamburg when we had bought my sea chest, and tiptoed out of the forecastle. The night was clear, and the stars above seemed to be part of the silent hills ringing Santa Rosalia. I tied the end of a rope around the bag and was going to lower it over the side when the watchman, one of the sailors, came out of the darkness. He knew I was going to desert and said quietly, "I'll lower it for you—just go to the pier."

I went down the gangplank, first making sure no one was aft to see me, then walked along the pier to where the watchman was lowering my bag. I untied the rope, waved a quick hand, then swung the bag to my shoulders, and without a glance back at the ship walked into the night. Nothing had been dear to me on her except the mighty rigging; there I had always felt happy and at ease.

I was at the time of average size but, according to the sailors, strong as a horse. I knew I had the endurance of a full-grown man and that I had been the only one on board of the whole crew of thirty who had been ordered into the hold every single day to shovel coke. For good measure the mate had made me trim the ballast as well. I liked to work, and no one could have shown more willingness and energy. And aloft, off the Horn in the fiercest gales, I had lain beside our best sailors on the tormented yards, clawing up the canvas and holding it down with our bellies. The voyage had pushed my age years ahead, and when I walked away with my few belongings on my shoulder, I felt that the umbilical cord holding me to the past and to childhood was broken.

I left my seabag in the friendly forecastle of a British square-rigger lying ahead of us and walked through the sleepy town and into the hills, to hide till the *Henriette* had sailed. I was afraid the captain would notify the police to look out for me, arrest me, and bring me back on board in irons.

When the sun rose over a glassy sea and burned down on the scorched hills that had not felt a drop of rain since time began and were as hot as any in the Arabian desert, I was watching the *Henriette* from behind a rock, wearing a big Mexican straw hat to disguise me as well as to keep the sun off. Some time in the morning I saw a tug come 'longside and haul her out to the roads where she anchored. I knew she was waiting for orders. That night I stole back into Santa Rosalia to the British ship where I had my gear. I was hungry, for I had been without food all day, but found nothing to eat except some hardtack and stale tea in an old tin half full of tea leaves, seemingly the dregs of weeks. Everything tasted good, however, and after eating my fill, I lay down beside my seabag, first telling the sailor on watch to give me a call before daylight, so that I could get ashore and into the hills again. I was happy, for the Britishers had told me that the *Henriette* got her orders during the day and would up anchor in the morning, bound in ballast for Vancouver where she was to load timber for Newcastle, Australia, thence to sail to Chile with coal and finally with nitrate to Europe. It would be at least two years before she was back home.

I was so tired from walking through the burning hills that I fell at once into a deep sleep. I awoke when a big hand grabbed me by the shoulder and pulled me out of the bunk into the dim light of the kerosene lamp hanging from a deck beam. Four sailors not belonging to the ship stood around me and told me that the *Bermuda*, a British four-masted bark, was lying out in the roads ready to sail in the morning. She was one seaman short, and they had come to take me out to her. "You better come," they said, "for she's the best ship in port, and then the police can't get you." I would sign on as able-bodied seaman with twenty times the wages I had on the *Henriette*. This quickly decided me, realizing what it meant in marks, and picking up my seabag I went on deck with them and lowered it into a lifeboat they had lying 'longside and which they had "borrowed" from some other ship in port. Then we slid down ourselves and pulled away.

The *Bermuda*, I learned listening to their drunken talk during the three-mile-long pull through the moonlight, was bound for Antofagasta in Chile to load nitrate for Europe, which was the way of most square-riggers in those days. I also heard that they would be able to buy at least four bottles of tequila with the money they would get from the *Bermuda*'s captain for bringing me on board.

As soon as we were 'longside, I was taken aft to the captain's quarters and signed on as able-bodied seaman.

I was now on a British ship where only English was spoken. After breakfast I went on deck. I had already found out that we had hardly more than half a crew, since the others had deserted and the captain had not tried to replace them—a practice indulged in by sailing-ship masters for the sake of economy; it also gave them a chance to make some profits of their own through faked wages. The boatswain sent me aloft to let go the sails while most of the crew went to the forecastlehead to heave up. When I came down again, the sails had been pulled tight, the yards trimmed, and we were catching the land breeze and standing away for the south on a course.

A brawny, middle-aged sailor, with head and face as hairy as any I had seen, said something to me.

I smiled and shook my head, then said in my best school English, "I do not speak English, sir."

"Blimy!" the hairy one roared in a voice as deep and resonant as a bell. "Not a bloody word of English and on a bloody British ship. And don't you give me that bloody 'sir' again. That's for the bloody bastards aft if you are foolish enough to hand it to them. They'll bloody well swallow it."

"I just understand a little," I said, grinning at this almost comical looking sailor whose long, heavy arms and the hair on his chest made him look like a bear.

"I'll bloody well teach you, me lad—bejaysus, I will," he roared, his eyes alight with friendliness. "Nothing but bloody squareheads and limejuicers on this bloody ship, and you couldn't hear a decent word of English on a bet. Look at that bloody Scotchman over there," he said, pointing a hamlike fist at a sailor near us and speaking loud enough to be heard over the whole ship. "If you think he speaks English, you're bloody well mistaken—a bloody dog couldn't understand him. Ireland, me lad, is the only country in the world where they speak English fit to be listened to, and I'll be teaching it to you. And there's that Liverpool bastard of a bloody coal trimmer on the other watch, with a jabber in his throat a bloody pig would be ashamed of."

I was in a different world from that of the *Henriette*. Every man seemed to be on his own and free to say what he wanted and do what he had to do his own way. There was no discipline seemingly, no iron-hard hand above any man, no sharp critical eyes to measure each move, no fear of being reprimanded and even being threatened. The sailors were a carefree lot who knew their work and did it according to their nature. All were seasoned square-rigger men. We had Scandinavians, Britishers, and Germans mainly. The carpenter was a Finn. We also had a young Australian and two Americans— one from Chicago, a Great Lakes sailor originally, and a half-breed Indian from Arizona who had worked a while in the copper mine of Santa Rosalia. If the *Henriette* had been like a prison, I was now at fullest liberty, and above all I was respected. I had never dreamed I could be so happy on a ship.

We sailed south, crossed the equator, caught the southeast trades, and with the yards against the backstays made our southing, then went on the other tack and stood for the coast of Chile. For two months we lay among other square-riggers out in the roads, getting our cargo of nitrate from lighters brought 'longside. When we finally sailed south, bound for Europe, we were a foot below the rightful mark, and the sailors growled, knowing the deck would be awash in heavy weather. We had shipped only one man in Antofagasta, though there were enough on the beach. "That bloody captain," Paddy roared, "it'll be our bloody sweat to bring her around the Horn and wintertime now, and the bloody ship lying stiff like a bloody barge in a river with the load in her."

We had bad weather the whole voyage, besides running completely out of provisions, and were months late coming up the Elbe. By this time I could speak English well, my still somewhat Oxfordian school accent overlaid at will with an Irish or Scotch brogue. Paddy had been my main teacher, besides Scotty, the young sailor from Glasgow who almost chewed his words out of shape before letting them go. Paddy was the chanteyman on our watch, and whenever we worked the ship, his deep voice rang out over the sea like a trumpet, and a man who didn't pull then didn't have it in him.

I came out of the British consul's office in Hamburg, having just been paid off in gold pieces, made my way through my drunken shipmates and the waterfront women already hanging on to them, and took a streetcar home. Time had been hard for my mother while I was away. From her letters to Santa Rosalia and Antofagasta, I knew what she had been through, and on the long voyage home I had come to a decision. I would quit the sea. Life on a square-rigger held out no future. I had learned to love the sea and the towering ships, the labor aloft and on deck, the storms and calms and the iron life, but it offered no inducements to continue. I had realized that the life of captains and mates was a mere physical existence which I felt would in time suffocate me. And the financial reward was a mere pittance. Besides I had learned that this was the twilight of the era of the big iron sailing ships, which had been designed and built near the end of the century to stem the tide of the ever-more-efficient-becoming steamships. To be able to compete, sailing-ship owners manned them with ever smaller crews than safety demanded, provided less and cheaper food, and also neglected keeping sails and rigging in a condition fit to stand up during the long and stormy voyages. The days of sail that had opened up the world were drawing to a close. A dying echo of its song of glory had struck my heart while in despair and now had faded away.

"Mother," I said, pouring my little hoard of gold coins in her lap, "I am going to take the first ship I can get to America, jump ship, work ashore, and save my money, then send for you and the little ones."

On the *Bermuda* I had learned something of the world. Most of the sailors had at one time or another jumped ship in the States, Argentina, Canada, or Australia, and worked ashore till they were tired of it and had shipped out again. I had listened to their experiences in those countries and asked endless questions about the people and wages. Finally I decided on the States, as sailors called it, as the land of my future—there I would work and earn the money which would enable me to take care of my mother and brothers.

A few days after being paid off, I went back to the waterfront and to a shipping office for British ships. It was crowded with seamen. A few jobs for sailors, firemen, and coal trimmers were marked up on a blackboard. The telephone rang, and the shipping master picked up the receiver and listened. After hanging up he bawled out, "I want an A.B. for the *Inkula*, Leyland Line, lying in Bremerhaven and sailing at midnight for Galveston."

"Where is Galveston?" I asked a British sailor standing beside me, never having heard the name before.

"In the bloody Gulf," he replied.

"What gulf?" I wanted to know.

"The bloody Gulf—Gulf of Mexico."

"Is it in Mexico?"

"In the bloody States—in Texas," he snapped, disgusted with my ignorance.

I held up my British seaman's book and with my square-rigger discharge had no trouble getting the job. I passed the doctor (my eyes had improved now), went home, packed my bag, and boarded the train for Bremerhaven. She left at midnight, went to Port Talbot for bunkers, and then crossed the Atlantic. Thirty days later I saw the low coast of Texas before me. We tied up and began to load cotton.

After ten days the holds were full, and we were due to sail the next day. I had been ashore every night to become acquainted with the land which I would henceforth call my own. My feelings had almost overwhelmed me when I stepped ashore the first time. I had thrown my chest out and, but for the people around me, would have warbled my joy to the sky. Now the big moment had come. I had purposely stayed on board to the last night to allay any suspicions and also to have time to find out what to do once I was ashore to make good my desertion.

A few of the seamen had already jumped ship and a watchman with a gun been put at the gangway to stop anyone else. This couldn't have kept me from the land of my dreams for, if necessary, I would have swum ashore. I went forward and, up on the fore-castlehead, took the rat guard off a bow hawser and made my way over it hand over hand while hanging on with my legs. Then I went to the railway station and boarded a train for Houston, then a sleepy little town with apparently no future, situated fifty miles from Galveston. I thought I would be safe there in case the police were looking for me. It was the height of the cotton-shipping season at the time, and Galveston was crowded with ships from which seamen were continually deserting, so that the police were on the lookout to pick them up and put them on any ship that needed men.

My first job was in the Brazos Bottom in the woods, felling trees, loading them on a wagon drawn by oxen, and sawing them into boards at a sawmill. I next cleared forest land and cut cord wood. Afterward I went back to Galveston, thinking I was safe now, worked on a dredge and then as coal passer and fireman on two United States Army transports, the *McClellan* and the *Sumner*. It was at the time of our trouble with Mexico, and the transports were on a war footing and loaded with soldiers. After it had been settled, I remained in Galveston, worked on a dredge again and then as longshoreman, which paid the best wages. I saved my money and, with the help of a little inheritance which fell to my mother from a sister who had died in Bohemia, brought her and my two little brothers to America. After looking around for a while, we bought a little ranch in Galveston County, and a new life began for all of us. Our contact with Europe was broken. It was then two years before the First World War.

3

THE land which we had bought, mostly unbroken prairie, proved when turned over not suited for farming, and to support us I went to Galveston, only twenty miles away, and joined the longshoremen's union. When no ships were in port, I worked on dredge boats, digging the Houston ship channel, sailed on fishing schooners to the Campeche Banks off Mexico, and followed the wheat harvests, beginning in Texas or Oklahoma and continuing north as the grain ripened to Kansas and the Dakotas. I also became a professional wrestler. My brothers in the meantime were growing up, and in 1919, to give them a better education, we sold our place and moved to San Francisco. Here one of my brothers died a few years later, after a short illness, while my mother lived until 1947, passing away at the age of eighty-three.

My wanderings now began in earnest. I crossed America from east to west, north to south time and again, working in lumber camps in Washington and Oregon, in shipyards, on rivers and on the coasts, on the plains and in the mountains. In Alaska I fished, built roads, and prospected. Then the trail led south again, up and down the Pacific coast and across to the oil fields of west Texas and Oklahoma, then just opening up.

In 1920 I almost lost an eye while working as a riveter in a San

Francisco shipyard, and a few years later, in 1922, I shattered my leg while loading cotton in a Japanese steamer on a Galveston pier. It meant crutches for almost a year. While convalescing with time on my hands, I turned to books again. I had been away from all reading since I shipped as a deck boy on the *Henriette* in 1908. I also wrote poetry, drew cartoons, and worked out a comic strip, and when I was able to walk again, went to New York and Cleveland to sell my idea. Chances looked bright in Cleveland where I became friendly with Donahey, the famous cartoonist of the *Plain Dealer*, but I changed my mind the last minute. I suddenly couldn't see myself sitting at a drawing board in a newspaper office. The world was too big, too wide—I had to see and live more. I shipped on a steamer and sailed till the Great Lakes froze, then returned to the Pacific coast. But my broken leg had made me a reader and student again and anxious to catch up, and after each job, I went off to some library and stayed till my money was gone.

My boyhood dream of perfect health and a strong body had been with me throughout the years, and I had followed many systems of physical culture and diets.

In 1938 I married. I had met Teddy, my wife, on a small steamer, the *Ingrid*, on my way to Devil's Island in French Guiana, to help an innocent prisoner escape.

I had heard about him from his mother, a Frenchwoman who was running a rooming house in New York where I had stayed while ashore, recuperating from an accident suffered on the S.S. *Western World*, a steamer of the old Munson Line. According to her story and several documents she showed me, she had been owner of a small hotel in France, having lost her husband in the First World War. Her oldest child, a boy of seventeen, was helping her with the hotel. One night there had been a brawl in the barroom between some youngsters of the small town and a group of hilarious officials returning from a party. Blows were struck, and an attorney, a prominent citizen of their community, fell and struck his head against a chair. A few days later he died. The widow's son and another youngster, an orphan, were tried and condemned to Devil's Island for the regular eight-year term. This meant a life sentence. Her son had then long served his time and become a *libéré* (a liberated man), but was not allowed to leave the colony. His mother was grieving her heart out for him, knowing only too well what life in the colony meant. I had received a sum of money in settlement for my injury and, not wanting to go back on a ship yet, decided to go to Devil's Island and try to help the victim of miscarried justice escape. I managed to get into the colony by way of Dutch Guiana and, disguised as a *libéré*, found the man, who by now had served almost twenty years. After some difficulties, I managed to get him on a smuggling sloop and off to Brazil.

Then I returned to New York and married Teddy, the girl I had met on the steamer on my way down to Dutch Guiana. She was in show business and ran a theatrical-booking agency. I quit the sea now and stayed in New York, becoming acquainted with the writing end of the show world—of singers, dancers, comedians, and acrobats.

In 1948 we went to the West Indies and bought a native sailing sloop, and after cruising for some months among the islands, making St. Thomas our headquarters, set sail for Miami, a distance of approximately two thousand miles. Our sloop had no motor. A hurricane caught us in the Caribbean and threw us through the Yucatan Channel into the Gulf of Mexico where, after riding it out, we sprang a leak. It was impossible to get at it, and we had to pump day and night to keep afloat. A ship finally saw our distress signal and came 'longside. It was the M.S. *Bonito* of the Suwanee Steamship Company of Jacksonville. The captain offered to take us off and land us in Havana, the port he was bound for, but this meant to abandon our sloop, which I wouldn't consider. I asked him to take Teddy off and send an SOS to the Coast Guard, while I stayed on board hoping to be towed in. Teddy refused to leave. "I'll stay if you stay," she declared, and there was no budging her. That was Teddy, small and even frail but iron all through. She was born in

New York where the houses stand thickest and had never been on a small boat before, having worked all her life in an office.

It was getting dark when the *Bonito* disappeared on the horizon. We continued to pump, hoping that the SOS, which the captain had promised to send, would be picked up. Our position was approximately 120 miles west of Dry Tortugas. I had thrown all our ballast overboard to keep us up, but the sloop was settling more and more, and around midnight her deck was almost awash. About two o'clock in the morning, a ship's lights bore down on us. It came up fast, straight as a bullet, and we made ready to jump overboard in case she didn't see us and ran us down. We had only a small lantern—all the hurricane had left us with—and no kerosene or gasoline to make a flare. Since we had no life vests, I tied Teddy to me, for she couldn't swim. The threatening lights swung off at the last minute, and I saw that the ship was a destroyer. They gave us a towline, and twelve hours later we tied up in Key West, where we heard that the Navy had picked up the SOS and ordered the destroyer to look for us. It had located us with its radar.

Teddy was a little wobbly on her legs, for we had been weeks at sea and in much bad weather, but after our boat had been hauled up and the leak fixed, she was eager to go on. Her love for the sea and ability to stand up under hardships was almost phenomenal. The native sloops of the West Indies are sturdy and good sailers but primitive in the extreme, since designed only for short voyages, and as for comfort, even a fly would balk being on board. But Teddy never complained.

A few years later Teddy was in a hospital in New York for a thyroid operation. I was sailing on the coast, making short trips, and every few days was in New York where I could visit her. One day I had the idea of building a raft and sailing it across the Pacific. I would go alone, and I would set a destination. It should be a raft that could hold its course and reach its port like a regular ship. Teddy said no. "One man and at your age—almost sixty—I can't see it."

After she left the hospital, I sailed on a number of tankers and had narrow escapes from collisions and explosions, besides being exposed day and night to gases escaping from leaking decks and through hatches and vents. We also had to go into the holds and clean tanks and more than once I tied a rope around a shipmate who had been overcome by gas to get him on deck and into the air. After two years Teddy realized that I might be in as much danger sailing on those ships as I would be alone on a raft and gave her consent for a solo raft voyage in the Pacific.

On June 22, 1954, she stood at the end of the submarine pier in the Peruvian navy base of Callao, Peru, and watched a tug take my raft out to sea. I had cleared for Samoa. The port captain, handing me my clearance papers, had said, "You'll be lucky to survive and fetch up on some reef no one ever heard of, never mind picking a spot almost seven thousand miles away."

A hundred and fifteen days after the tug let me go fifty miles off the coast, I landed in Samoa. I had long been given up for lost.

After my return I wrote the story of my voyage, lectured in America and also in Europe. I was sixty-four now. One day I discovered that my body was showing signs of wear.

Diabetes, arthritis, and digestion and kidney troubles began to plague me, not to mention other symptoms of which one was consuming nervousness, which I felt was an indication of some other serious and still hidden condition. Age was catching up with me. It was a shock. The man who I had thought was unbreakable was breaking up.

I had studied health methods all my life and, once I realized what was going on in my body, knew what to do.

After I'd talked it over with Teddy, we retired to a quiet spot in the hills of southern California, dug up a patch of virgin ground for a garden where we raised our own vegetables, and I went to work on myself.

I tried everything in the way of natural healing I had learned in my wanderings and studies. I did breathing exercises, I took water cures and other treatments, and rigged up a steam bath; I drank herbal teas and sometimes only distilled water; for weeks I lived only on cereals, then only on fruits and vegetables. I also fasted and, as it was often the case with me, went to extremes. Teddy, always beside me, kept counseling moderation, thinking I couldn't live through my experiments. "Don't expect the impossible," she said. "What are you trying to do? You are an old man nearing seventy." And so on. But I was certain that my knowledge, my insight, and will would carry me through. At last the tide turned. After a final fever, lying on sweat-drenched sheets and blankets and with even the mattress soaked, I said to Teddy, "I have it licked." It took a year however before I was fully on my feet.

We lived about ten miles from the Pacific and used to go to the beach a few times a week for a dip and to sit on the sand. One day, sitting beside Teddy under a beach umbrella and looking out upon the blue water, I felt something stirring within me. Thoughts of my raft voyage arose, of my 115 days alone on those same blue levels— far from here but on the same ocean, seeing no human beings, alone in thousands of miles in space. I had forgotten all about it almost, it seemed so long ago—those glorious days and nights when the whole world was mine, the sea and sky from the highest star to the dark depths beneath, with not a soul near of all the earth's millions.

Teddy got up and went in for a dip, and I watched her, for the undertow was strong and it was dangerous to go in deeper than one's knees. I sat there dreaming, living through those days again. I saw the flying fishes and sharks and the lightning dashes of the dolphin (fish) and my two little shipmates—Meekie, my black cat, and Eekie, my green parrot. Meekie was still living and quite near, in Long Beach, California, and in perfect health. I had forgotten so much. The whole voyage appeared like a vision that had almost faded amid the crowded scenes of the life I had led since I was a boy. But today was a day for remembering, sitting in the warm and lazy sun, drowsy and in harmony with creation.

It had been a glorious voyage on that balsa raft, which I had hewn out of the jungles of Ecuador, though there had been mishaps and nearness of death and even despair. Man easily forgets what was bad. The sea lay calm before me, calm and hot as on the days when the sails of my raft hung like scorched rags from yard and mast, and the logs grew foul with moss and seemed to sink lower into the sea; days when the horizon was empty but for some solitary bird far away winging its way out of the walls of anchored clouds that encircled me, the prisoner. Sickness also I had. For a day and a night I had lain on deck writhing in agony, turning my pain-crazed eyes to the sky or pressing a distorted face against the bamboo deck, broken, subdued, and even wishing for death. I had crawled to my transmitter and cranked, knowing it did not work but in my agony hoped that a passing ship might hear. My eyes had gone to my razor-sharp fish knives stuck above the cabin door, to cut into the seat of the pain—the pit of my stomach—and stop the relentless tightening up. I had scrawled a last message to Teddy on a piece of paper and tacked it on the door. Then, senseless, I had lain on deck, alone with the hours, the sun's coming and going, and the seas' washing over me. Everything had disappeared, and only my body lay there, a rope keeping it from slipping over the side.

When I had awakened, the pain in the pit of my stomach was gone; miraculously as it had come, it had disappeared. Not a trace of it, though there was a dull pain when I pressed against the spot. What had been the cause? I wondered, for I had never had a pain of any kind in my stomach. For days I was so weak that I could not get to my feet unless I pulled myself up by a rope, and my flesh dropped away from my bones, and my face was a mask to frighten. I never fully recovered on the voyage. Back in New York I found out that I had suffered from a perforated stomach ulcer. A doctor, who had warned me before leaving that I might be stricken with appendicitis or something of that sort, said to me, "You boasted that you couldn't get sick, remember. You could easily have died out there."

Another mishap was when I lost my water supply. I had it in five-gallon tin cans, lying on the logs beneath the deck and exposed to the wash of the waves. The tin was thin, had rusted through, and the water leaked out. I discovered it in time to save what amounted to about ninety cups. On the *Henriette*, my first ship, I had learned to drink seawater to keep my bowels functioning, since we lived mainly on a starchy diet with no fresh fruit or vegetables. It had been a lesson I never forgot, and throughout the years, whenever I was on a ship, I turned to seawater for the same medicinal reasons. Later I came to the conclusion that there were other, as yet unknown properties in seawater of medicinal as well as nutritive value.

What terrible moments when I discovered that my water was gone! At first I was stunned. Then I picked up the empty cans, light as feathers, and threw them one by one over the side. I watched them strung out behind me in my wake, bobbing up and down and bright as silver, for they were brand new and only the seams had rusted. Slowly the hours had gone by. The sun had burned her way across the sky, and I stood waterless on my logs except for my little hoard of ninety mugs. The Marquesas, nearest land, were more than a thousand miles away. I knew I could reach them with what water I had, but it meant smashing the raft on its steep shore and giving up, for Samoa, my destination, was almost three thousand miles farther. I knew I had only myself to blame for putting water in such frail cans and then storing them on the water-washed logs. At last it was evening. The sun had set, and the stars tiptoed out into the night and looked down on the sea. It was calm, and a greater peace than usual lay on the water. It fell also on me, sitting by the wheel. Suddenly the answer came. I got up, took my tin mug from the nail, and kneeling at the edge of the raft dipped it into the sea. The bitter draught went down—I felt it inside of me, and I felt that it did no harm. I knew I could continue my voyage. Twenty days later, while seventy-five miles north of the Marquesas, a torrential rain fell, the only rain of the voyage, and I filled what containers I had.

Teddy was still on the beach, walking up and down where the sand was wet and firm from the receding tide. There had been other mishaps. I had put out a fishing line baited with a flying fish that had fallen on deck during the night for bait. Dolphin (fish) were around the raft, and I wanted one. When I looked at the line again, it was tight. As I began to pull in, I knew it was not a dolphin—which tear through the water like bullets when caught—but a shark. I pulled him up on the logs, slimy and moss-grown. He had turned on his back, and his jaws with the two rows of teeth were wide open. Wanting to save the hook, I held him with my gaff and began to work the hook loose. The gristle in a shark's jaw is tough, and I had quite a job, but at last the hook came out. At the very same moment the shark, which had been almost motionless, became alive and began to thrash violently about and struck the gaff, on which I leaned, with his breast fin and knocked it out of my hand. I lost my balance and fell headfirst over the shark into the foaming wake. Frantic with fear, I turned around to get hold of the raft again, but it was too late. It was sailing away. Then came a jerk. The end of the fish line, with the hook which I had taken out of the shark's jaw, had caught on the sleeve of my woolen shirt as I fell. I grabbed it and pulled myself to the raft—slowly, for the line was an old one and bitten almost through in places. It had been given me by the captain of a tuna clipper lying in Callao. As I pulled and swam, blood spurted from a severed artery in my left hand. I had cut it on the shark's teeth as, falling overboard, I reached out for something to hold on to. When I was back on board, I put on a tourniquet, but the wound required a needle. I tried a sailing needle but it was too big and too painful, and a sewing needle had to do the job. A hundred days later when I landed the wound was still open.

Memories of hardships and adversities overcome—of a man tested in battle—the great moments of life ... I was smiling into the blue eyes of the Pacific as one smiles at an old friend with whom one has shared a glorious past. Teddy came back and sat down. "The water is wonderful. You ought to go in," she said.

That night in the lonely hills of the Santa Margarita range, I was walking up and down in front of our bungalow. Teddy was inside reading. There was no sound; only now and then the dry rustling of the avocado leaves of a nearby grove came like a low murmur out of the night. The Pacific was still talking to me of my seven balsa logs lashed together and sailing through storms and calms. Suddenly the silence was shattered by yells, screams, and shrieks as of madmen trapped in a fire—a band of coyotes in a nearby canyon smelling a rabbit. Then all was still again, so still that the stars seemed to be talking. Back and forth I walked, my eyes on the western hills, for just a few miles away above their rim lay the Pacific. Suddenly I knew that I would make another raft voyage. Always my revelations had come like this—with the same suddenness and finality.

The days went by, Teddy not knowing what went on in my mind. The thing was born though as yet had no real shape. I knew, however, that I would want to leave from Callao as in 1954, and I knew that this time I would want to sail nonstop to Australia, to Sydney if possible. It meant crossing the whole Pacific, from east to west—at least eleven thousand miles of sailing, alone again and without touching land. Was it a dream begotten in silly idleness never to become reality? I asked myself a hundred times. Could it be done? I lived through every day and night of my other voyage again, looking for flaws—for my weaknesses and strengths and the merciless moods of the sea. Was it plain madness or a disordered outburst of long-pent-up physical energies demanding action? Was it my inherited hunger reaching for what was beyond the horizon? The idea didn't let go but stood up under all questioning, all analysis.

One day I told Teddy. She looked at me as if I had lost my senses. To convince her was like attacking an Egyptian pyramid with a pickax, prying out stone after stone till the ground was level again. I had to bare my very insides to make her understand why I had to go. One day, quite unexpectedly, after listening to me again, she said, "There will be no living with you if you don't do it—go ahead."

I sent a letter to Ecuador and asked about balsa logs. Could I get them and when and could they be shipped to the States? I wanted them in New York to build the raft where it would be easier to get everything needed for fitting it out. From New York a steamer should take it down to Callao.

I remembered what I had been through in 1954 locating trees big enough for a raft. For months I had flown in small, single-motored planes, over swamps and creeks impossible to get through on foot. It was in the rainy season, and the woods were often shrouded in fogs and mists or beaten to roaring seas of leaves by equatorial squalls. Time and again we were lost above the wilderness. Once a wing tip caught on a tree, and the plane was jerked around and began to drop, but the pilot by some miracle pulled us out, out of a crash. Finally we came down almost out of gas on a strip of grass hardly visible in the semidarkness of the storm.

But I had found my balsas at last, not by spotting the trees from the air but through the information obtained from an Indian living in the jungle near Quevedo, hundreds of miles up the Rio Playa from Guayaquil. "I know some big trees," he said simply. "Come with me." We hacked our way, swinging our machetes through miles of dense vegetation. The trees, blue gray and with smooth barks, stood like columns in the semidarkness waiting for me. There were seven within a radius of three hundred or four hundred yards, all of the size I needed. Since they stood so near together, like one family, I later called my raft the *Seven Little Sisters—Siete Hermanitas* in Spanish. They were big trees, two and a half feet in diameter at the butt. As a rule balsas die and crash before reaching this size. After locating them, we had to cut a path through the jungle for the oxen to drag them to the nearest road, where one by one they were loaded on a banana truck and carried to the river for the three days' drift down to Guayaquil. There I hauled them back on land and tied them together into a raft.

A few months passed with no news from Ecuador. I wrote again and finally had an answer: There were no logs around Quevedo, but they might be found way up in the interior. I had to wait, however, till after the rainy season since all the creeks were dry now. Nothing could be done for at least eight or ten months. I was also told that the logs would have to be strapped for shipment to New York to keep them from splitting. I knew that balsas split wide open soon after taken out of the water. I was also warned of the danger of them breaking or otherwise being damaged while transported. Balsas are notoriously fragile.

"Let's go down to Ecuador and look for them ourselves," Teddy said. She was always ready for travel or adventure.

"Into the jungle?"

"Yes. I always wanted to go there."

"You don't know that jungle down there."

"I'm not afraid. Women have been in the jungles before. I'd love to go. And you may find logs somewhere without having to wait for the rainy season. You didn't wait for the rainy season in 1954."

I shook my head. "You don't know what I went through flying over the jungle—and afterward to get them out. I was lucky I could get oxen and that there were no big swamps right there. The trees have to grow beside a creek or on the bank of a river, so that they fall into the water, and the water must be deep enough to carry them. Otherwise I couldn't get them out. I have to wait, that's all. I really would hate to go down there and look for them myself— takes too much out of a man. Fever, mosquitoes, and always *mañana* if you want something done. *Mañana.* Next year—that's what *mañana* means."

"I wouldn't mind to go—really."

"You will go anywhere, I know."

"I don't think you'll get your logs unless you go and look yourself—that's what I think."

One day when going to the beach again to spend a few hours lying in the sand, we had to step over a pipeline laid down by a dredge digging a yacht basin a mile or so up the coast near Camp Pendleton. As I put my hand on the big pipe to climb over it, I saw a way out of my dilemma—pipes!

"That's it, Teddy," I said. "Pipes—pipes for my raft. Here are my logs, right here."

Teddy looked incredulous. "Will they float? Iron?"

"Do iron ships float? Do battleships float with steel plates a foot thick on the sides?"

"They are different."

"They'll float, don't worry about that. A wonder I didn't think of it before." I picked up a pebble and struck the pipe. "That's it. Simple—every bit as good as logs."

I stood looking at the miles of pipe stretching along the beach all welded together, heard the water, the sand and rocks rushing through and clattering. The whole line was humming. "These are heavy pipes," I said. "I don't need them that thick. That's it, all right. Funny I hadn't thought of it before."

In New York a few weeks later, we called up all the companies selling large pipes we could find in the telephone book. We became busy from morning to night. Our tables and dressers and even the floor became desks littered with letters, advertisements, telephone numbers, and hundreds of notes to remind us of what to do. Our typewriter clattered away into all hours of the night. I went out to City Island and asked the sailmaker who had made the sails for the *Seven Little Sisters* if he knew of a place where I could build the raft. "Across the street," he said. "That's the only place I know of here."

It was a large boatyard with rows of cradles outside and in the sheds, full of sailing yachts and power cruisers, all under canvas for the winter. The yard had other sheds but used only for new construction. "The place is yours," I was told. "You can start your raft tomorrow." It meant working outside, however, which was impossible, for the ground was two feet under snow and the bay full of ice. I would have to wait till the end of April at the earliest. It was just before Christmas now.

Later we found a place in New Jersey. After deciding to build a trimaran—a type of craft used since ancient times and very much in vogue now—and settling on the dimensions, we went to work.

The raft consisted of three pontoons, each twenty feet long—two aft and one in the center and each having a somewhat flat shape like the hull of a power boat. The length at the waterline was approximately thirty-four feet and the width about twenty. A six-inch heavy steel pipe encircled the three pontoons on top and, together with girders running from side to side, welded the whole into a solid mass. To this frame a deck of the best two-inch Oregon pine planks was bolted, of the same kind as those used on our plane carriers. The mainmast, straddling the raft with its two legs, was almost thirty-eight feet high. From it hung the eighteen-foot-long yard with the mainsail. The after mast was twenty feet high and the jibboom holding the forestay and jib sprang out ten feet beyond the bow. Aft was a cabin to house provisions, charts, sextant, chronometers, cameras, and film, and everything that could not be left on deck. The cabin gave me headroom and was about seven feet long and five feet wide. The pontoons were filled with polyurethane, a chemical which, when poured in as a liquid, expanded and filled the space with a corklike substance impenetrable to water. This would keep the raft from sinking even if the pontoons rusted through on the long voyage or I struck rocks or a reef. I had two rudders, one on each of the two after pontoons; otherwise the raft was similar to the *Seven Little Sisters*.

Teddy wanted me to see a doctor, a cousin of hers. I knew him. He was still young, in his forties, successful and versed in the latest methods. I didn't think it was necessary, but Teddy insisted.

"It would be unforgivable if you went on such a voyage without a checkup," she argued. "Half a year alone on a raft, maybe longer . . . Why, Bill, where is your common sense? Anything can happen. Anything could develop from some hidden weakness. Remember what happened in 1954—you almost died. Do you forget that? What if it should happen again? You are all worn out now from running around. If something is wrong, Bernie will find it and warn you. He can also give you something so you wouldn't have to suffer like you did in fifty-four if something really serious should happen. Do you think I could have one easy moment while you're away if you went like this? You are seventy, you know—regardless of what you think. Seventy is seventy and not thirty-five or something like that. Now don't be foolish."

I grinned, knowing that Teddy would force me to see her cousin.

"In 1954," she went on, "when the doctors of the navy base in Callao wanted to examine you before sailing, you refused."

"I had just been ruptured leaving Guayaquil, a few weeks before," I retorted. "I didn't want them to find out and stop me."

"They certainly would or at least would have ordered you to get a truss. It was a crime you didn't get one yourself. The most terrible thing could have happened. Okay, Bill, I'll call up Bernie right away and set the date."

I went for several blood tests and other tests—tests I had never heard of. Bernie obviously knew his business. He had promised Teddy to "give me the works," she later confessed and, if he found anything wrong, to tell me. One day I lay on a table with wires fastened to my head and feet, arms and other parts of my body, all leading to a rather formidable-looking machine with a panel of dials and indicators of different colors and lights coming and going. Bernie was taking a cardiograph. I was breathing evenly as he had told me to do, listening to the low hum of the motor and watching his face. It was expressionless. Finally he shut off the current and looked at the scroll or graph that had registered my heart action. He was frowning. "Damn it," he said.

"Anything wrong?" I asked, thinking he had discovered something terrible and the voyage was off.

"You are dramatically—let me say fantastically—healthy," he said, shaking his head, and after another look at the graph, took off the wires and told me to get up.

Then he picked the graph up again and studied it. "That's for my record. I'll see what the story is after you come back. This one here I'll show to a friend of mine—a heart specialist." He kept shaking his head. "Looks like it was made by a machine—I can't understand it. Anyway you have the heart of an ox."

When the raft was almost ready, I had to look for a cat and dog to take along on the voyage. In 1954 I had a cat and a parrot, but there had been bad blood between them from the beginning, and at the very end of the voyage, when we had already sighted a few of the Samoan islands, Meekie got into the cage and killed her little green shipmate. It was during a stormy night, and I was at the wheel when it happened. And so this time I wanted a young cat and a young dog which would become friendly.

A telephone book gave us the names of the animal shelters in the city, and we started out, beginning with the one farthest uptown. There were plenty of cats and dogs to be had, but we saw nothing we liked. Most of them were friendly, particularly the cats, gazing at us from behind the bars of the cages, some giving plaintive little meows and plainly wanting to be petted. The dogs were more cautious though some barked a friendly welcome and, wagging their tails, shoved eager noses through the bars. We finally came to the last shelter on our list. It was in an old, dark, and narrow building. An attendant took us down into the cellar, where we began with the dogs—big, small, and of all breeds, colors, and ages. Again some were friendly while a few were frightened, retreated into a corner, and even growled. Those obviously had seen hard times or cruel treatment. We came to the cats, going slowly from cage to cage and looking at the little prisoners. I felt as if I were in an ancient slave market sizing up the wares. There was the last cage already. "That's it, Teddy—that's the one." I stopped, my eyes on a tortoise-shell-colored, fully grown cat. She came to the bars and rubbed herself against them. The attendant opened the cage, and purring loudly, she went into Teddy's arms and snuggled against her as if she had been waiting for her. She was a gentle and beautiful cat seemingly part Persian, dark brown with lighter touches, black belly and dainty

45

little black feet. Her eyes were large and golden, and her face was strikingly appealing. We were told she was about two years old and had belonged to an old lady who had died, had had one litter but now was spayed. Her name was something that sounded like a mix-up of Japanese and Italian, but we called her Kiki to make it similar to Meekie, my black cat of 1954. We left her at the shelter to be inoculated for admission into Peru and, a few days later, brought her to the hotel, where she at once became the center of our little makeshift household. I still needed a dog, but after a few more fruitless trips to the shelters, our time was up in New York, and I decided to get one in Peru.

4

ON May 2 the raft was ready, and a
Moran Company towboat took it down the Passaic River to Port
Newark where the *Santa Margarita* of the Grace Line lay ready to
sail the next day to South America and Callao, my jumping-off
place. It was a gusty, clear day with white rags of clouds drifting
rapidly across a blue sky, and when we loosened the mainsail to
hoist it for the photographers—it had *Age Unlimited,* the name of
the raft, on its face in large black letters—six of us hanging on to it
were almost hurled to the deck. "You'll have your hands full with
that sail by yourself," I heard someone say just while I was thinking
the same. The raft rode very low, and even while we were coming
down the sheltered water of the river—a creek really—the deck forward was awash. I realized I would have to cut off the steel cabin
and replace it with a wooden one, something I had already anticipated. This and quite a lot of other work I had discovered would
be necessary to make the raft seaworthy. It would have to be done
in Callao in the Peruvian navy base, where free labor had been
promised me by the Government. In 1954 Peru had also treated me
royally, giving me all the material and help I needed besides the
good wishes of the whole nation.

The raft was hoisted on board the *Santa Margarita* on the afternoon of May 3 and lashed down on number three hatch in front of the bridge. The masts and jibboom had been taken off the day before and put into the lower hold. It was getting dark when the ship with Teddy, me, and Kiki on board steamed through the Narrows and out to sea.

The voyage to Callao with stops at Norfolk, Panama, and Buenaventura was pleasant. We had the best of food, a good crew, and congenial passengers. Captain Hokansen had been port captain of the Grace Line in Callao in 1954 when the *Santa Cecilia* brought my raft down from Guayaquil, where I had built it, and so knew me. Kiki of course became the pet forward and aft, and the way she leaned over the side and looked into the water streaking past made me think she had waited for this new experience all her life. I knew she would feel at home on the raft.

Much of my time was spent on the bridge with the navigating officer, for I needed freshening up badly, not having looked at a sextant or chart or worked out a latitude or longitude since 1954, when I had packed everything away after reaching Samoa. Except for a few Atlantic crossings, I hadn't even been near a ship. A new angle for me on the coming voyage would be the navigation after crossing the international date line, which runs through Suva in the Fijis. I had never navigated east of Greenwich. But vast stretches of sea would have to be crossed before I came near the Fijis and the 180th meridian, marking the date line. (Callao was on the 77th.) And after the Fijis came the run to Australia—past the New Hebrides and New Caledonia. Standing in the chartroom of the ship, I was now and then a little staggered by what lay ahead. It struck me a bit like reading about the distance of the moon from the earth and was hard to visualize. Had I bitten off more than I could chew? There were doubtful moments as the ship made its way south, through the Panama Canal and along the coast of Colombia, Ecuador, and then Peru—many moments when I stood on deck and looked at my raft lashed across the hatch and small like a toy.

48

We docked in Callao on May 16 late in the afternoon, and the raft was lowered into the sea during the night. The next day a Grace Line tug towed it to the Peruvian navy base. Peru opened its arms in welcome to Teddy and me. It was like a homecoming after an absence of nine years. I was, however, a little apprehensive about the attitude of the military government which had some time ago been established by the heads of the armed forces after the President had been deposed. The first morning I paid my respects to the commander of the navy base, Admiral Juan Luis Kruger. He was very friendly and assured me of fullest assistance. The next day Teddy and I went to the Minister of the Navy, one of the three heads of the junta government. He embraced me warmly. "Señor Willis," he said, "I beg you to remember that Peru is your home now—the people, the Government, and the navy base are yours. We are proud of you, proud that you sailed from our shore nine years ago and have come back to sail from here again. All Peru prayed in 1954 that you would safely reach Samoa, your destination. All Peru will pray now that, with the help of God, you will reach Australia." He was so friendly and warm that Teddy had to brush away a tear.

Lima had changed. It was in an upsurge of growth. There were five-and-dime stores and supermarkets, and the streets were crowded with automobiles struggling through traffic jams—all the hustle and bustle of a big city.

We had taken rooms at the Gran Hotel Bolivar where we had lived in '54, and every morning I went to Callao, the port of Lima eight miles away. Callao had been founded by Francisco Pizarro, whose mummified body lay in state in the Cathedral in the Plaza de Armas of Lima, showing the almost severed neck where the assassin's dagger had struck the seventy-year-old conqueror.

The road to Callao used to run through open country—through sugarcane, cornfields, and banana plantations—but now was almost solidly lined with houses. To my further surprise, when nearing the port, I could see the high bows of fishing trawlers above the roofs.

49

They were built all along in open lots and backyards, and they were mostly of iron, though some were of wood, and all of approximately fifty tons. A miracle had taken place in Callao. From a port which only had a few small fishing boats handled by one or two men, it had within the last few years become the biggest fishing port in the world. Five thousand trawlers streamed through the breakwater before dawn each morning and came back in the evening loaded to the point of sinking with fish. They didn't have far to go to lower their nets, for the nitrogen-rich water of the Humboldt Current sweeping up the coast from the Antarctic was alive with seemingly inexhaustible schools of anchovies. For ages they had been untouched except by sea birds—especially pelicans, which, feasting on these riches, had multiplied to such numbers that they fairly covered the coastal islands of Peru and Chile, where they had their rookeries, with their droppings. Finally these droppings, called guano, rose to mountains. It was the world's finest plant food, and countless ships had filled their holds and carried it away beneath the clouds of birds that darkened the sky. Then suddenly the world had begun to cry for food for the new millions born every day. Their hunger had to be stilled. And here in the Humboldt Current was food—food, fish oil, and fertilizer.

My raft had been lifted out of the water in the navy yard and work on her begun. First the iron cabin was cut off and replaced with a wooden one; then slots to hold the centerboards were forged and fastened to the deck. Sheets of split bamboo were nailed to the deck to cover the cracks between the planks which had been put down one and a half inches apart to lessen the impact of the seas from beneath. The outside of the cabin was also lined with split bamboo to help keep the rain and spray off and also for looks. The looks were important, for my raft was almost wholly of steel, and I knew that in the long months of solitude ahead my eyes would hunger for the sight of bamboo, banana leaves, and wood to remind me of the land I had left behind. It would help, I thought, to keep me sane. For this reason also I put a thick layer of banana leaves on the roof of the cabin. There were endless things to do, and one week after another went by. When everything seemed finished, I had to get busy with my provisions. I had to figure on eight or nine months' supplies. From first to last Teddy had shared all labor, even as in New York, and without her aid I never could have managed.

The Peruvian press was with me every day, in Callao or in Lima at night, clamoring for a story, asking just what I was doing at the time and when I would be ready. I was called *El Navegante Solitario*, a name originally given me by the Argentine press in 1954 while I was still in Guayaquil building my balsa raft. Few people really believed that I could make the voyage. At the navy base they were betting pro and con. The general opinion had it that it was impossible for a man to make a raft voyage alone halfway around the world through the changing seasons—through winter gales and summer hurricanes—from South America to Australia. Some thought of course that I wasn't quite sane. There were others however who wanted to come along—career officers, enlisted men, and day workers at the base, who knew me from 1954. Some were tough, practical men whose forefathers had built and sailed the first galleons that crossed the Pacfic and explored this vast emptiness of space, sailing as far as the Coral Sea, two centuries before the first Dutch, French, or British ships plowed through, coming from the Cape of Good Hope or following Magellan's track around South America. They came to me almost every day while I was working on the raft, sizing me up and willing to risk their lives. Some didn't speak English. They couldn't understand why a man would want to go alone. "Is it true that you are seventy years old?" they all asked. Fifty was old in Peru. I sometimes had to flex my arms and let them feel my muscles. But they doubted my ability to stand up alone. I was pretty well worn-out after my long preparations—four months in New York and now two in Callao getting the raft ready—and not much of a specimen to look at. Oh, I was anxious to get going and deliver myself body, soul, and spirit to the tides of nature—to whatever came down from above or rose up from below. I knew I would recover easily enough but was worried about Teddy. She had had a long breakdown in New York and now several attacks of fever and been under the care of a doctor. And still she kept working, running around for me, doing countless little jobs. What would happen to her after I left?

I had begun to look around for a dog, a companion for Kiki and me, but it seemed even harder here in Peru than in New York to find one. The dogs were all big sheep or cattle dogs that had strayed into the city, or they were pups of the same breed and so not suitable for a raft, since I couldn't take enough water or food for them along. Kiki, living in the hotel with us, had become the pet of the help and the press as well, and there were few days when she didn't have her photograph taken, down in the lobby or out on the Plaza San Martin, walking beside Teddy and me on a leash. She always stopped the traffic since she looked so different from Peruvian cats, and often we were asked, *"Es un tigre?"* (Is it a tiger?)

"No, no—she's just a little cat," Teddy always answered, but no one seemed convinced. Perhaps people had a better insight than we into Kiki's true nature, but it was not till five months later and only once that I saw gentle Kiki turn into a bundle of fury and show that she had indeed a tiger or two inside of her.

Our search for a dog continued. There were enough Americans in Lima who had dogs I would have liked to have, but I was always refused. It was always the same: At first I was told, "I have just the dog you want—he loves water, likes to play with cats," and so on. I had to listen to all the dog's virtues, and when I thought he was as good as mine and asked for him, it was, "On a raft—my dog? Never. I couldn't sleep nights afraid of what might happen to him ... my husband would kill me ... I couldn't do it to my little daughter—she takes him in bed with her ..." etc.

I finally decided to take another cat. All our American friends had cats, and I thought I would have little difficulty now, since cats usually have one litter after another—someone was bound to have a half-grown kitten to spare. They didn't. A cat, I was told, didn't belong on the water, since it hates it. I should have a dog. It would be cruel to put an animal on a raft, knowing it couldn't possibly survive. It had been the same in 1954. When it got around then that I was looking for a cat, the SPCA of Lima protested, saying it would be the height of cruelty toward a helpless animal. Meekie was really sneaked on board the very moment of departing, a gift from the submarine captains. After a few days at sea, she became the best little four-footed sailor I had ever seen or heard of, standing, coal black from head to tail, on deck and sniffing the sea air, a picture of utter contentment, taking the rise and fall of the raft as if she were part of it. And when flying fish started to fall on deck nights, she was positively in heaven. She was still alive today, in Long Beach, California, ten years old, a slim black beauty and not looking older than a few years.

At last we heard of a hacienda near Callao that had some kittens and would let me pick one. A friend drove us out to the house almost hidden among corn and cotton. We met the whole cat family. The father of the mob was a murderous-looking marauder, coal black, lean and long of body and legs, and with glowing eyes, a real demon. The mother was a comfortable-looking gray tabby with black stripes and white belly. There were half a dozen generations of her offspring around, some slinking black devils taking after the father and others favoring the mother. We picked a gentle-looking kitten about three or four months old, gray with snow-white, downy belly and feet, and supposedly a male, and we at once named him Aussie after the land he was bound for. All the animals of the little hacienda seemed to have gathered around to see little Aussie carried off. There were a few llamas, half a dozen sheep, and a gang of savage-looking red-eyed dogs. A donkey brayed disconsolately under a nearby tree, a bull rubbed himself against a shaky fence, his eyes bulging, and a brown and white goat, slick as a glass statue, looked at us with an expression as if foreseeing a gloomy future for

the kitten Teddy held in her arms and getting a devilish kick out
of it.

When most of the work was done, the raft was put back in the
water and moored in the submarine base. The next day it was chris-
tened. A large crowd from Lima had come out for the ceremony
and stood, together with the officers from the base and the U.S.
Navy mission and men from the embassies, on the pier. Teddy took
the beribboned bottle of champagne and raised it, while the photographers stood ready.

"I christen you the *Age Unlimited*," Teddy said.

"In Spanish—quick," I whispered.

"What is it again—gee, I always forget."

"*Edad Sin Limite.*"

"*Edad Sin Limite*," Teddy shrieked. It sounded like Chinese, but
the bottle smashed beautifully against the iron jibboom amid the
spray of Peruvian champagne, and the crowd applauded.

"That bottle was heavy," Teddy said gleefully. "But you know
what I did—I said a little prayer while smashing it."

"You did?"

"Yes. I said, 'Please, little raft, take Bill safely to Australia.' "

One day, while I was working on the raft, a smart-looking seaman in full uniform, holding a boy of nine or ten by the hand, came
to me. I recognized him as the boatswain's mate who had been in
charge of the sailors helping me with the raft in 1954. "This is my
boy," he said proudly after we had shaken hands. "He was born
the day you sailed from Callao. After I came home from the base
that evening, he was there—in my wife's arms. 'What shall we call
him?' she asked. 'William Willis,' I said, 'that shall be his name.'
'No,' my wife cried, 'no—William Willis, no! That man will drown
with his raft—I wouldn't have my child named after him.' But I had
my way—I knew you would make it."

"How about this time?" I asked.

He hesitated avoiding my eyes.

ABOVE: Just after cutting towlines fifty miles out of Callao, July 5, 1963. LEFT: Sail is raised for the first time on the *Age Unlimited*.

A meal in the cabin of the *Age Unlimited*.

The author takes a nap in the "bedroom" of the raft.

ABOVE: Kiki in her favorite spot: the kayak mast. BELOW: Kiki and Aussie on deck of the raft after landing in Apia. Both enjoyed the ocean voyage.

ABOVE: Block and tackle steering after the rudders broke. BELOW: A shark that had bothered the author while swimming.

ABOVE: The raft lands at Pui Paa, Samoa, after 130 days at sea, November 12, 1963. RIGHT: The author and an aborigine friend near Tully, northern Queensland.

ABOVE LEFT: The author and Kiki getting Time-Ticks on transistor radio.
ABOVE RIGHT: Aussie and the author inspect dried fish, midships centerboard. BELOW: Sailing through Sydney Heads, Australia.

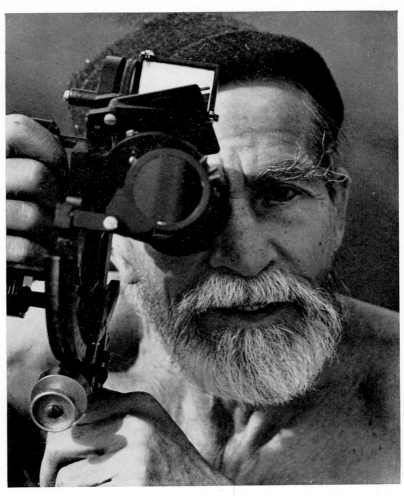

The photographer's photographer: author taking sight.

"You wouldn't name your boy after me this time, is that it?"
Again he said nothing.

I laughed. "It's a long jump to Australia, I know, but—I feel ten years younger. And, if you say the word, I'll take your boy along."
He grinned and shook his head.

One day a tall, aristocratic-looking man was standing on the pier watching me work on the raft. He stood so quietly and seemed so interested that after about half an hour I invited him down to look around. He did and surprised me with his knowledge of rafts. What also struck me was his quiet, dignified bearing and manner of speaking. He spoke no English. After looking all around the raft, he said, pointing to the banana leaves on the roof of the cabin and rustling in the wind, "If you want more leaves, I can give them to you."

"Why, have you an hacienda?" I asked half in jest.

"Si, señor," he replied

"Do you also have vegetables?" I had been on the point of ordering my supply for the voyage but didn't know just where.

"To be sure I do," was the answer. "I raise them for the market."

"I need potatoes, onions, carrots, and cabbages."

"I have everything you want."

"I'll pay you the market price, of course."

He smiled and made a movement with his hand. "You will have everything on the pier tomorrow morning. Just tell me how much of each you want."

True to his word, he was on the pier early in the morning with a truckload of market baskets full of produce, enough for six men. Everything was fresh out of the ground and obviously the pick of the fields. He smiled when I offered to pay. "You will make me very happy if you accept them from a man who admires your courage," he said. The baskets were of loose weave which let the air through and so ideal for my purpose. After we had everything on board, I invited him to be my guest on the trial run which was due the following day. So far I had decided to take only Teddy along and two brothers I had become acquainted with, students at the Lima

55

university, who had given me considerable assistance and now were on the lookout for a carrier pigeon for me to release during the voyage. Needless to say, the haciendero gratefully accepted my invitation.

That night he came to the hotel with an album. *La Balsa Siete Hermanitas* (The Raft Seven Little Sisters) was written on the cover and the whole album was full of clippings he had cut out of the Lima papers in 1954 while I lay in the navy base getting ready. Without knowing me, he had cut out every item the papers published about my raft, pasted it into the album, and preserved it these ten years. Here was a raft enthusiast, a true aficionado if ever there was one. This quiet man was a dreamer of raft voyages—that was his passion. He told me he also had an album with the clippings of Eric de Bischop, the French voyageur who twice tried to cross the Pacific with a crew of four on a bamboo raft and during the last attempt lost his life on a reef in the northern Cooks. After handing me the album to read at my leisure, he said, "Señor Willis, I now must beg you to write at once a letter to the Minister of the Navy, for I just found out that no one will be permitted on your raft except you, your wife, and the two students you invited. I just received the news from the navy base. It is all on account of safety measures. The navy doesn't want to be held responsible if something should happen to anyone while on the run. We have a junta government, you see, and they have to be very careful on account of the press blowing everything up."

"I understand that well enough," I said, "but at this time—it is almost eight o'clock. How can we get to the Minister of the Navy?"

"Señor, he is dining at my brother's house this very moment, and I shall take the letter directly to him."

I wrote the letter, and he rushed off. An hour later he called me on the phone and told me that the minister had granted him permission to be on the raft. "You must have said something very nice about me," he said.

"I just wrote that you were the only man I knew whom I would choose as companion on my voyage if I took one along."

"You said that?" he exclaimed. "I thank you very much. Do you know, Señor Willis, that I would gladly give you my hacienda if you would take me with you?"

"Perhaps the next time I go," I replied, laughing.

"Please take him up on that," Teddy whispered. "I always wanted to own a hacienda."

I could just imagine him standing on the shores of Spain when Columbus, Cortez, or Pizarro picked their companions. How he would have stepped forward with sword and plumed hat or in armor and offered his services!

The next day was the trial run as scheduled. We also wanted to work out the compass compensation—an important factor since the raft was of steel—and an officer of the base and a sailor with a walkie-talkie had come on board for this purpose. I had used the same compass in 1954 on my first raft voyage and before that in 1948, when Teddy and I almost went down in a West Indies hurricane on our sloop *Hold-together*. The tug took us out twenty miles, but there was no wind and therefore no point in letting the towline go. It was ideal for checking the compass however, and while the tug was making three slow, mile-long circles, continuously giving its heading to us over the walkie-talkie, the officer standing beside my compass jotted down our readings on the same course. The difference in the headings were later worked out on a chart and given to me. My compass incidentally was nearly perfect, meaning its deviation from the true magnetic was negligible.

I was lying in bed and listening to Teddy's labored breathing. She had had fever now for over two weeks but still went out every day into the fog and raw winds to see that I got everything I needed, running from shop to shop through miles of traffic. It was June and the middle of the winter in Lima, south of the equator. Since our arrival in Peru, we had not had a single day of sunshine, and in New York the winter had been long and exceptionally severe. I was afraid of what might happen to her after I left and wanted her to take it easy. But Teddy wouldn't give in. "I'll be all right after you're gone," she kept saying. "I'll go to the mountains and get some sun. I'll just lie there and soak it up. You are so long getting ready." I was afraid she would collapse completely the moment I was gone. I reached over and felt her pulse. She moved in her sleep. I lay there, listening to her laboring lungs. She tossed and turned toward me as if I could help her.

I got up and began walking up and down. The street lay dark, narrow, and gloomy beneath, everything wet from the drizzling fog. I would be gone for six, seven, or even eight months and have no news from Teddy. And she would not hear from me. No passing ship would report me, for my course would be far from shipping lanes, just as in 1954. She had done too much. Wild thoughts leaped through my mind—perhaps I should take her along. I had thought of it before, but remembering my 1954 voyage, I knew it couldn't be. Her heart might give out in the solitude—anything could happen out there. I could never forgive myself.

"Can't you sleep?" I heard Teddy's voice behind me. I turned around and saw her sitting up in bed.

"I woke up and walked up and down a little," I said.

"You should get all the sleep you can while you are on land."

"How do you feel?"

"All right. You know what I just dreamed?"

"What?"

"I saw you on the raft out at sea—all alone. It seemed to be far from land. There was sunshine all around, and I was talking to you. I liked that sunshine, believe me."

"Where were you?"

"I was right there—on the raft. I dreamed it just now before waking up."

I went to the night table and gave her some of the medicine for her throat and chest.

"You know, Teddy," I said then, "I just now had an idea—just now. I guess you gave it to me. Listen, you know about telepathy, don't you?"

"Yes . . . but nothing in particular."

"But you know how often we get each other's thoughts, don't you?"

"Yes, every day we do."

"If we could do that while I am at sea—something like that, communicate with each other, I mean."

"That would be something," Teddy said.

"I would only want to know if you are well. That alone worries me."

"I'll be all right, but you—what about you out there? It's you I am worried about."

"We ought to try it, Teddy."

"You mean try to get each other's thoughts?"

"Yes."

"Over thousands of miles?"

"The distance wouldn't mean anything—distance means nothing in electricity and in thought even less. Thought travels faster than anything, and thought is something definite just like electricity. That is known, and there can be no doubt about it. The point is to know how to make use of it."

"What an idea—if it only worked. But it couldn't, it couldn't." Teddy lay down again. "I don't see how. But don't you worry about me, I know I'll be all right. I'll get over this. All I need is sunshine. And now you go back to sleep."

I dressed and went down the corridor and the broad marble steps of the great hotel. It was a little after five o'clock. In the lobby they were at work already, rolling back the thick red carpet, cleaning and washing and moving chairs and tables. It was drizzling a bit, and on the Plaza in front of the hotel the equestrian statue of San Martìn looked dark and forlorn. This idea of mine, I thought, walking around the square, if it only worked a little—only a little ... People had practiced telepathy for thousands of years—all races, no matter in what stage of development. The Yogis, I had read, practiced it scientifically, at night when everything was quiet. Distance meant nothing. All primitive tribes knew about it. Generally the priests and witch doctors were the ones who practiced it. Getting someone's thoughts—everybody experienced it at some time. My trip would be hell otherwise, month after month and no news from Teddy. And she in the same fix. I at least would be busy. We'd had hundreds of examples of it, Teddy and I—every day almost, sometimes several times—and hardly paid any attention to it, just took it for granted. I went back to the hotel, made myself a cup of instant coffee, ate an orange, and took a taxi to Callao.

It kept going through my head all day. Science, not only metaphysical science, accepted telepathy as a fact, just like with reservations, premonitions, clairvoyance, hypnotism, mesmerism, and such —though, as with everything else, much of it was distorted by ignorance. It was all a matter of mathematics, of two and two makes four, with not a trace of the miraculous and no more out of the ordinary than an apple falling out of a tree. But one had to know how to practice it to get anywhere. One had to be relaxed, of course, and know how to concentrate. And who was ever really relaxed in our world of tensions? And who could really hold a thought for more than one second? It all depended on knowing how. Perhaps I could work out something. I certainly would try. Teddy would be receptive to my thoughts, I knew that. It just depended on me. They had all practiced it—the Romans, Greeks, Egyptians, and ancient Persians, all of them, even the Bible was full of it. They believed in forebodings, foretelling the future, and all that, and didn't make a move without it. Some voodoo priests from Haiti or some Yogi should be here to teach me. For that matter, there were enough witch doctors in the jungles of South America.

60

In the afternoon I went to Lima and had the postmaster stamp some envelopes for me to carry to Australia and mail from there—the world's first transpacific solo-raft-voyage mail. I had carried twelve letters on the *Seven Little Sisters* in 1954, commemorating my voyage from Callao to Pago Pago, American Samoa.

5

THE piers of the base were crowded with onlookers and the ships, from truck to deck, lined with blue-jackets. Crowds had come out from Lima—ambassadors, consuls, men of different embassies, and the officers of the U.S. Navy mission who had assisted me from the day of my arrival. I was ready to sail. It was two thirty in the afternoon, July 4, 1963.

A launch pulled the raft out of the slip and 'longside of the *Rios*, the big navy salvage tug which had taken me out for the trial run. Three sailors jumped down to the raft from its deck, and the tow-line was made fast. One of the sailors had a walkie-talkie, and they were to stay with me till I was turned loose the next morning about fifty miles off the coast.

The tow seaward began, slowly at first, for the harbor was crowded with boats. All the ships were beflagged and blowing their whistles—Callao, oldest port on the west coast of America, was giving me a great send-off.

I stood by the wheel as the raft plowed through the gray water. Fishing boats were coming in through the breakwater loaded with their catch, and oilskin-clad men were waving, while small boats followed in our wake and crowded close for a last look at my strange craft and perhaps at the equally strange *Navegante Solitario*.

The clouds hung low, almost down to the top of my mast, and the air was heavy, the wind raw and cold. I felt no joy at coming to grips with my big experiment of proving that I had conquered old age, for the picture of Teddy was before my eyes, standing at the end of the pier less than a mile behind me, a small frail figure huddled against the wind and waving a handkerchief, her face wet with tears.

"Oh, Bill," she had said, "shall I go to dinner tonight with Dell? She wants me to. She's going to drive me back to the hotel and wants to be with me all day and then wants me to sleep in her house, so I wouldn't be alone. What shall I do? I don't want to stay with anybody today—I want to go right back to the hotel and—and..." Her face was quivering, fighting back tears.

"Lie down and cry, I know. Do that, do that, Teddy," I said and added, "and don't forget: I'll be in touch with you all the time —you know what I mean." Then we parted.

We were at sea. The big tug was wallowing ahead, big as a battleship. The grayness of sea and sky was dense, almost like a solid, and visibility was less than a mile. Hour after hour went by. At dusk I went forward and tied a lantern to the jibboom. A powerful floodlight already lighted up the stern of the *Rios*. Night was upon us. The three sailors, one hugging the walkie-talkie, lay forward on deck huddled in pea jackets and half under their blankets. I sat aft by the wheel, my knees drawn up to my chin.

Hours went by. Bound for Australia at last. The day before I had cleared the raft for Sydney. Suddenly I was awake. The raft was shaking violently and then lifted high into the air. It remained a few awful moments on the height, then began to sink and sink. The sea around us seemed to be dropping away, and I had the feeling that some tremendous catastrophe was happening. Sea and sky seemed to have lost their cohesion and be in a state of disintegration. The sinking had stopped, and the raft was rising again—higher and higher. It was incredible. There was no wind, and a strange silence lay on the water. I looked towards the *Rios* and saw that she was deep

63

below us, as on the very bottom of the ocean. The sailors were hanging on, white in the face. We rose and fell a few times more, though not to such heights; then the strange agitation ceased. I went forward and checked the towline and found it all right.

A while later an excited voice came from the walkie-talkie, asking if we were all right, and then told us that we had been in the grip of a tidal wave caused by an earthquake originating directly beneath us, and that Lima and Callao had been shaken to their foundations. Later we were told that the people had rushed out into the streets expecting another tremor, fearing it might bring the city down in ruins. They still remembered the big earthquake of a few years before which had originated in the same spot off the coast and leveled whole towns and villages for miles in one of the greatest disasters in Peruvian history. This time there had been no damage to the city, however, and no further tremor was expected. So Teddy no doubt was all right, but she would worry a bit when she found out that the raft had been right above the upheaval. The *Rios*, we were also told, had had a harder time of it than we, having almost turned over. The shocks had begun exactly at 12:45 A.M.

A gray dawn emerged almost imperceptibly out of the night. The three sailors were asleep in their blankets, even their heads covered, for the night air on the coast was supposed to be deadly for the lungs. The sea rose and fell with bleak regularity. The *Rios* labored ahead, unwieldy, big with its many turrets and booms, its black smoke mingling with the somber sky. Soon they would let go and I would be alone and bound for Australia. Few thought I would make it. It did seem impossible this morning in the gray dawn. Was it all a dream I had dreamed and now had awakened from? The whole world had taken me seriously, and now I was on a raft, had water and food on board and two little shipmates, and was on my way.

It was brought fully home to me what I was setting out to do, and I could not help but look at myself—at the motives and urges behind me. I went back to my earliest boyhood and from there to my very roots, before the breathing began, and then beyond, into my ancestry. I roamed into the dim spheres of prehistoric Europe and Asia, and finished by saying to myself and then to all men as if in justification: If this is folly, it is your folly also. But it is no folly, only a dream that cries for fulfillment. We are all dreamers on this earth and by the nature of our oneness have the same dreams, foolish ones and sound ones, but only a few men go on to make them come true or have the courage to go down trying. Teddy understands, and that alone matters.

Later the three sailors and I sat together beside the cabin for what little shelter it gave, since the wind was penetrating, and wet and spray came over the bow.

"*Mal tiempo,*" one of them said, staring ahead.

No one spoke for a while, then another sailor said in English, "Bad time of the year."

All three looked at me, their dark eyes probing. They couldn't understand why I wanted to go alone. "I should have been on my way six weeks ago," I said.

"You will have storms," the one who had spoken last remarked.

I nodded, thinking of the western Pacific. "*Es nada,*" I said. "A seaman goes to the sea, storms or calms, alone or with others. *Asì la vida.*" (Such is life.)

"And you are really seventy years old?"

"Seventy is right."

"My father is an old man, and he is only fifty-two."

"A man of fifty-two is a mere child," I almost snapped, and all three broke out laughing. The one who had spoken was twenty-five and the others twenty and twenty-two.

El Viejo del Mar (the Old One of the Sea, a name given me by the Lima newspapers), he has no sense, they thought. I could see it in their eyes.

It had always been impossible for me to think in terms of age, and I often wondered, as I saw the years go by and the world change and people grow old and sick, why I should remain as I was.

Was it my way of life—my way of thinking? Never a day of real tiredness to warn me that it was time to slow up and square off for the armchair or just puttering around; never a let-up in energy, physical or mental, and in zest for life. And that explains the shock I suffered when I felt myself breaking up. How I had taken myself to task for a miserable weakling and then fled into the hills of California, vowing I wouldn't come out till I was strong again!

An hour later, at eight thirty in the morning, the *Rios* stopped her headway, and the raft slowly drifted toward her. Her poop was lined with photographers and reporters of the Lima press. The raft was still a dozen yards or so away from the heavily rolling ship when I became worried, for if we bumped against her we would be damaged; certainly the projecting jibboom would be bent or broken. Before leaving Callao, I had spoken to the captain of the *Rios* about this and asked him to lower a boat to take the sailors off after they let go the towline, and he had agreed. I shouted again and again, but no one on deck moved, and we came closer and closer. Then we smashed together.

"Captain," I now roared at the top of my voice, looking up at him standing on the bridge and calmly gazing down, "one more bump, and you'll have to take me back to Callao for repairs. The whole press can see what you're doing!"

There was action now, and after a few more smashes the *Rios* pulled away and lowered a boat. We now let go the towline, and my sailors jumped into the boat. I was alone on my raft. I hoisted the mainsail and mizzen, and took the wheel. The *Rios* had turned about and was astern, her afterdeck crowded with sailors and men of the press taking their last pictures. Farewell shouts drifted over the water. A long-drawn, droning toot hovered in the air and died away.

"*Adiós, amigos!*" I shouted into the wind. The *Rios* was heading back for Callao.

The sea had come up considerably and was full of whitecaps. Heavy clouds darkened the sky. The raft rolled as if possessed and sat low in the water, and I threw some sacks with vegetables, which I knew I wouldn't need, overboard to bring her up, but it helped little, and water kept coming over. In the afternoon I lowered the mainsail and hoisted the jib; I also put a reef in the mizzen. Kiki cried now and then and looked beseechingly at me, as the day advanced and the atrocious jolting continued. No doubt she was asking me to take her back to Teddy. Aussie was crouching in a sheltered spot among the piled-up provisions, his eyes closed but alert. My two carrier pigeons were snug in their little wooden cage in the cabin and didn't seem to mind being at sea. Now and then they pecked at the cracked corn or took a sip of water. The next morning, as I had promised their owner, I would take the cage on deck, open it, and set them free. One was a female who had been sitting on eggs and was therefore expected to fly back at once.

> Logbook entry, July 8, 1963
> D.R. long: 79° west
> D.R. lat: 11° south
> Course: northwest

Sky thickly overcast. Fairly high sea. Wind southeast. Raft laboring heavily. Impossible to stand on deck without holding on. Water spurting up between planks and through the bamboo. The split bamboo with which I covered the planks in Callao keeps the raft from being completely awash in this kind of weather. Temperature at seven was 60 degrees. So far haven't seen the sun.

Kiki and Aussie were in good condition after a two-day fast. I had them both tied up so they wouldn't be washed overboard. They weren't a bit afraid of the sea, however, and sometimes stood with their forefeet on the board I nailed to the edge of the raft, gazing into the foam streaking past and almost touching their noses, but

67

ready to jump back when a wave threatened to come over. Occasionally they got drenched but didn't seem to mind.

I sent my first message two hours after sunset last night, giving
my dead-reckoning position and saying everything was well. If someone picked it up, I knew Teddy would be notified. My transmitter
was operated by turning two handles which activated the generator;
then I let go with one hand and tapped out the message with the
other. Since I wasn't a trained radio operator, I first wrote down
the message on a piece of paper—vertically, one letter to each line,
and beside it the Morse-code equivalent. While cranking with one
hand, I then tapped away, copying one line of code after another.
The whole operation, on account of the cranking, was really a two-
man job. My call letters were Salvita III and my wave length 8364
kilocycles.

I had baskets with fresh fruit on deck but grated a raw potato
and ate it mixed with a chopped onion and lemon juice for supper.
This was my idea of something highly antiscorbutic. Then I opened
a can of beans for something more substantial.

The raft was not sailing nearly as fast as I expected, and I realized
that I was in for a long voyage—most likely six or eight months,
since my sailing distance would be approximately eleven thousand
miles. I had decided not to shave, and gray whiskers were sprouting
out, reminding me I was no longer the youngster of 1924 when I
had raised my last crop—a long time for a face to lie fallow. I had
been in Alaska then, fishing for salmon and prospecting. Alaska was
real frontier country in those days with some of the 1898 Klondike
sourdoughs still left. Klondike Annie was also still around—in Juneau
at the end of an uphill street and really the last rose of summer.
Some of the girls said she had been old already when she left the
Barbary Coast in San Francisco to try her luck at the northern
diggings.

On the 1954 raft voyage I shaved every day, only omitting it in
bad weather. I think it had been an instinctive clinging to one of

the customs of civilized life in a now almost fantastically primitive existence.

Kiki amazed me. She seemed to be absolutely fearless, standing with her forefeet at the very edge of the raft and leaning halfway over the side, gazing into the foam, the tip of her tail moving slowly back and forth as if she just had spied something amid the shadows trying to scurry away from her. Little did I dream when I first saw her in a cage in the animal shelter in New York that she would so quickly adapt herself to the rugged life on a raft. Teddy had cried when she said good-bye to her on sailing day. "You must bring her back, whatever you do," she said. "And you must be kind to her. You must always talk to her no matter how busy you are. And you must stroke her and keep her purring and watch that her nose is always wet. She has the cutest and wettest nose I ever saw on a cat, and you must keep it so."

Logbook entry, July 10, 1963
D.R. long: 80° 11′ west
D.R. lat: 10° 45′ south
Course: northwest

No sun and am still navigating by dead reckoning. This morning found a large diving bird among the banana leaves covering the top of the cabin. It was asleep, and when I came near, lazily opened one eye, then closed it again. To judge by the mess it made it must have been on the roof all night. Perhaps it took the raft for a Peruvian guano carrier. Had little sleep since leaving Callao but feel good.

I had become aware of a sense of power as I overcame one difficulty after another. The little worries of life had all fallen away, washed off by the even flow of the sea which now covered all my visible earth. It meant that I was becoming used to life on a raft again and the solitude of the sea, and that I felt the elements had accepted me. The period of transition from life on land, where I had

69

lived for almost ten years, to that on the sea was over. I was really on my way. There was only Teddy now to worry about.

I had kept the American flag on my masthead since leaving Callao, just to see its bright colors fluttering in the wind and to cheer me up, but today took it down, rolled it up and put it in my suitcase with my shore clothes to protect it against mildew. It was the same flag that had waved from my masthead during the voyage of the *Seven Little Sisters* and had lain since my return from Samoa in a trunk in a warehouse in Manhattan, together with my sextant, compass, and cameras. Most of our more valuable goods lay in warehouses, for that matter, scattered here and there over America. Occasionally Teddy complained and said, "I don't know if I'll ever have my own home with you," to which I always replied, "Remember that when a man has built his house and the last nail is driven in, it means he has driven the first nail into his coffin—into his and that of his wife. We aren't ready for that yet, are we?"

> Logbook entry, July 12, 1963
> D.R. long: 80° 35′ west
> D.R. lat: 9° 3′ south
> Course: northwest by west

Night blustery with almost gale-force gusts. Solid mass of clouds in the morning and continuing wind. Heaviest weather so far. Temperature dropped to 59 degrees during night.

I still had to get used to the jolting and laboring of the raft. Its motion was violent and continuous and quite different from the action of a boat, and therefore it put a great strain on me to retain my balance. To get around the deck I sometimes had to be quite an acrobat.

Life on a fore-and-aft rigged sailing boat is a lot easier and more comfortable. There it is mainly a question of sitting it out—in the cockpit or even below in the cabin. Nearly all the necessary work can be done in the cockpit, such as hoisting and lowering the sails, reefing, and, of course, steering. A well-built and properly rigged boat often holds its course for one, two, and even three thousand miles without a hand touching the wheel or tiller. And there are automatic steering devices these days to make it still easier for the lone voyager or a small crew. On a square-rigged raft one has the sheet, tack, and the braces to handle, and the steering has to be done standing, since it requires considerable strength which cannot possibly be applied while sitting. A device for automatic steering would therefore be out of question, since it would have to be operated by power.

When a fore-and-aft rigged ship, such as all our yachts are, goes into the wind, the boom swings over to the other side, and it continues to make its way. The man may be in the cockpit or asleep in the cabin at the time, only to find out when he comes on deck that his boat is on the other tack with no harm done. When a square-rigged raft goes into the wind, a maneuver requiring exact timing and considerable hauling, besides much running around, is necessary to handle the sheet, tack, and braces as well as the steering to bring it back on its course. I knew very well that a square-rigged raft should have at least a three- or four-man crew, but having successfully and against all the advice of experienced seamen sailed the *Seven Little Sisters* for a record voyage across the Pacific in 1954, I had decided to do it again. It should again be a test of endurance, of continuous labor, speed, and alertness from the moment of sailing to dropping my anchor wherever it might be. I also knew that I would have to go for days and weeks with very little and even no sleep, depending on the weather, and often only have time to gulp down a hastily opened can of soup. The *Kon-Tiki* raft, I knew, had six men, and Eric de Bischop, the French navigator, on his two fore-and-aft rigged rafts had five, which enabled them to divide the day into three watches. The ancient Peruvians, sailing their rafts along the coast of South America, also had large crews.

Already in the first moments of my decision to build another raft,

71

I had the idea of calling it the *Age Unlimited*. This should express my rebirth to health. But why go alone? I had been asked again and again. To me the real test of the voyage was the solitude and all it implied: man on his own, depending solely on himself under all conditions, with no one near except his Creator, and every fiber—physical, mental, and spiritual—put to the test. I had been through it for 115 days in 1954 and, though near disaster more than once, had never felt so keenly and gloriously alive. For this I longed again. To go with others, even with only one man, would in my eyes have watered down the expedition to a routine job, even to drudgery. I also intended to keep a careful record of my physical and mental reactions, to bring back if possible something of value—not only for the elderly or so-called senior citizens but also for men in their prime, and above all for our youth whose physical condition has been the object of so much concern in recent years.

> Logbook entry, July 14, 1963
> D.R. long: 83° 42' west
> D.R. lat: 8° 40' south
> Course: northwest

Discovered a crack in both my rudders where the tiller part comes out from the blades. At closer investigation found that the two rods which form the tiller are made of thin tubing instead of solid iron as I had thought. Serious matter since I have neither the tools nor the material to make repairs. Also would be difficult if not impossible to do anything while the raft is in the water, for seas are breaking continuously over the stern. Approximately 500 or 600 miles from Callao, and there is no chance of turning back against the wind and current. Nearest land is Punta Aguja about 225 miles north-northeast.

I had been eating a lot to keep going, even eating nights. The night before I devoured two cans of baked beans and fifteen or sixteen bananas and drank two cans of evaporated milk, yet still felt hungry.

The weather continued stormy, and the raft was having a hard time of it, crashing and tumbling through the seas like an empty drum dragged behind a steamer. The weather side was taking seas almost continuously, and the mainsail was wet from spray halfway up to the yard. I hadn't seen the sun yet and was still navigating by dead reckoning. Handling the ropes and other gear kept me busy, and my arms felt as if pulled out of their sockets.

Logbook entry, July 15, 1963

After thinking it over, decided to run into Guayaquil and have the rudders rebuilt or others put on. Perhaps, if logs are available, will even consider building a balsa raft, for I am far from being satisfied with my trimaran. Changed course to northeast for coast of Ecuador.

I had dozed at the wheel when I was awakened by Kiki who was no longer tied up, racing around the raft as if she had gone crazy. She was fairly flying into the cabin and out again and with frantic leaps tried to get to the top. Turning on the flashlight, I thought that perhaps some monster like a giant octopus had come on board and was trying to catch her, when I heard a tremendous panting and blowing beside the raft and saw that the water was full of large porpoises tumbling about, their bodies bathed in streams of flames in the phosphorescent sea. Now everything became clear. Kiki, who had been staring into the water for days and had never seen anything to frighten her, must have thought these monsters had risen from the depths to get her. Aussie, on the contrary, still tied up, was sitting calmly at the edge of the raft and watching them, seemingly not interested. Coming from Callao and raised in the open with snorting bulls, braying jackasses, devil-eyed goats, sheep, and dogs, he was used to weird sounds and sights.

It had rained a little last night, and I hurriedly made a chute from a sheet of corrugated tin left over from the roof of the cabin but

73

caught only a few quarts. In the morning I heated it and gave myself a good soaping down, the first one. Then I made a bundle of my dirty clothes and let it trail in the sea for a few hours. Clothes once exposed to seawater never dry again completely on account of the salt they absorb, even if all day out in the sun, and nights become quite damp, almost wet.

The raft was rolling from beam to beam at its regular rate, smashing its sides into the sea as if it wanted to pitch the masts out of their sockets and overboard. They always fetched up with a shock that jarred the whole raft and made me wonder how it could hold together. The rolling reminded me of a day when off the Horn as a boy. We had been rolling for days in tremendous seas, and it was almost impossible to lie in the fore-and-aft bunks. "Nail your seaboots to the bulkhead before you lie down," a sailor said to me. "Then stick your feet into them. That'll keep you in your bunk. That's the way to do it."

"And when they call all hands?" I asked timidly.

"Oh," he replied, "then you just tell the mate to wait a while, because you're not quite ready." By this time I knew he was spoofing, for I could just imagine the mate bursting into the forecastle with a rope's end or even a belaying pin and dragging me out by head or heels if I wasn't on deck within ten seconds after being called.

> Logbook entry, July 16, 1963
> Long: 84° 38′ west
> Lat: 7° 10′ south
> 220 miles from Punta Aguja

Sun came out this afternoon and took four sights and worked them out. Guayaquil out of the question—have not made any easting, merely drifted north pushed by the wind, heavy seas, and the Humboldt Current. If I continue, would most likely sail into the Galápagos Archipelago, be caught by the northward-setting currents among its islands, and finally be marooned in

74

the calms north of the equator from which escape might be impossible. The only thing I can do is go back on my original course, keep my eyes on the rudders, and if possible, work out a way to strengthen the defective parts. After clearing the Galápagos, have appr. 3,000 miles of open sea to the Marquesas, and if the rudder situation becomes hopeless, have to land on one of the islands of that group.

Another misfortune befell me when my transmitter stopped working. I hadn't expected much from it, since I never thought it was rigged up right in Callao. When originally installed by the Marconi people in New Jersey, it had worked perfectly. But even under ideal conditions, its maximum range had hardly been over five hundred miles, and Teddy, well aware of this, would not have expected any messages to come through.

I was sitting aft by the wheel and listening to the seas pounding the raft. It was long after midnight. The wheel jerked violently as the seas smashed into the rudders, and sooner or later they would break under this treatment. Well, I wouldn't get excited about it. I stared into the darkness, into the black sky and almost coal black sea, and thought of the *Seven Little Sisters* making her way over this same course almost ten years ago. I saw myself lying on deck, crazed by almost unbearable pain in the pit of my stomach, at another time imploring the empty sky after losing most of my water supply, and on still another occasion holding my arm high above my head to keep from bleeding to death and finally stitching up the severed artery. I had come through it all and spent some of the happiest hours of my life on that lonely voyage. And so it would be now, no matter what happened—whether the rudders broke or not, I felt certain.

I believe that he who has been in lonely seas will go back for the peace he knows he will find. But it is not his for the mere asking. Each day, each moment, must by the nature of his being be one of suffering, for he has to tear out what binds him to his kind and

75

above all to his father and mother, his wife or child—the blood anchors which hold him to time and space—and stand naked and shorn in anguish. At last, if it is so willed, he may gaze into the solemnity of silence and see himself. If he becomes frightened at his own smallness, he screams for help until he becomes mad. Then the revelation is not for him.

The sea was quite heavy today and spurted up through the split bamboo, as through a sieve. There were a lot of birds around, no doubt coming from the Galápagos. Sometimes they flew listlessly along, as if tired, then suddenly became rigid and sped over the water straight and swift like arrows. Sometimes they dropped to the surface in fluttering, screaming masses to pick up something not visible from the raft, perhaps a school of anchovy. Others sped along over the waves, rising and falling evenly with them, often deep in the troughs and banking continuously to keep from being engulfed. Some indulged in jubilant flights as if excited to ecstasy by the wild waves tumbling beneath and the consciousness of their own mastery. Many were frigate birds, large black birds with saber-narrow and crooked wings disproportionately long, which made them look like aerial spiders. When scanning the sea for prey, they soared high, hanging like crosses nailed to the sky, then dropped suddenly and, when near the surface and maneuvering to pick up their prey, went into series of contortions that made one think their wings would break off.

I had been thinking a lot of Teddy. How was she getting along? I saw her before me almost constantly, in New York now and picking up her old life again while all her thoughts were in the Pacific. Fortunately she had sound nerves and was not given to idle worrying, nor did she believe in omens, and so the earthquake incident would have been forgotten by now. I should really have concentrated on contacting her, as I had told her I would, but the nights had been as stormy as the days, and it would have been hard to fix one's thoughts, under the windy sky and with the blows of the seas pounding the raft in one's ears. I wanted a calm night for that with a clear sky—one of those silent nights as poets called them. I knew of course that I couldn't expect proof of anything, but I did know that, somehow, if I persisted, there would come a feeling of her nearness.

6

THE weather had been warm, and I had taken off my clothes, poured a pail of seawater over my head, and scrubbed myself with a stiff brush which Teddy had bought for me to scrub the floor of the cabin with—occasionally, she had pleaded. Afterward I stretched out on deck and warmed my sun-starved skin until a ton or so of cold Humboldt Current, fresh and unpolluted from the Antarctic, came over the side, lifted me up like a babe, and deposited me not too gently against the cabin.

For supper that day I cooked a pot of vegetable soup—cabbage, potatoes, onions, and carrots, everything chopped up fine to make it boil quickly on my little primus stove. I also tossed in a liberal dash of cayenne pepper, a few cloves of garlic, and caraway seed. A ham bone would have made it a dish fit for a king, but I had taken no meat along, figuring I would catch fish. A lot of my vegetables had spoiled already, but I hoped my potatoes and onions would last, especially potatoes since they were my antiscurvy preventive even more so than my canned lemon juice. I also had ten dozen fresh limes, packed in sawdust to keep them for a month or so, and two quarts of boiled lime juice, which was supposed to last well preserved the Peruvian way.

As I looked at the cartons of food in my cabin, I could not help thinking back to my 1954 voyage, when my main food consisted almost solely of raw rye flour mixed with a little water, the same flour which was used by the Indians in the high Andes. The monks in the Tibetan monasteries as well as the Himalayan burden carriers lived on similar flour, I learned later, also eating it raw. Besides this flour, I had a sticky raw-sugar product used by Peruvian and Ecuadorian Indians called *chancaça* which contained all the natural molasses. This meager diet had been supplemented by the fish I caught, but unfortunately during the last three thousand miles of the voyage I seldom caught one.

My first experience with a different diet was forced on me after I had left my frugal home and gone on board the *Henriette*, my first ship, among bearded and husky men with fists like hams and heavily muscled arms hanging down almost to their knees, chewing tobacco and roaring sea chanteys while hauling on the ropes. None of my mother's light cooking for this herculean crew. Three times a week our fare was pea soup and three times beans, always served thick as mush. The cook got everything back, with a curse or two and a warning of a kick in the pants, if a spoon wouldn't stand up in it. And three times a week it was salt beef and three times pork, while on Sundays we were given canned meat. One meal a day was all, and sometimes I was hungry enough to cut a strip of leather from the rigging and chew it. Besides the daily thick soup, each man got a potato or two while they lasted, always served in the jacket. In the morning, even if we had worked all night aloft, there was nothing but an atrocious buckwheat cereal which no one ever touched and of course hardtack, or "belaying-pin bread" as we called it, since it took a hammer or belaying pin to break it. Evenings we occasionally had a hash of meat and potatoes left over from noon, mixed with ground ship's biscuit and perhaps, while they lasted, an onion. But the food must have been right for that sort of life, and there must have been enough, for no one ever complained of sickness. The idea of the ship owners seemed to have been to keep us as hungry and lean as wolves, fit to climb to the royal yard ten times during a watch if necessary. That had been long ago, but on calm nights I sometimes saw myself a boy again, climbing aloft clearing yard after yard till I was lost in the darkness above the ship and so high I thought that by reaching out I could almost touch the stars.

For a number of days I had felt a bit stuffy around the middle and sluggish mentally, and I drank some seawater—about half a mugful, approximately the equivalent of an average cup. Since I always believed in its medicinal as well as nutritive value, it went down easily enough, and I made up my mind to drink it every day from then on. My technique of drinking was to pour it quickly down my throat and then inhale quickly a few times with open mouth till the gall and salt taste had disappeared.

As I watched the seagulls around me today, I wondered whether the two pigeons which I had released on the second morning after leaving Callao arrived safely in Lima. They had been given me by a breeder of carrier pigeons, and following his instructions, I set them free on the second morning. I had kept them in the cabin but, an hour before the appointed time, put the cage on deck to get them used to the air and sight of the sea. They had been trained on north and south flights along the coast of Peru and had never flown over water. At nine o'clock sharp, when it was fully light, I fastened a string to the door of the cage and took up a position with my movie camera. Then I pulled the string. One bird came out as soon as the door opened, raised its head, lifted its wings, and took off. The other followed. They flew close together, rising quickly and heading in the direction of land, then turned and circled the raft. After circling twice, they disappeared among the clouds, flying straight east as if they had looked at my compass and chart.

Kiki and Aussie were becoming friendly. Aussie had often tried to snuggle up to her, expecting her to take the place of his mother, from whom he had been so unceremoniously parted, but Kiki remained aloof and sometimes hissed frightfully when he came too close to her. All that seemed changed now. Last evening, when checking the deck for the night, I found them both huddled in an empty carton as close together as they could get, Aussie pressing against the thickly furred Kiki for warmth. It had been another raw and dreary day for little Aussie to be all alone on the wide sea without a friend, seeing nothing but the gray combers moving past and hearing the endless thundering of the waves against the raft. I took another look at them later and saw Kiki licking Aussie, like a mother cat its young, and Aussie, though pulled almost out of shape, submitting and seemingly in heaven.

It had given me a lift also, I think, and after the deck was clear and the ropes hanging from the cleats ready for instant use, I sat down beside the wheel and started to sing some of the old songs I knew, taking up a habit again acquired on the *Seven Little Sisters* nine years before. When I got tired, I took out my brand-new harmonica. I had never played a harmonica, but Teddy had bought it and suggested I try during the voyage. I was just managing to coax some sort of tune out of it when the raft threatened to run into the wind, and I had to grab the wheel. I hung on to the harmonica, however, and kept on practicing, steering with the other hand and both my knees while seas came over and washed my feet. When I got tired, I sang again and afterwards took another look at my little shipmates lying side by side in the carton. They opened sleepy eyes at the intrusion of my flashlight in their dreams and listened patiently when I told them that everything would be all right again, that life on the raft wouldn't always be as tough as now, and that one of these days the sun would come out and warm all the stiffness out of their bones.

The night continued cold and miserable with occasional rain and strong gusts of wind, and at last, after a long spell at the wheel and lowering and raising centerboards trying to get the raft to behave, I thought of a bottle a kind lady friend of Teddy's had handed down to me from the pier in Callao at the very moment of letting go from

81

the dock. She had almost fallen into the slip in her eagerness. "It's a very special Swedish punch, and you should keep it for a cold and bad night when you really feel low," she had said, smiling. "But be sure to heat it before drinking to get the full flavor out of it." I had the right setting for it now—a cold and miserable night—and opened it. After one smell I decided that it needed no heating.

In the morning, as soon as it was daylight enough to see what I was doing, I fed Kiki and Aussie. They slept in a large crate lashed to the forward part of the cabin in which I kept a lot of my stores and gear, but sometimes I let Kiki sleep in the cabin, since she was very clean. She had begun to eat what I gave her with relish which was all canned food until I could catch fish. At first, no doubt, she had longed for the tidbits Teddy used to bring back to her from the hotel dining room wrapped in a napkin. She had lost a little weight by now and no longer was *gordo* (fatty), as the hotel people and journalists in Lima called her. Aussie, only four months old, wanted mainly milk and often. He slept a lot, was used to sleeping outdoors, and always found the smallest hole on the raft to crawl into, and seemed to be quite capable of taking care of himself no matter what lay ahead.

> Logbook entry, July 29, 1963
> Long: 93° 46' west
> Lat: 03° 6' south
> Course: west-northwest

I was now about 180 miles southwest of the island of Isabella, largest of the Galápagos group. The first part of my voyage lay behind me, getting away from the coast and across the Humboldt Current and the danger of being pushed into the Galápagos, to be either wrecked on the rocks or driven by the strong northward currents into the windless levels of the equator beyond.

Twenty-five days out, and I had sailed approximately fourteen hundred miles, allowing for my zigzag course. The weather had been stormy throughout, and my rudders had me worried. I had worked on them a number of times already but was limited in what I could do, for everything broke again in the endless smashing of seas. What made it worse was that the steering gear couldn't function right with defective rudders; I had to bring the wheel hard over now to move the rudders twenty degrees, which more than doubled the work of steering and in case of sudden squalls could become a serious problem. Perhaps I would finally have to steer with my centerboards and sails alone, which on a cumbersome raft couldn't be very dependable among the islands and atolls of the western Pacific. Anyway, I thought I could write off the Galápagos now as my first important milepost passed and change course to straight west as soon as the wind let up a little and the sea went down. It had been blowing with near gale force for over a week, and I realized that the boys at the navy base had certainly known what they were talking about warning me of bad weather.

Today I saw a dolphin (fish) chasing a flying fish near the raft where I could watch almost every move. It had always given me a thrill to watch these five-feet-long tigers of the sea tear through the waves, a streak of foam showing their path. They were all speed and intensity, and their enormously high and thin foreheads, shaped like the blade of a shipwright's ax, throw the water up in spurts. Their whole bodies, from head to evenly forked tail, also were thin, resembling a slab split from the side of a log. Flying fish, most elusive of prey, often did a complete turn while in flight to shake them off. It wasn't easy and sometimes took many flights, for the dolphin hunts with wide open eyes and can see where the flying fish comes down for a second or two to wet its wings. This it must do to fly again. Before long the hapless fish becomes tired, and its flights shorten, and with a final rush the killer's jaws close over it. It is swallowed headfirst. I caught a dolphin with four full-grown flying fish all caught shortly before in the stomach, lying side by side in a tight bundle as if packed by a careful hand. Dolphins, like greyhounds, have small stomachs.

More deadly to the flying fish are the spidery winged frigate birds. There are more of them, and since they soar high like eagles, little escapes their telescopic sight. After spotting a school of flying fish, perhaps by the streak of foam of a pursuing dolphin, the frigate bird hurtles down and, in a series of fantastic banks, brakes its descent, its eyes on the prey. Then begins the maneuver to pick up the flying fish, which in frantic fear to escape the pursuing dolphin, continuously changes course. It becomes a race of which shall get it. Often the frigate bird picks it up in front of the dolphin's already opened jaws. Frigate birds seemingly devour fish after fish, which in these waters are from six to eight inches long. Proof of the enormous destructiveness of sea birds to fish life is seen in the mountains of guano on the islands off Peru and Chile, their ancient rookeries.

The birds around me, frigate birds, boobies, and ordinary gulls, made their homes on the nearby Galápagos, generally flying against the wind in the morning to reach their hunting grounds quickly and in the evening returning with full bellies and tired beating of wings with the wind. Watching them day after day, sometimes able to distinguish certain ones by their markings, I was led to believe that no matter how far from land, each mile of the ocean was patrolled by birds, and even that each section had its own hunters. Often I saw the same birds in the vicinity of the raft in the morning, watched them move away in their search for food till they became mere dots on the horizon, then disappear from sight, to come back in the evening from another direction. The birds nearly always flew in pairs.

From the moment the sun lighted up the sea until it went down, the struggle for survival went on. Hunting continued even at night, for I could hear birds crying to each other on the dark sea while searching for their prey—perhaps shrimp or cuttlefish or such that had come up from the depths. Or I could see, when the moon was full, their silhouettes streak black across its silver disk. I also heard and saw the short, convulsive struggles beside the raft when a shark had seized a careless dolphin or bonito.

I had a real Peruvian dish for supper—chopped onion and raw fish, soaked in lemon juice and a little olive oil and spiced with garlic. In Peru they use sea bass for this national delicacy, while on the raft it was dolphin, fully as good. The dolphin that I refer to throughout is a fish and is not the much larger porpoise generally called a dolphin, which is a mammal and belongs to the whale family.

My provisions were all staples—beans, lentils, rice, flour, oatmeal, dehydrated potatoes, dehydrated soups, lemon juice, prunes, raisins, honey, butter, ship's biscuit, and shortening for frying fish. I also had condensed and evaporated milk. My water was in three wooden barrels lashed to the portside of the cabin, each one holding fifty-five gallons, enough for eight months or more in case of necessity. I intended of course to catch rainwater also.

A flying fish had landed early in the dawn. At first I wanted to divide it between Kiki and Aussie, who hadn't had one all night for I found no telltale fins on deck, but then I thought I might catch a dolphin with it, and we would all have a good breakfast. I put it on the hook and threw the line out. I never used more than forty or fifty feet of line on account of the sharks, which generally appeared as if by magic when I began fishing and often took my fish from the hook before I could get it on board.

A dolphin struck the bait like a bullet, and I pulled in. It was a full-grown male with a battle-ax head, which hurled itself against the pontoon in almost suicidal frenzy till the hook tore out of its jaws and it got away. Nothing could have stopped it except a shark cutting it in half. I admired it too much to be sorry I had lost it, but Kiki and Aussie, who had watched me pull it in and expected it to come on deck, wondered what had become of it.

A little later I saw a dolphin pursuing a flying fish make eight tremendous leaps, one after another, to keep it in sight. The fish, shining like a silver dart in the morning sun, kept changing its course in midair, but its flights were becoming shorter. Suddenly a frigate bird banked down out of the clouds and with the usual acrobatics maneuvered for a pickup. The flying fish dropped to the sea to escape this black phantom out of the air, and with a rush and burst of foam the jaws of the dolphin closed over it. The hunt was over. The frigate bird rose easily, like a rag tossed up into the wind, and a few minutes later was hanging motionless in the sky, almost a mile away, head down and eyes on the sea, like a thin black cross.

As mind and body became used to the work and solitude, an increasing sense of freedom came over me. The sea was bringing out what was necessary to survive. The world I had lived in, the companionship of my fellowmen, had become dim and appeared more and more like a dream through which I had wandered without having really been part of it. Now and then friendly faces loomed up out of the dimming haze, shining and speaking with gentle voices while what was petty and mean was forgiven as not important.

The sun was down and night falling—another day was coming to a close. The waves looked tired as they rose and fell, moaning some ancient lullaby of the deep. A few clouds stood forlorn in the sky, and a solitary white bird lifted itself from the somber-looking waves and with slow beat flew away into the dusk.

I had eaten little for supper and was sitting by the wheel which was lashed. Occasionally I got up to check the heading and see how we were doing and, if necessary, change the centerboards, raising or lowering them, each differently to make the best course, for my faulty rudders made accurate steering difficult if not impossible.

Time passed, and suddenly, as if she had come on board, I saw Teddy before me. I sensed that the time had come. Slowly I turned and faced back over the stern, toward New York. "Teddy ... Teddy ... Teddy ..." I called. "Can you hear me? Can you hear me, Teddy? I can see you clearly. I can see you, little girl. Yes, I can see you clearly. And you can see me too. I know you see me—I know ..."

Time didn't matter. I sat there on the raft making its way west-

86

ward and saw Teddy ailing and saw her weeping, and tears came to me also. "It will pass, Teddy," I said. "You will get strong again. I am all right—see, out here and sailing. Don't worry about me."

It was like a seeing and talking over thousands of miles, and there was no doubt in my mind that it had been a real meeting. A while later, I got up and went around the raft, pulling in a little on the tack and lowering the starboard centerboard a foot.

The sea had been quite heavy the last four days, and the raft rolled more than usual, and it seemed impossible to make more than forty-two miles a day. The wind was southeast, and I was steering west by south. I had been feasting on flying fish which had fallen on deck nights by the bucket. Since dolphins don't hunt nights, I thought that they had been washed on board while asleep. At daytime also the sea was full of them, perhaps because we were getting away from the Galápagos, and it was too far for most frigate birds and the divers to make a daily trip. There were still enough around, however, and I could see them plummeting down all around the horizon. The dolphins of course now had things their own way with no competition from the sky.

My day as usual began with a saltwater rubdown and a few loosening-up movements. There was little chance of neglecting them with my two little shipmates to remind me throughout the day how flexible the body should be.

The solitude had really closed down on me, for I began to hear voices—those of my mother and Teddy. On my 1954 voyage I had heard them only nights, but now I heard them in the daytime also and much more often. I heard them clearly and always speaking quietly and only one appeared at a time. The impression of face and body was quite distinct, and I took their appearance for granted and was never startled. They were always concerned about me and sometimes offered a gentle warning when I was on the point of doing something dangerous, like going overboard to work on the rudders.

They never contradicted me, only confirmed me in my decisions, and were always gentle and full of understanding. I considered their voices echoes of my innermost craving for companionship—even a form of communion with the two human beings who have had the greatest influence on my life. When they awakened me during the night, as they occasionally did, I was more definitely aware of them than otherwise, and the impression of their reality was so vivid that it took a few moments to realize that I was alone on a raft and thousands of miles from the nearest shore. Then invariably the knowledge of being so utterly alone came with a shock, followed by a definite feeling of having been unjustly abandoned by them. This always produced a sense of resentment.

A big moon was shining, and while I was on the weather side to slack away on the port brace, a swarm of flying fish rose out of the sea like a silver rain, struck me full, and fell on deck. There were a few dozen flapping around on the bamboo. Down I went on my knees, picking them up with both hands, when a sea came over, threw me against the water barrels, and washed most of them off again. Kiki and Aussie both were asleep, having eaten their fill already.

At dawn I had put a flying fish on the hook and thrown the line out. The half-grown dolphins which had made the underside of the raft their home had not left yet for their morning hunt and were ravenous. Four of them streaked to the bait. As I jerked the line in, several bit into the fish, but their mouths were too small to take it whole. Dolphins have very small mouths and tiny teeth. Just when I had the line 'longside to try another cast, a grown dolphin shot in like a torpedo and was hooked. I swung it on board. Kiki and Aussie, watching with great interest, jumped to the top of the cabin to be out of the way, knowing there would be a rough-and-tumble brawl all over the deck, with the chance of them getting smacked by the crazed fish.

88

For three days I had not been able to take a sight, since the weather had been stormy and sky full of clouds. My last sights, taken on August 4th, had put my position at longitude 99 degrees 24 minutes west and latitude 00 degrees 31 minutes south—just thirty miles south of the equator. Then it started to blow up strong, and before dark I had to lower the mainsail and put a reef in the mizzen. For three days I was driven north under a cloudy sky; then the wind slackened, and the seas began to go down. Throughout the storm there had been no sun, and I put my dead-reckoning position at 1 degree 10 minutes north latitude—seventy miles north of the equator. My farthest north, I hoped, thinking of the nearby doldrums with its calms, where a sailing vessel could be trapped for weeks. Then the wind shifted, and I headed southwest. After a day of light winds, it kept increasing till it blew with near gale force, and I scudded south, driving the raft for all I could to get back on my course. Two days later, it began to let up, but I could still make good time. On August twelfth I had a clear sky and worked out my position:

Logbook entry, August 12, 1963
Long: 105° 11′ west
Lat: 2° 14′ south

On the run south, sailing full before the wind and taking a chance of having the mainsail blown out of the boltropes, I had made the fastest time I had so far. While the raft was under this strain, which had the stays and rigging whining and the deck awash, two of my centerboards had broken off with the sound of explosions. Fortunately I had others. Six heavy iron sockets, forged in the Callao navy yard and bolted to the deck, kept the centerboards in place, but I used ropes also to hold them steady.

A friend of mine, a marine architect in City Island who incidentally later built the America's Cup winner *Constellation*, had told an old ship chandler that I would be in his shop to look around for extra rope and other gear I might have use for on the raft. When

I came in, he showed me his stock—Irish linen rope, white, smooth as silk, and very strong. I knew the price of linen rope and said I couldn't afford it. "You can!" the old man shrieked and marked the price down to fit my pocket and, after the deal was made, tossed in the same amount as a present. "You may need it," he had said. "I haven't seen the ship yet that had too much gear. You can't buy anything out there, you know." He knew the sea and had done some of the big salvage jobs on the New Jersey coast, made fortunes and lost them again. He also gave me two staysails, used but in good condition, besides turning buckles, shackles, blocks, and clamps as well as coils of marlin and rigging wire.

On a sunny and rather calm day, I had taken the two sails out of the bag and spread them out on deck to let the air and sun at them. I intended to cut them up for awnings, chutes for catching rainwater, and for patches. Both were in good condition and bore the name of a well-known sailmaker on City Island. One was of Egyptian cotton and had been made for a famous yacht whose owner had died. As I looked at them lying on deck, I thought it was a shame they should be jammed into a bag or be cut up for this or that, for to me sails were living wings made to stand full in the wind.

That night, while I was at the wheel and the stars were playing hide-and-seek with me over the top of the yard, I had an idea. I would make use of one of those sails. My mainsail, the one hanging from the yard, cleared the deck by a full eight feet, which allowed a lot of good wind to pass beneath without helping the raft. It had been a thorn in my flesh since the beginning and was due to a mix-up in the specifications. I would change that—I would take the larger of the two sails and hoist it in front of the mainsail and fasten it right down across the deck, just far enough away to clear it and so catch at least some of the wind that now was lost. I lashed the wheel, pulled the sail out of the bag, spread it out on deck, and measured the leeches. It would do. I would use the jib halyard for hoisting it and fasten the sheet and tack hard down across the fore-deck, giving it always the same set as the mainsail.

I was all on fire, for an extra sail would help me cut down the miles to Australia—still from eight thousand to ten thousand miles away, with my bad rudders most likely more—and, when dawn came to the sea, made a cup of tea and got busy. Everything had been worked out during the night, and with a few hauls the peak of the sail went up on the jib halyard. Then I brought sheet and tack across the deck, right down to the split bamboo. It billowed out at once and stood full in the wind with not a wrinkle on it, as if sewn for the spot. I doubted if it ever felt better on the mil-lionaire's yacht it had been made for. The old ship chandler must have had a premonition when he said, "Take it—you have no extra sails and may need it."

When I lowered the mainsail, the extra sail would go down also, of couse, the halyard taken off and put back on the jib. I watched the newcomer to my rigging all day and, checking my speed by tossing a piece of crumpled paper over the side, calculated that I gained perhaps two or three miles on a day's run.

Then I thought of using the other sail also. It was a beauty, hav-ing hardly been used, but was much smaller. There could be only one place for it—as an extra mizzen. It was almost exactly the same size. I climbed up on the mast, rigged up a block and halyard, and hoisted it aloft. It also stood as if made for the spot—the peak as high as the mizzen, the throat fast to the foot of the mast, and the other corner across the deck to the rail. Hanging six inches away from the mast, it didn't fill with dead air but drove as much as the mizzen. I had two extra sails now—extra miles—and the raft looked more like a ship, though was still a dancer and a roller.

For the first time on the voyage, I felt that I was really sailing and almost shouted for joy. Now I was surrounded by canvas curv-ing white and beautiful around me, every thread doing its work. Now the wind sang a happier song, and the sun shone brighter. It wasn't only the added mileage, which did not really amount to so much, but the joy of getting the most out of the wind. Ever since leaving Callao, I had been thinking of a better-designed raft with more sails, and made a few drawings which perhaps some time in the future I might make use of. But Australia first—sailing into Sydney Bay. But those miles still ahead, how slowly they dropped behind.

7

SOLITUDE chastens a man, for he sees himself in his true little stature, whether he wants to or not, when standing alone. What am I really doing out here? I asked myself now and then, and always answered: I am on a long and wide trail, a trail made by millions of dreams, and so I am not alone. How small I am and yet so bold—but how incredibly small.

In the woods, hills, or mountains, the solitude is gentle and not absolute. Each tree or blade of grass, each fragment of stone, is a living thing, gloriously near to you; and the distant peaks, around which the stars gather, and the rays of the sun are but temples where you worship even though miles away. But on the sea the solitude is a window opening into naked space. You see the sky and clouds and the evenly driven waves, but you are aware that they are only a mask to hide the emptiness of space behind; you are aware always that a few miles from you begins the region where man's mind can be destroyed by the gazing.

Logbook entry

Quite heavy sea. No sun. Raft rolling and hard to make way over deck. A few rain squalls in morning. Water coming over bow and sides. Still lying on port tack. Through the rain saw

93

a number of large whales cavorting like a flotilla of submarines
—sperm whales according to the angle of their spouts.

I missed Teddy, missed the quiet evenings in the cottage when
she used to read to me—she was a marvelous reader—or the long
walks along the canyons and across the hills through the purple sage,
and the clear nights when the coyotes yelled like demented Indians
on the war path. All that I missed. Then I thought smiling that I
hadn't paid this month's rent yet. That was one blessing out here—
no landlord to put you out. When the lord of the sea puts you out
here, he feeds you to the sharks.

Kiki came to be petted. She just seemed to know when I needed
her. She had found a daily addition to her diet—a little piece of dried
banana leaf from those on top of the cabin forever rustling in the
wind, probably to supplement her fish-and-canned-food diet with
something grown on the earth. Meekie did something similar on the
1954 voyage when nibbling at the sea moss that had grown on the
logs. Kiki also lapped up a little seawater now and then which Aussie
does regularly. They were both in wonderful shape without any
sign of sickness and, I know, wouldn't forgive me if I got sick and
neglected them. "What kind of a lone voyager are you?" they would
have asked and with their tails up walked away in disgust.

I had finished my last fresh limes and opened one of the two quart
bottles of boiled lime juice given me by two friends in Lima. The
boiling, I thought, had taken away only a little of the strength.
Besides these two quarts I had three cartons of lemon juice in small
bottles put up in California, so there was little danger of scurvy.

The weather had moderated considerably the last few days, and
I had a chance to do quite a bit of repair work. Things cropped
up every day that had to be done. The big problem was, of course,
the rudders. I had been using thin steel cables for lashing but with
only temporary success.

A number of dolphins had made their home beneath the raft
and seemed to have decided to stay with it, blow high, blow low,

in fair weather or foul. I hoped they would remain all the way to Australia, for I liked their company. Most of them were grown females with young ones from three to twelve inches long. There were also a number of half-grown ones, about two and a half to three feet, which came out at all times of the day from underneath to practice their leaps but hadn't the strength yet or the speed to run down flying fish. They always swam in groups of three and four for protection against the sharks. I saw one of them make a leap of twenty feet close to the raft, taking to the air on a rising sea. On a straight upward leap they reached four or five feet, while a grown dolphin could clear the surface as high as ten or twelve. When coming down, they often turned on the side and struck the water a smashing blow audible for a considerable distance. This I thought was used as a signal and also as a means of keeping the body hard as steel and streamlined for the fantastic speed necessary to run down flying fish.

In landing a grown dolphin that had taken the hook, the trick was to lift it out of the water just before coming 'longside, for if it had a chance, it would hurl and hammer itself against the raft until the hook was torn out with or without part of the jaw. A dolphin is perhaps the most gorgeous fish to look at when pulled out of the water. The body then is a blazing jade-blue mass, with golden and green overtones toward the silver-white belly, the whole encased in streams of glittering drops like a veritable robe of diamonds. Peruvians called them *dorados*, the golden ones.

I saw a few frigate birds and a white booby today. The booby was curious about the raft and flew over it between the mainmast and the mizzen. With its long thick neck and level held wings, attached well back on the body, it looked exactly like a miniature jet plane. Sometimes they dived straight down from a great height and, with wings folded back, smashed into the sea like stones; at other times they plowed in at a slant to pick up their prey.

The sea had been rough, and it was impossible to write in my log-book, and I thought of the feature writer of a Lima newspaper who had come to the hotel one night. He spoke good English, had been in the U.S. Navy, and said he wanted to come along on my voyage as the official chronicler. All Spanish expeditions had chroniclers, he explained. "If you don't take one, the full story of your voyage will never be told," he went on.

"What else would you do besides writing if I took you along?" I asked.

"That's all," he replied. "I ask you questions, and you answer, and I put everything down."

"How many questions would you ask during the day?"

"I would ask you every time I thought of something."

"What sort of questions would you ask?"

"Oh, mainly how the solitude affects you—a man of your age, you know. Don't you see the world would be very interested in that?"

"But there wouldn't be any solitude with the two of us on the raft," I retorted.

"There would be plenty—plenty enough for me, at least," he confessed with a grin.

"Have you ever been alone?" I asked.

"Me? No, never,"

"But you think you can take it?"

"With you, yes."

"And if I should fall overboard or get sick and die, you would be alone anyway."

He looked a little frightened for a moment, then smiled and said, "I wouldn't let you fall overboard."

"You would look out for me, wouldn't you—for the old man of seventy?" I asked.

"I certainly would," he said patronizingly.

"And who would do the cooking?"

"I don't know anything about cooking," he said sharply.

"How about washing the dishes and peeling potatoes?"

He made a grimace and shrugged his shoulders and was very disappointed when I turned him down. He came around almost every day afterwards, together with the paper's photographer, until the very moment of my departure, asking whether I had changed my mind.

Long before sunrise each morning, I knelt at the edge of the raft, scooped up water from the sea, and, tossing my head back, drew it up through the nose a number of times till the nasal passages were clear. Then I gargled the same way and worked a bit on my ears, as Kiki and Aussie did to keep them at top alertness. After that I put my face in a bucket of seawater and, while holding my breath, rolled my eyes to the left and then to the right. I repeated this for a few minutes. I also focused them on a point on the horizon and afterwards, as intently as I could, on something near me on the raft, though this was generally difficult on account of the rolling.

I kept a short line trailing from Kiki's collar as a sort of a restrainer—nights when the moon was out, the air warm, and flying fish fell on deck, and the flame-bathed bodies of the dolphins shot out like rockets from under the raft and set her blood tingling, so that she leaned dangerously far over the edge to watch them. Her usual hideout was in the stern of the kayak or just anywhere on top of the cabin among the banana leaves, from where she could overlook the deck and see if a flying fish had come on board or perhaps think she was in a jungle. Occasionally she got her leash all tangled up in some gear and, trying to extricate herself, put knot after knot into it until there was room for not one more. I had counted as many as twenty knots in her little lifeline. When totally helpless, she would let out a single plaintive meow—one that could be plainly heard. I knew at once by the sound what it meant and came running—or rather climbing. The moment I began untangling her, she was beside herself with gratitude and lavished her caresses on me with paws, body, tail, and tongue and loud purring. Around ten o'clock in the morning, she generally retired from the heat of the day after a last wrestling match with Aussie—they generally wrestled to a draw— and found a hiding place among my charts and plotting sheets. Aussie watched everything she did and learned fast. Occasionally she jumped on him, obeying some sudden impulse to battle or to caress, and pinning him to the deck seemed to crush him. It was all done in fun, however, and Aussie never complained.

I noticed that the tubular sections on the rudder blades holding the rudderposts were of such thin material that they had almost worn through. This looked as serious as any of my other rudder troubles, since the blades would become useless if they couldn't be fastened to the hull.

I had a feast of boiled fish, potatoes, and a big frying pan full of mustard sauce, using my Australian butter, dark flour, evaporated milk, and plenty of mustard, which was a splendid tonic for the stomach. I boiled them sometimes but mostly fried them and always used plenty of lemon juice. Cooking, however, when the raft tried to throw her rigging which she seemed to do habitually, became a juggling feat with pots, frying pan, the stove, and all the other paraphernalia.

I was out months now but hadn't used any salt yet, since I had no craving for it. All my life I had used very little salt, having a nature to reject all but the smallest amount. My mother, I remember, always used it sparingly. So it was perhaps a family trait. Later I came to believe that the main source of the salts needed to retain health should come from properly prepared vegetables—through steaming in their own juices, meaning without addition of water, and also through baking. Teddy agreed with this theory, and so our consumption of table salt became almost nil.

My ability to drink so much seawater on my 1954 voyage, after having lost most of my water supply, had most likely something to do with my normally almost salt-free diet. In Alaska years ago, where I had no fresh fruit or vegetables, I craved salt if my diet consisted mainly of lean caribou meat, but when I ate it in a stew with bones, fats, and other parts, the craving disappeared or lessened. From the Indians I had learned to add a little of the animal's bile when eating only lean meat. This bitter secretion seemed to hold the balance between health and disease or perhaps even death when one was living under conditions where nothing else but meat could be had and was foolish enough to eat only steak, the so-called choicest cut. The Indians of the Great Plains, I read later, also followed this practice of eating a little of the bile. The white buffalo hunters, on the contrary, when forced to subsist on buffalo meat alone for any length of time, partook only of the leanest cuts and became stricken with disease and often died.

I had waited until I had worked out my noon latitude, then got my tools ready to go overboard and work on the port rudder again, which was the worse of the two. Everything I thought I could possibly use was, as usual, put in a wooden box where it could be reached while I was in the water. The box also had a lot of iron in it to keep it from being washed overboard in case a sea came on deck. It had begun to cloud up, and after tying a line around my waist, I went overboard without taking time to eat, in order to do the job as quickly as possible.

It took longer than I had expected, and I was getting tired from the continuous pounding and submersions and hanging on while the seas tried to tear me off. As usual I had been gashed by the rough edges of the broken iron I had to work with and was bleeding. Another sea came over, and grabbing the rudder with both hands while holding a pair of pliers between my teeth and with a wrench stuck in my belt, I hung on beneath the foaming surface, holding my breath. The raft must have gone off course, for it wallowed and rolled, taking one sea after another, and I wondered how much longer I could hold out. When it eased up at last, I saw, looking into the shadows beneath the raft, a long dark shape within a few feet of my naked legs. It was a shark, hardly discernible. White was the color that attracted them, white flesh or the white belly of a fish to sink their teeth into. I lost no time pulling in my legs and climbing back on board, wondering what I would have done if he had taken my foot or leg. He was big enough to do it, and it would have been easy enough to sneak up, for while working I sometimes had to hold my leg well away from the rudder to keep my balance. I realized that I had to find a way of protecting myself while overboard. Perhaps a sort of cage would do it, something made of bamboo slats at least to check any sudden rushes. The rudders were in an exposed position, with the open sea on each side, and in the churning wake, as well as the darkness beneath the raft, it was hard to see anything, especially when engrossed in the work I was doing. Sharks, being primarily sneaks, are masters at remaining hidden till it is time to strike.

All night long the raft had been surrounded by dolphins gliding lazily, seemingly in their sleep, through the water. There were so many that I thought they had come here for a rendezvous. The water was exceptionally phosphorescent and, when churned into flaming beads by a suddenly darting fish, looked surprisingly like a miniature firmament with all the stars and the Milky Way. Once a large porpoise came out of the night, panting like an elephant looking for trouble, and in a flash all dolphins disappeared. They returned after it had left and stayed till dawn, then suddenly were gone. I thought some might still be around and threw out my fishing line but after trying for half an hour had no bite.

Logbook entry

Sultry and squally during night with occasional showers. Sky cleared early in morning. Not much wind but fine weather. First real trade-wind weather I had. Replaced dolphin head on my shark line with a fresh one.

Today was lentil day. I had soaked them for thirty-six hours, which caused germination and greatly increased the nutritive value besides speeding up the cooking. Mixed with fried onions, mustard, and garlic it was a fine dish. My potatoes, standing forward on deck in an open, loosely woven basket and fully exposed to the weather and spray, were holding out well. I had about three bushels left. My onions, however, were going bad, and I used them three times a day to get the most out of them.

When checking my fishing lines and hooks, I discovered several packs of small hooks and wondered how they got there, since I hadn't bought them. Then I found this note attached to one of the packages scribbled by Teddy: "I bought the small hooks in case the raft should be wrecked somewhere, and you found yourself alone on an atoll. With small hooks you can get fish you couldn't with your big ones. Please keep them and don't throw them overboard, for you don't know what is to come. It's a long way to Australia. Teddy."

Teddy was right, of course. She always kept the fundamentals in mind. Small fish could be caught easier and were more plentiful in a lagoon, also more apt to come to a drifting life raft or a kayak. I then thought if I should find myself wrecked on some uninhabited island I could survive almost indefinitely, for I had more tools and other equipment than on my 1954 voyage.

It was well after midnight, and the raft was making its way as if asleep. I also was asleep on my rubber poncho beside the cabin. In my dreaming I became aware of Teddy being on the raft. I awoke with a start and stared into the night, deeply disturbed by the vividness of the impression, then realized that she had called me—called me from New York—called me across the Pacific. . . . After these meetings, I see her almost constantly before me for a few days till she fades again behind me in the sea.

On August 16 I saw a small cloud in the sky, which looked surprisingly much like a plane. It was in the northeast and quite clearly defined, light brown in the sun and moving fast in a southeasterly direction, while the larger cloud masses nearby appeared motionless. For quite a few moments I thought it was a plane and that it was looking for me. It was about eight miles away, and finally lost its shape and disintegrated.

About half an hour later, at 2:45 local time in the afternoon, while standing beside the compass and looking in the same direction, having entirely forgotten the plane-shaped cloud, I saw a ship heading straight for the raft. It was a steamer, about four miles away and seemingly coming at full speed. I broke out my American flag and hoisted it, and the steamer, less than a mile away, then hoisted the British colors. She slowed down when approximately four hundred yards away and began to circle me, while I waved to the white-clad officers on the bridge and the sailors on the forecastlehead. Her name, which I could make out with my glasses, was the *Whakatane*. I was doing about two and a half knots at the time. She circled me twice. For a moment I was tempted to ask for assistance in repairing my rudders but then decided against it, for the sea was moderately heavy and contact by boat would have been difficult. Besides, work on the rudders, such as the necessary welding, would have been impossible, since they were too deep in the water. Nothing of lasting value could be done without taking the rudders off entirely and having the raft on dry land. This applied especially to the brackets or sleeves holding the rudderposts which were paper thin, so that I expected them to wear through any time and the rudders to fall off. Even if some sort of help could have been given, it would have meant heaving to by the steamer for many hours and so the incurring of a considerable loss of money to the owners, which no captain would consent to. I was happy, however, that the ship had sighted me, for I knew she would radio to the Coast Guard in Hawaii and that Teddy would be notified I was alive and well. After completing her last circle, the *Whakatane* went back on her course. It was about three o'clock then and time for my afternoon sight. After I had worked it out, I looked for her again, but she was already beneath the horizon.

Incidentally Teddy was not notified till over two months later, due to a mistake somewhere. Following is the report which finally reached her from Washington, D.C., and dated October 25, 1963:

ON 17 AUG SS WHAKATANE/GRKY REPORTED FOL QUOTE LAT 02.4
SOUTH LONG 108.6 WEST SIGHTED RAFT WITH NAME AGE UNLIMITED
ON MAINSAIL FLYING UNITED STATES ENSIGN RUNNING BEFORE THE
WIND AT COURSE 280 TRUE STOP CIRCLED AT TWO CABLES ONE MAN
ON BOARD HEALTHY NO SIGNALS OF DISTRESS UNQUOTE.

Logbook entry, August 16, 1963
Long: 108° 6' west
Lat: 0.2° 4' south
Course: southwest by west

At 2:45 in the afternoon sighted the British [New Zealand]
steamer *Whakatane*. She approached from the northeast, slowed
down when appr. 400 yards away, and circled the raft twice.
I waved to show I was all right—even went out on the jibboom.
I was making appr. 2½ knots at the time. She then continued
on her course, which was about west southwest.

8

THE night was clear, and sitting by the compass, I thought of the ancient Polynesians making their way over these same seas in their big double canoes. How their navigators must have gazed up at the constellations, measuring as best they could the height of the large stars above the horizon, aware that if they calculated wrong they might never see land again. There was, besides, the ever-present danger of squalls and headwinds, of gales and shifting currents and days and nights of cloudy weather, to wipe out all possibility of seeing the sun or stars and so computing their position. Once lost, there was no going back, since they didn't know which way to turn, not having a compass; they had to sail on, even when food and water had given out and the dying had begun—the weaker first and then the strong. Sometimes a few survived to crawl up on a beach from a canoe wrecked on a reef, on land perhaps never trodden by a human foot before. If women were in the canoe, they would build huts, the same kind of huts they had built for countless generations, and within a few decades another island in the vast Pacific would be inhabited. Those who had come first would have died by that time, and the story of the voyage would have become a saga of courage and suffering and of an indomitable leader who would be glorified and worshipped. Each storyteller and singer, as generations came and went, would embellish him with new attributes, until he rose like a god out of the dreams of their past. But the road back to the home isle would remain closed forever, for the sea washes away a vessel's wake once it has passed, and the stars are not fixed on mountain peaks to steer a course by. Memories of other island homes lost in the shadows of time would have mingled with the last, and soon little would be left except the realization that they were a race of wanderers flung across the Pacific by hurricanes or gales or the many hazards of the sea.

Where did they originally come from, these great canoe builders and dead-reckoning navigators? Who knows their story? Who can tell by gazing at the stars what happened beneath them when the earth was young? Perhaps they did see canoes or rafts of logs lost on the waters beneath, trying in vain to come back to a coast after being blown away. The oceans are vast but also small, for man's endurance is incredible, and he could well survive drifts to Polynesia from Asia as well as the Americas, both north and south. This is the story the faces and bodies of the Polynesians tell, as well as occasional words brought ages ago from a distant shore and now distorted by the usage of time. I had spoken with Polynesians, and while many thought they came from the northwest, others claimed the rising sun guided their forefathers. Others as firmly believed that they were living on the summits of a sunken continent.

The raft was rolling from beam to beam, smashing bow and stern into the sea while the mast was whipping the sky and trying to jump out of its fastenings. I remembered when I sat in the office of the cable manufacturer in New York who supplied me with my stays and how he said that, though he had a much larger yacht and a mast about three times as high as mine, he carried no stays near as heavy as those I wanted. "Those cables will hold fifteen tons," he said dubiously, "but I'll give them to you." I knew why I wanted heavy gear from 1954 but had not anticipated such violent and ceaseless rolling as was the fate of this iron trimaran. In the old square-rigger days the greatest danger to a ship, besides being caught on a lee shore in a gale, was to be becalmed in a dead swell and rolling till the backstays gave way and the masts went overboard. Many a ship was lost in the calms. They used to rig up preventer stays but chains, cables, and rope could stand only so much, when towering masts with yards and many tons of rigging fetched up with a shock after a forty degree swing.

The night after sighting the *Whakatane*, while sitting more asleep than awake beside the cabin, I was startled by a low humming roar which quickly increased. Jumping up, I saw a big ship aglow with lights coming up astern on the starboard side and dangerously close. I snatched up my flashlight to light up my sail, but the ship had already passed my beam. A change in the steamer's course of only a fraction of a degree or a momentary dozing by her quartermaster might well have finished my voyage right there. Teddy's greatest fear had always been that I would be run down, in 1954 and now. I had carried a light at the beginning of the voyage, but all my lanterns had become useless from rust.

> Logbook entry, August 19, 1963
> Long: 111° 35′ west
> Lat: 2° 32′ south
> My 70th birthday.

My stoves were beginning to give me trouble, no doubt from their continuous exposure to sea air, and after using a lot of matches and precious alcohol, I decided to forget about a hot supper and settled for a can of cold beans. I had been without hot food before in my life, sometimes for months and once for days on the *Henriette* when our galley was flooded, a sea having smashed the iron door. No food for the sailors then except the hardtack biscuits, and they were full of maggots. We generally put the biscuits in a canvas bag —with the maggots of course—and smashed them with a belaying pin, then eased them down with a drink of water. Since the fore-castle was always half dark, it was easy to ignore the maggots we swallowed. I remembered a day when we had been aloft in snow and sleet for hours and were sitting on our sea chests, faces sunken, salt encrusted, and gray, still in oilskins and sou'westers, and smash-ing up biscuits. Suddenly one of the sailors, the biggest man in the forecastle, roared out, "I don't mind eating biscuits, but if there's more maggots to them than biscuit, what the hell am I eating? Can you tell me? And if I start picking out all the maggots, I'd starve to death before I finish. These damn biscuits are five years old if they're a day. I know it—I saw them come on board. The Old Man bought them from some other skinflint of a captain who had held them out on his crew. Belly robbers!" He pounded his big fist on the two boards fastened to the deck and overhead that served us for a table. "I'm going to get off this ship as soon as we hit port. To hell with them all! I'm quitting the sea—I had enough!" His blue eyes were blazing, and with his straw-yellow beard and rugged face, one could take him for a Viking standing in the bow of one of their snake-limbed ships ready for a raid on a coast. Then his eyes fell on me. "Son," he said and let his heavy paw fall on my shoulder like a weight. "I went to sea when I was twelve. Cook on a schooner in the Baltic. You know what that means? Don't think you're catching hell here—the Horn is nothing. Cook... I was on the bloody deck more than in the galley, and when the others lay in their bunks snor-ing their heads off, I had to cook. Yes, my boy, at fifteen I was a full-grown man as tall as now and not a runt like you." He grinned, and his iron fingers gripped my flesh hard. "But what I want to tell you is—quit the sea. Quit her before it's too late." Then he burst out singing:

> "Clouds and winds and oceans
> I chose my fate to be...
> Whom the sea has taken
> Never shall be free."

His booming voice shook the forecastle and mingled with the sounds of the seas smashing against the deckhouse.

To keep my mind alert I practiced memorizing lines of poetry and prose and, what was more important, numbers. I had found this to be a good habit even when ashore.

After almost a week of cloudy weather, it had cleared, and I had a night of stars of such beauty it almost overwhelmed me. They stood above the dark sea like clouds of light massed around the big constellations. The North Star was just a little lower than I expected, proof that I had made some southing. A little to the west of it, standing straight up, were the three handle stars of the Big Dipper. The Milky Way showed up clearly, crossing the sky a little aft of the raft. Venus had gone down early. By midnight Orion had climbed up to the zenith like a separate firmament and stood wide and gorgeous in space, reminding me of a vast butterfly.

Sometime during the night Kiki tiptoed to the wheel and asked for water. She only meowed when she wanted something, and I always knew that it was important. After lapping up a little she and Aussie went aft around the stern to check the weather side for flying fish. Seas were coming over, and they had to be quick to get them before they were washed off again.

I had felt the lack of fresh food in my diet for a few days, and in the morning took three large cloves of garlic, chopped them up fine, and dropped them in a saucepan simmering with a cup of evaporated milk mixed with water. After ten minutes I took it off and drank it. I then didn't eat till noon. Teddy had bought me a whole pound of garlic in the Lima market, to the astonishment of the market woman who, taking Teddy for a homeward-bound tourist, had asked, "No have garlic in the United States?"

Last night I had waited to the last minute to lower the mainsail, thinking the squall that had kept me busy was about over, when another one came out of the darkness tearing up the sea, and I knew

I was in trouble. I had to bring the sail down. It hung up a few times on the mast, and I had to go up and clear it. When I finally had it on deck, it ballooned out in a wild mass, all the way to the jibboom, threatening to tear itself into shreds on everything forward, especially the centerboards. It took a full half hour of hard struggling before I had the gaskets around it and got it lashed to the mast legs. When the deck was finally cleared up and I was aft again, I thought of Paddy, our chanteyman on the four-masted bark *Bermuda*, who used to say after coming down on deck from hours on the yards, "And now, bejaysus, the Old Man will be calling us aft to splice the main brace, me lads, but he bloody well wouldn't, being the bloody bastard he is, and that settles it. But will he guzzle it!" I too needed a stimulant, for I felt all empty and worn inside and my legs a bit shaky, and opening a can of beans, I ate it to get back to myself, for the night was far from over, and if it cleared, I would have to raise the mainsail again.

My appetite continued good. I think this was not only due to the long hours of work and little sleep, but also because my body missed the vital food it had been used to and tried to make up by quantity. My vitality seemed little impaired, however, for I was never really tired, and my mind was keen, though a slow drain on my strength was at times noticeable.

For a few nights already I had noticed large patches of phosphorescence coming up from the depths and thought they might be masses of minute living things, as well as small shrimp and squid, risen from the ocean floor, for I frequently found specimens on deck in the morning. The depth of the sea here was, according to my chart, about fourteen thousand feet.

It had been a fine day with the trade wind blowing evenly and strong. The big white clouds came drifting up from the horizon and tried to tarry and build their castles in the air, but the wind kept the billowing masses moving. There had been very few fine days since leaving Callao; mostly it had been stormy.

Whom the Sea Has Taken

Logbook entry, August 30, 1963
Long: 125° 5′ west
Lat: 02° 40′ south
Course: west by south

Am on a 3,000-mile open stretch of sea, between the Galápagos and Marquesas. Wish the whole distance to Sydney were
open with no reef nor island near; then I would get there, somehow—with or without rudders.

In the southeast it looked threatening, but above me a few stars
were shining. I was sitting beside the compass and playing my harmonica. So far I had learned to play four or five tunes—far from
well, but they helped me through some lonely hours. My best one,
or the one I enjoyed playing most, was the old English chantey,
"Rolling Home Across The Ocean." I sang and played it to my own
words:

> I dream of the Horn on a winter's morning,
> High aloft amid ice and snow,
> Calling to the deck below me,
> "Hoist away and let 'er go."
>
> Westward, westward, ever westward
> To the setting of the sun—
> I am steering ever westward
> Since my raft the trail begun.
>
> Hail all you men and women—
> I am outward bound once more;
> I will sail through Sydney's headlands
> And drop my anchor on your shore.

When I got tired playing, I sang, while flying fish fell on deck
around me and hit the cabin with a thud, and the raft rolled and
shook and thundered. Seven or eight months of this, perhaps more . . .
They say the noise in our cities shatters the nerves and destroys our

health and can even drive a person to insanity. My raft would have been an ideal place to make experiments. I had analyzed its sounds in every sort of weather and thought they included almost the whole hellish range of what was inharmonious, unbearable, maddening, and even deadly. Sometimes they even had my little shipmates puzzled and on the jump.

The sky was almost clear and the sun shining bright. The sea was running high, and there was a considerable swell, and after rising on the back of a sea, the raft would slide down into what looked like a mile-long valley. A few sharks were clearly visible inside of distant seas, since they looked brown in the water when seen from the air though their true color was gray. They generally kept at a distance of twenty to fifty yards from the raft and were very elusive. Even when they were not visible, I seemed to know whether they were around and sooner or later spotted them. They glided through the waves with undulating, easy movements a few feet beneath the surface, rarely changing their pace, the dorsal fin showing now and then. Occasionally they shot forward like submerged surf-board riders. What attracted them mostly to the raft were the families of dolphins living beneath in the shadows where they felt safe. These raft dolphins had been with me now for a few thousand miles and were like old acquaintances. I even knew their ways. The tiny ones, for instance, only ventured out when the sea was calm and the water exceptionally clear and never swam more than a few yards away from the raft. All the dolphins I caught came to the raft from the open sea and so didn't know my way of fishing. The meat which I didn't use I sun cured and salted down for future emergency.

The other day I watched a large flying fish near the raft hard pressed by a dolphin. It soared almost like a bird. They glide with all fins spread out, using the large pectoral fins for the glide and the others for balancing and steering. The body is held up at a slight angle. A beautiful, almost fourteen-inch long specimen, the largest

I had seen so far, fell on deck a few nights ago. They are beautiful fish, streamlined like jet planes with vivid blue bodies, transparent and camouflaged wings and silvery white bellies. Their eyes are like black pearls and very large, as are those of the dolphins. A shark's small eyes in contract are lurking and pus yellow and lie in slits under the shovel-shaped head.

> Logbook entry, September 3, 1963
> D.R. long: 130° west
> D.R. lat: 03° 30′ south
> Course: west by south
> Wind: east-northeast

Distance out of Callao appr. 4,000 miles. Am on the same meridian as Pitcairn Island, 1370 miles away to the south.

Kiki and Aussie had become inseparable companions. Aussie was growing at a good rate and apparently came of a hardy breed. I noticed clearly defined ridges of muscles on his shoulders. His whole body was unusually hard for a cat, and I thought this might be due to the almost continuous balancing necessary on the raft. Their liveliest times were on moonlight nights when the seas slid past like silver-splashed hills and dolphins streaked out like flaming arrows from beneath the raft and, maddened by the beauty in which they lived, tried to leap at the moon. They wrestled a lot now since Aussie was becoming stronger every day, and it was a treat to watch them. Both were born wrestlers and always finished a bout, no matter how fierce it appeared, on the friendliest terms with Kiki licking him almost out of shape like a bear's cub. Incidentally I had never seen Aussie back up, though Kiki still outweighed him considerably.

I had rigged up a jury steering gear with blocks and tackles a few days ago which carried me through a bad night. Unfortunately even the best three-quarter-inch rope wears through in a day when in the sea and running back and forth through a block.

Whom the Sea Has Taken

Logbook entry, September 6, 1963
Long: 134° 15' west
Lat: 03° 31' south
Course: west
Wind: southeast

It had been a bright day when this came out of space and stood before me. I was in Sydney, having just tied up my raft, and climbing up to the pier, I saw a friend come towards me. His face was serious and still. "How is Teddy?" I asked anxiously, alarmed by his expression. He hesitated a moment, then said, "Teddy is dead. She was killed in an auto accident." It was terribly real and would not go away. Was it a revelation and true? Teddy is dead. . . . It couldn't be, of course—it was just my imagination. Was the isolation beginning to work on me and break me down? Teddy was still weak and ailing, that I knew, for I was fully convinced that my telepathic contacts with her were not figments of the brain. She was still sick and perhaps even struggling for her life, but I did not believe that there had been an accident. This vision of my friend bringing me the tragic news on my landing in Sydney, though always rejected by me, came back for many weeks and with startling clearness before it faded away.

My mind was set on potato pancakes for supper, and though the sea was quite high and the raft rolling, I wanted to have my way. I picked three large potatoes, scrubbed them, and kneeling beside the cabin grated them skin and all. I added a little flour, a dash of cayenne, caraway seed, a pinch of mustard, and as usual was liberal with garlic. My best stove had gone back on me again, requiring almost incessant pumping, but I hoped for the best, not having had anything hot since morning when I wheedled some boiling water out of it for a cup of tea. My frying pan was hanging from a nail outside the cabin, black, greasy, rusty, and unwashed since the beginning of the voyage except by spray coming over when the wind was northerly. I put some butter in the pan and, when it was hot, ladled in the mix. All my cooking was done on my knees, the only way possible in the narrow space, and I had developed thick calluses on them since I only wore shorts. Trousers would have slowed me up too much, racing around the raft, climbing aloft, and handling the endless gear.

The pancake was just beginning to smell buttery when I heard the mainsail flap. I looked at the pan with the browning pancake, the stove, and all my cooking gear spread out around it and, hoping the stove wouldn't fall over and start a fire, jumped on deck and pulled the wheel over. The raft took a long time obeying but at last nudged over; the flapping stopped, and she lay rolling and stamping before the wind again.

The cabin was in a mess. The stove had gone out, and the frying pan lay upside down and tangled up with everything I had on the floor, the half-cooked pancake in a sorry-looking paste beneath. I was hungry, picked up my pancake, put some honey on it, and ate it. It couldn't have tasted better. Then I started the stove again, and when the pan was hot, put in butter and potato mix. Before it was done, I again had to rush to the wheel and on my return found the same mess on the floor, and another raw pancake was devoured. Once more I started the works and had everything going nicely when I heard the ominous flapping outside. This time I got mad and roared, "Steady out there—steady! What the hell is the matter with you? Steady, I say . . ." But the raft wasn't in a mood to take orders, and I had to jump out. I was too late, however, and she went into the wind, and it was almost dark before I could get back into the cabin. There was still plenty of mix left, and I was hungrier than ever, and lighting a lamp, I started the stove once more. I ate the last pancake sitting in the door with the stars looking down on me. The potatoes must have done their work, for I was in a state of almost ecstatic happiness.

Logbook entry, September 11, 1963
Long: 140° 10′ west
Lat: 03° 22′ south
Course: west by south
Wind: southeast
4570 miles from Callao

Checking my position on the chart, I found that I was 330 miles north of Nuku Hiva in the Marquesas—much further north than I liked—but the wind had been strong and consistently from southeast, and it was hard to get back south. On my 1954 voyage I passed the 140th meridian in latitude 5 degrees 38 minutes, only 190 miles from Nuku Hiva. I had considered the voyage half over then and started to level off for the final stretch to Pago Pago, the destination I had cleared for, and changed course to west southwest. This time I was handicapped with almost useless rudders and looked at my charts with increasing apprehension as I saw the atolls and reefs ahead of me, though for the next few thousand miles I anticipated little trouble. The nearest reef ahead now was the Filippo Reef, approximately six hundred or eight hundred miles away in latitude 5 degrees 30 minutes south, with breakers reported as far south as 6 degrees 20 minutes. I hoped to pass to the south of it, unless the southerly wind continued and made it impossible.

For a few days I had not caught a dolphin, and in the early dawn I took my flashlight and checked the deck to see if any flying fish had fallen on board. There were none, but then I saw Kiki crouching over something—a flying fish, already half-eaten. I took it away from her, giving her a little pat for compensation, put it on the hook, and threw the line out, hurling it high to make the bait hit the water with a splash and attract any dolphins that might be near. It was still very early, and the sea lay dark and still. No bite ... I pulled the line in again, thinking it was still a little too dark for dolphins to start biting but tried once more. A bite ... A big one, for he almost pulled me overboard. Then he zigzagged and tore through the water, continually changing directions as if dodging something. Dolphins are like trapped tigers when hooked, but this one was the hardest to hold of any I had had. Close to the raft he went berserk. Suddenly I saw why: A big dark shape hardly discernible was behind him— a shark. The dolphin, I thought, had most likely been aware that a shark was around when he took the bait but, sure of his lightning speed, thought that he could get away. Now he was caught. I tried to pull him out of the water, but the shark was on top of him, and the line, tight as a wire from the pull of the crazed fish, became slack—I had only a bloody head on the hook. I'll use that for bait for you, Mr. Shark, I thought and tried to lift the head on deck, but a shadow streaked through the water, and the line became slack and hung loose. Another shark had taken the head, hook and all. I tried three more flying fish and hooked two dolphins, but the sharks got every one. There was a whole mob of them around, some quite big, patrolling the raft all day, coming up from astern and moving ahead as tireless and unchanging as the waves. No dolphins were to be seen, but I knew that all my families were below in the shadows, hugging the pontoons.

Later in the morning I noticed a bird flying unusually high and alone, and taking my binoculars I saw that it was an albatross. It was flying south by west. I thought it might have come from the Galápagos and was on its way to the stormy latitudes of the fifties and beyond. I had seen them as a boy when rounding the Horn, hanging motionless in the air, often no higher than the poop. To me, the wide-eyed youngster, their flight seemed almost incomprehensible, for in hours of watching I seldom saw them move a wing, riding the air like master sledders the rising and falling slopes of an endless mountain. I had plenty of opportunity to watch them, for at the end of each watch I had to go aft, take the reel with the ship's log line out of a box, hold it high overhead, and facing the wake let the line run out. The mate, standing by the rail with an hourglass, watched the sand run down, and the moment the last grain disappeared cried, "Stop!" I at once turned the reel to keep any more line from running out, and the mate checked the nearest marking on it and so computed the ship's speed. High on the cliffs of the Galápagos and other lonely rocks the albatross lay their eggs, perhaps putting their feet on land for the mating for the first time in a year. Thousands of miles of unbroken flying lie behind them, circling the earth in her stormiest regions again and again. They rarely sit down on the sea, since their long wings make it hard for them to rise again.

When the albatross egg is hatched, the fledgling opens its eyes to the sun and watches her course through the sky. Nights it sees the darkness laid out in a vast pattern of lights moving slowly across the firmament. Night after night it watches them from its stony perch and gradually they become engraved in its brain as signposts that will guide it over the sea. A few weeks later it totters to the edge of the cliff, drops off into the void beneath, and begins to fly. A royal wanderer is on the way.

Men who have lived on the Galápagos told me that they have seen the albatross pick up its fledgling when the time had come for its flying, carry it high up into the air, and drop it, then stay beside the hurtling youngster till it opens its wings and flies.

Last night while asleep beside the wheel, I was awakened by the staccato beat of a fish flapping on deck. It was exceptionally loud, and thinking it was a big flying fish, I jumped up to grab it before it had a chance to get back into the sea. A new moon was in the sky, and what I saw on deck was not a flying fish but a snake, wriggling and slashing about fiercely like a streak of silver. Was I seeing things? I snatched up my flashlight to make sure. It was a snake, about three and a half feet long with vicious-looking head and eyes and the undershot jaw of a barracuda. Four disproportionately long and foul-looking teeth protruded from the open mouth, each at a different angle, two above and two below. I grabbed it by the back of the neck and flung it into a box to scrutinize it at my leisure in the morning. The same sort of fish had fallen on deck in 1954, and I later learned it was a mackerel shark. The next morning I photographed it and opening its stomach found a number of tiny inchlong flying fish inside.

The sea was actually alive these days with small flying fish, and the young dolphins beneath the raft were feasting on them from dawn to dusk. Wherever I looked, I saw their gulping mouths break the surface. The tiny creatures looked like silvery splinters of glass blown about by the wind as they rose and scattered. They were still slow in the water, however, and could only fly a few feet and so fell an easy prey to their pursuers. There were millions of them, and each morning the deck of the raft was covered inches deep.

Kiki and Aussie ate from the same dish, but Kiki, a little lady, always backed away when Aussie, who was obviously brought up in catch-as-catch-can surroundings, pushed his little hungry face into the bowl. Perhaps it was the mother instinct in Kiki to give to a youngster first. When Aussie had had enough, she came back and leisurely ate her fill. She ate comparatively little. If anything was left in the evening, Aussie always took care of it during the night.

I had to go overboard again. It was a windy day, and the sea rather high. As usual I went over with a line around my waist, which proved quite necessary, for I was washed from the rudder to which I clung with arms and legs twice and once turned upside down and around so rapidly that I lost my bearing. I had rigged up some sort of contraption of bamboo slats to protect me, at least a little, from sharks while in the water. There were four sharks around me that day, and anyone not knowing them might have thought they were quite gentle and even friendly. I had no bait at the time for my big hook; otherwise I would have caught one to feed the others. The sharks out here as a rule will not blindly take any bait. I had seen them swim several hours behind a chunk of dried dolphin meat I used occasionally as bait, almost touching it with their noses, and

118

still not take it. My sharks were of the gray tipped variety, deep-sea rovers which as a rule are not scavengers.

The raft was at this time making its way over the ancient cross-roads of the Pacific, over the courses of the Marquesans, Samoans, Tahitians, and Hawaiians. Here their big double canoes sailed and sank in squalls and hurricanes perhaps long before our European time began. Here, some scientists say, was once a vast continent, until the earth one day went into such convulsions that it threatened to break apart. When it was over, after ages of fiery eruptions that hurled great landmasses into space and filled the sky with smoke and flames, the continent with its millions of people, its civilizations and cities and fields lay miles deep in the slime of the Pacific. So scientists say. The depth beneath my raft, according to my chart, was six thousand fathoms—thirty-six thousand feet.

> Logbook entry, September 17, 1963
> D.R. long: 149° 24' west
> D.R. lat: 5° 30' south
> Course: west
> Wind: southeast

Stormy weather during night and at sunrise red sky. Quite high, wallowing sort of sea. Sky in the southeast overcast.

I had been in a depressed and agitated state of mind the last few days, very unusual for me. It had been coming on for a week or so, and last night was quite noticeable. Perhaps it was the realization of my worsening condition—the broken rudders, the increasingly bad weather, the endless distance ahead, and above all wondering how Teddy was getting along.

The wind had been northeast for a day or two and given me a chance to steer south but then switched to southeast again. The

Filippo Reef was still 340 miles away. I saw many sharks around the raft today.

Some people believe that sharks have to turn on their backs to bite. I have never noticed anything like it, though I certainly had plenty of opportunity to watch them at a distance of a few feet. They would starve to death, I think, if they first had to turn on their back after sneaking up on some unsuspecting dolphin or plump little bonito which move as fast as bullets. If their prey is something dead, floating in the sea, they nose it a few times and then strike with a convulsive jerk of the whole body. Should the object be big, like the body of a whale, they tear off with a violent and quite awful-looking twist what the teeth have hold of, which has reminded me of tearing a chunk out of the trunk of a tree.

Teddy and I were on our Virgin Island sloop, coming from Guantanamo Bay and bound for Miami, when we were becalmed off the southern coast of Cuba. This was in 1948. There was a slow set towards the shore, and we had dropped our anchor in about thirty fathoms. The water was exceptionally clear, for it was after two days of storm, and we noticed a porpoise near us teaching her young how to tumble and dive. It was a large female. A shark appeared and then a few others, and they began circling the mother and its young. Some were pretty big, ten and twelve footers and perhaps even more. The cow tried to get away, but the sharks closed in, and then one attacked the young. Soon they were all at it. The mother tried to fight them off turning from one to the other. There were at least five or six now, but we couldn't tell exactly amid the thrashing bodies and now bloody water. After the calf was torn, they attacked the mother. We saw her leaping out of the sea, trying to escape the killers, a bloody mass with sharks hanging on to her side and twisting like enraged demons as they tore out her vitals. Suddenly another porpoise streaked through the sea, plowed through the sharks, touched the doomed cow, and was gone. The male, we thought. The cow was almost in shreds but still fighting when the sea became churned into foam by a solid line of porpoises, perhaps ten or fifteen coming on like fiercely panting horses with high arching necks and streaming manes. They smashed into the sharks. Porpoises use their heads like pile drivers. Some of the sharks were knocked partly out of the sea, while others were driven on the shore to be smashed in shallow water. We were still becalmed during the night, and several times could hear a porpoise blowing near the boat. "Probably the male mourning for its mate," Teddy said.

9

I WAS getting closer to the Filippo Reef and hoped for more wind to take me to the south of it. For the last few days I had been in a more than usually meditative frame of mind, wondering about life and mankind and the riddle of the universe, giving free rein to philosophical speculations.

In the evening sea and raft were in good temper, and she held her course more or less. I had put the lashings over the spokes and, after watching the compass for a while, let her go. She swung off, steadied up, and came back—and so on and on. I lost a lot of mileage that way but had become used to it. West by south was the course to Australia—as faraway seemingly as the sun that had set ahead of me a few hours before. That's where I was bound for. I had water and food and patience. I could always sing, and I had my two little shipmates. Mentally I was at ease.

> "Westward, westward, ever westward
> To the setting of the sun ..."

I had sat down on the sturdy little box given me in Lima for Kiki and Aussie to sleep in, which neither would do even once. It had been a long day in the blazing sun, sewing sails, fighting the shifting winds, and going overboard to work on the rudders. Dozing off again and again, I was sitting with my back against the cabin. Suddenly I became wide awake and saw the earth before me, sort of spreading out with all that was in it. I saw it faraway but very clearly, as if looking at it through a powerful telescope. I saw towns and villages and highways and the big crowded cities. I saw New York, square tower beside square tower, square boxes with miles of windows reaching up so high that they shut off all light from the earth, and a thousand trains roaring through iron-ribbed bowels deep beneath, flinging its millions of dwellers back and forth through dust and darkness. I looked into the homes also and saw white-faced men and women gazing terror-stricken at something. Cancer . . .

One day while living in California I had gone to a neighboring farmer to buy grapes. I had been there before and knew him. He was out in the field, and his wife told me with tears in her eyes that he was dying of cancer and didn't have long to go. I had been under the shadow of the scourge myself, and my father and mother had succumbed to it, also Teddy's father and several relatives. My grandmother also. Almost every home on earth was threatened. I went into the vineyard where the farmer was puttering around and, after chatting a while about the weather, told him I had recently read that by living on grapes one could cure cancer or at least check it. I had heard of it before, I mentioned. I said I didn't know that it was anything like a cure, but that it would be something to stop it and check further inroads. "You wouldn't have anything to lose trying," I said, "you with your grapes. You have the best grapes in the world. All you have to do is stretch out a hand, and you have a bunch fit for a king, warm from the sun, and just crying to be eaten—like gold flowing into the body. The finest fruit grown anywhere on the face of the earth. You got it, man, all around you." I went on saying I had read that some of the big and expensive sanitariums in Switzerland, Austria, and Russia cured cancer that way or stopped it dead so it couldn't go farther.

He looked at me out of his doomed eyes, his whole doomed, lined,

123

and sagging face, then asked bitterly, "What do you mean—just eat a bunch of grapes every day?"

"You must eat nothing but grapes—nothing else, no coffee, tea, tobacco, or liquor, nothing but grapes. All you can eat."

"That's out," he growled, his face setting hard.

I persisted. "They'll find a cure sooner or later—the doctors I mean —with all the experimenting going on, all the billions put into it; but in the meantime I'd sure as hell try anything that might stop it or slow it up." But he wasn't interested.

I heard the sail flap and got up and looked at the compass. The wind had shifted a little, and I took the lashings off and brought the wheel a couple of spokes over.

The next day was sultry and unusually warm. There was little wind, and the sea was sluggish with quite a swell, and I was wondering about bad weather. There had been a ring around the moon for a few nights and yesterday a bad-looking sunrise. I had been asked why I didn't take a barometer along. There was nothing I could do out here if I knew a storm was coming, no shelter to run to; besides with my almost rudderless raft I would have a hard time getting into a harbor if there was one. The sky told me accurately enough what the weather would be like, and it was up to me to be ready. A hurricane always took a while to blow up, and if I saw a squall coming really fast, I could drop my mainsail within seconds. Incidentally I had found ways to secure or let go sheet, tack, and braces with a single move or two.

> Logbook entry, September 24, 1963
> D.R. long: 149° 46′ west
> D.R. lat: 06° 15′ south
> Course: west
> Wind: southeast

No sight for 2 days. My dead-reckoning position puts me within 45 miles due east of the breakers of part of the Filippo Reef, and if the strong southeast wind holds for another day or so, may well pile up, and the voyage come to an end. Have been trying for 2 weeks to get south. I'm appr. 675 miles due north of Tahiti.

I was watching Kiki today, walking along the deck and as usual stopping after each careful step to look, sniff, and listen as if she had never been on the raft or anywhere else in this world before but had just descended from some other planet. When she came to a pail of seawater standing on deck, she stopped, got on her hind legs, sniffed the water, and began to lap it up. Three times she stopped to catch her breath and lick her lips, then began again until she had enough. I checked her water bowl, which was forward, and found it full and so was led to believe that she had drunk seawater for medicinal reasons. I had seen Aussie do the same and also at a time when fresh water was available. Since Kiki was very careful about what she ate or drank, I was convinced she knew what she was doing. Aussie definitely seemed to need seawater and had his own place on the starboard pontoon where he could lap it up fresh from the sea any time and quickly get back on deck.

It had been curry sauce with potatoes for supper. Curry was a favorite dish of mine, first tasted on the four-master *Bermuda* over fifty years ago, and I had it at least twice a week. If I had onions to go with it, I wouldn't have traded it for a Waldorf handout cooked by an imported chef, but unfortunately by this time my onions were gone.

A new group of gray-tipped sharks was escorting the raft now and keeping the dolphins under cover. Sharks are the true masters of distance swimming, and with their great size and strength, their formidable teeth, and cunning are the true monarchs of the sea. I never tired of watching them swim, lazily, effortlessly as if asleep. But the muddy eyes beneath their shovel head moved from side to side, I knew, and a dangling leg or foot would quickly have become a bloody stump if held over the side. One could compare them to the albatross, which also glided through its element with no noticeable effort and like the shark could probably go weeks without food.

It was quite easy to believe, watching the fish around me swimming day after day and month after month and seemingly quite at home, knowing where they were, that surface fish like sharks and dolphins, which have seen the stars above them since their emergence to their present state, could use them as the birds are believed to do also by means of sensibilities beyond our knowledge, as signposts to find their way across the seas.

Man forever tries to master the solitude to help him solve the riddle of life but always falls back, for he cannot live in isolation for any length of time and remain sane. He is born of flesh and needs the companionship of flesh to keep alive. Every moment of his life he takes from his fellow beings and in return gives. A continuous exchange takes place—has taken place since the beginning—which binds all men into an insoluble mass. Even a hermit hiding in a cave lives on men, for his thoughts can only be of men or of a god formed like a man.

Man with man beside him can face death easier than if alone. A condemned man stands firmer on the gallows if the hangman whispers a kind word or a cry of courage rings out from an onlooker. He will even smile at a joke. If a friendly hand touches his shoulder, he feels all mankind in his heart and annihilation does not appear final. Perhaps a few hours before, while in the awful emptiness of his cell awaiting the fateful opening of the door, he screamed in terror at the very thought of what was to come or tried to smash his head against the wall. Man belongs to man, and if he ever reaches the stars, all must go together. There is no salvation for one—Nirvana is the escape of the weak. That is the lesson taught out here, on the threshold of the infinite.

I cleared the Filippo Reef, when the wind shifted to northeast, with little room to spare, for my last dead-reckoning position had put me very close to it, and at the coming of night I had been up on the mast with my binoculars looking for breakers.

The rudders had needed fixing again, and I tied my few slats of bamboo together again to form a sort of screen, fastened pieces of iron to the ends, and lowered it into the sea behind the rudders, hoping it would keep the sharks off. It was a very makeshift affair in the churning wake but the best I could do. I also had my harpoon ready. When I was nearly finished, a ten-foot shark decided to barge through my flimsy handiwork and get hold of me somewhere, most likely one of my dangling legs. He was very persistent. Back I climbed on deck, and chopping up a flying fish that had fallen on deck during the night, I wrapped it up in a slab of dried dolphin meat, rubbed some of my blood from a gashed arm on it, and put it on the hook. My ten-footer was interested, but it was a while before he had the scent of the blood. Then he lunged in, excited enough to grab a keg of nails. I shot him at the rail and let him trail behind the raft for his partners, while I went back overboard and finished the work.

Fresh food had been one of the main problems on board since the first log raft or canoe left a shore to tackle the unknown beyond the horizon. Scurvy, caused by lack of fresh food, is perhaps the most dreadful of all mankind's diseases. In a fully developed case a human body turns to loathsome, red-flecked mud, screaming at the slightest movement. Cholera, yellow fever, all the big plagues which have devastated the earth are merciful compared to this scourge of the sea.

Personally I think that, besides lemon or lime juice, a daily drink of perhaps half a cup of seawater would keep scurvy from breaking out. I had also read of an American whaling-ship captain of the old days who kept scurvy from his crew by giving them a daily ration of sauerkraut of which he had several barrels. The big Galápagos turtles taken on board by whaling ships in hundreds and kept alive also did their share in keeping seamen healthy.

For my lunch today I had dehydrated vegetable soup with dolphin meat and thickened with wheat germ. Sometimes I made the same dish with a grated potato or a broken-up ship's biscuit.

It sneaked up on me one day while the raft lay becalmed in the sea, rolling from beam to beam, and I realized that I still had many thousands of miles to go. I had been becalmed for four days—becalmed or with a mere pittance of wind—and nights there had been one squall after another coming from almost all quarters. All at once it stood before me, filling all space, and struck me to the marrow as it said: "Get out of it! You can't make it—get out of it," and forced my eyes to the rail.

Had life become unbearable? Endless work, endless sleeplessness, and the fact that I had worked for months on the rudders but that everything had been useless and had to remain useless, had brought this on. I had a raft, sails, and provisions and plenty of water, and I had a goal—but I was adrift and by the looks had to remain adrift in midocean far from where I wanted to go. I fought this thing down, this all-pervading summons, after I had recovered from the shock. I even grinned at it, but the fact that it had appeared made me wonder at myself. It had been an entirely new experience in my life. You are vulnerable, boy, I said to myself. Yes, you didn't know that was in you.

The next day, with the raft like hot cinders around me and rolling under the pitiless sun, the thing was there again, coming wide out of space. "Get out of it," it ordered quietly but with the weight of the whole sky behind it. It came every day thereafter, and every day I forced it back, always laughing in the end at its presumption of finding me weak. I realized that it was the specter of the solitude created by myself and had to come, like a toothache or bellyache, when conditions were right. I accepted it and was not afraid—even when it came several times a day. But I could see clearly that this voyage would test me to the last fiber.

I had watched the squall move toward me, coming in a large black mass and looking bad, but decided to keep the mainsail up, hoping

I could keep the raft before it for some extra miles. I had been having bad weather, lowering and raising the mainsail many times, and being pretty well worn-out was willing to take almost any chance. The squall was quite near, and I was standing with my hands on the spokes ready to turn the wheel when I heard Teddy's voice. She was forward, and her face was calm as usual, and she said quietly and very distinctly as was her way, "You are ready for that squall, I see." I was not the least surprised; it was rather as if she had to come out of the emptiness around me to console me with her presence. The echo of her voice rang through me till I came to grips with the wind. After a while the sail had to come down, and I had to go in and slug it out—headfirst and arms flailing to subdue it and secure it to the yard.

My medical tests showed no pathological condition, and from all observations I thought I was in perfect health. I had speed, endurance, strength, and mental keenness after ninety days alone at sea. Now and then a sluggishness set in and lasted a few days, but I put it down to my deficient diet. My daily ration of seawater I thought helped me, and also a quick, rugged washdown and thorough pounding with my fists from head to toes, reaching every muscle, artery, organ, and joint. I also increased my deep breathing when I felt sluggish. But diet is life—man is what he eats.

I found that the pilot and current charts issued by the U.S. Hydrographic Office were quite accurate as a whole, though they certainly made no mention of the fantastically mixed-up and stormy weather I was experiencing. Whenever I had a day of fair weather, it was like a holiday. My little shipmates seemingly felt the same way, for then they played and ran around the deck and sprawled in the sunniest spots. Occasionally when dozing nights, I woke up thinking a hurricane had struck, only to find Kiki and Aussie chasing each other through the dry banana leaves on the cabin roof. They were masters of balance and agility. The other day Kiki had looked rather sluggish, and touching her nose, I thought it was a little warm and wondered what I could do for her. She was lying on deck like a heap of tawny fur, and I imagined all sorts of gloomy things. Then Aussie appeared on a nearby box, saw her, and jumped on top of her as if he wanted to tear her apart. Kiki came to life in a flash, and they put on almost half an hour of one of the best wrestling matches I had seen anywhere, I think. It was fought to a draw and ended in a licking-each-other match where the honors again were even.

Frigate birds were fishing far off, having probably come from the Filippo Reef or perhaps south from Vostock Island. I was steering west-southwest and heading for the 12th parallel to clear Rakahanga, where Eric de Bischop had died, and Manikiki which lay at approximately longitude 161 west and latitude 10 south. The two atolls were still faraway, but I couldn't be too cautious. Incidentally I had my 1954 logbook on board and could compare my two voyages.

The raft had developed a new set of noises, one of which, a long-drawn shriek as of something in extreme agony, was especially trying. I finally traced it to one of the mast sockets and almost buried it in grease, but it only seemed to make matters worse. Since leaving Callao, I had lived in this pandemonium of noises with my little shipmates. Occasionally even they looked around as if afraid the raft was coming apart.

> Logbook entry, October 5, 1963
> Long: 155° 16' west
> Lat: 10° 16' south
> Course: southwest by west
> Wind: north-northeast

Out 3 months today and covered appr. 5,700 miles. Weather continues bad. Don't seem to know the Pacific of 1954.

I had thrown out my fishing line in the early dawn, and a dolphin took it. The fear and fury of the hooked fish fairly leaped from the line into me, as if I held its body with my bare hands, and

I had a time pulling it in. When it was about ten feet away, I saw another dolphin near it—a bull with a tremendous head. First I thought the two fish had been fighting, then realized that the other was its mate and trying to help it. I swung it on board in all its beauty and saw the gasping mouth with the hook in the upper jaw, the big, limpid eyes full of agony, and its mate, utterly maddened, leaping against the pontoon trying to follow it to the deck. After I had landed it, I stepped back, letting it smash about till the hook was out of its jaw, for I had decided to spare it. The next moment it was back in the sea and speeding away beside its mate in a mass of foam, a piece of upper jaw left on the hook. When we were on our West Indies sloop, Teddy never ate of a dolphin if she had seen its eyes after it was hooked or when it lay dying on deck, its gorgeous colors turned gray.

The moon had come back, and its magic was upon the sea and every wave. I watched its nightly progress across the sky, watched it rise through the clouds, stand serene on high, and gradually sink, generally embattled in a squall, into the sea.

Long before the sun came up, I felt in my bones what sort of day it was going to be. Sometimes I could also tell by the flight of the birds or the ways of the dolphins—how they darted out from beneath the raft, how they jumped and moved through the waves. On a sultry, squally day they barely stirred in the morning.

The Tokolau group was the nearest land now, about eight hundred or nine hundred miles to the west if I followed the 12th parallel as I intended to do.

Quite often when alone at the wheel nights, I saw long processions of the elderly, which we name a little condescendingly our senior citizens, in the sun of southern California, on the south shore of Long Island in New York, or in Florida in ever-widening ranks, heads and backs bent and shuffling aimlessly to their end. I had spoken to many, always hoping I might utter some word of advice on health which would fall on fertile soil. Sometimes I thought that I had.

This had been a day for thinking, and as usual I put down a few of my thoughts in my log book among other impressions and observations. I had gone back over the seventy years I lived on earth and lumped them all into one mass—a mere drop given me out of the stream of eternity. Having a mind, I could lengthen them as I wished or contract them to one flash. There had been no terror in me at its beginning, and there should be no terror at its normal conclusion or the approach of it. One is almost forced to think of the end out here in a solitude so vast and unbroken that the world of men has lost most of its significance. The great tragedy of life, it appeared to me, would be to become old mentally. The ancients, realizing this, discovered early that the mind could not remain young if the body aged before its time, and systems of health were devised to overcome this. But seventy years are seventy years, I thought, taking stock of myself, and asked, How much longer could I expect to live on earth? Ten, twenty, or perhaps thirty years? So little time—even thirty. So little time and yet so much, since one second has the substance of eternity. But the thing was fulfillment while living—the quiet ecstasy of creating, of doing something constructive whatever it might be, each to his own temperament and gifts. One should add that the advantage was with him who could do something with his hands, for man was given his hands primarily to bless himself with. This was the normal state of man, and life without it was but a dying regardless of age.

So far I had had little rain. There had been frequent showers coming with the squalls but never lasting downpours. Last night, however, it rained heavily, and I filled all my buckets and containers. In the morning the weather cleared, and the air became dry and clean, and the trade-wind clouds streamed high and like the washed fleeces of snow-white sheep across the sky.

Whom the Sea Has Taken

Logbook entry, October 16, 1963
Long: 159° 16′ west
Lat: 11° 24′ south
Course: west-southwest
Wind: northeast

110 miles east southeast of Manikiki and appr. 610 miles due north of Raratonga in the Cook Islands where my 1954 message that I had sighted Samoa, my destination, was picked up by the British amateur Doug Cunnold and relayed to Pago Pago, seat of the American government.

I continued to hear the voices of my mother and Teddy, and they were as real in a way as everything else around me, just like the summons that came out of space and told me to make an end of it.

Today the raft was rolling so much that I couldn't take a single good sight, though I tried thirty or forty times, both from the deck and the top of the cabin. Incidentally I took an average of from twenty to twenty-four sights every single day when the sun was out to get a fairly accurate latitude, such was the rolling of the raft.

I wondered what the world was doing and debated whether to turn on my transistor, which so far I hadn't done, using it only for my time signals. I decided against. There wouldn't be a war, I figured, for the big boys were afraid of their own bombs. Besides, if they turned one of the jumbos loose, no matter where on the face of the earth, I would see the smoke and fire. It would be time enough then to tune in and see what was up and how they had lined up.

I was sitting flat on deck at the edge of the raft, letting my feet hang in the sea; just had a hankering for a good long soak of my feet in the middle of the world's largest ocean. My harpoon was beside me to discourage any sharks from coming too near. The water was pleasantly warm and yet fresh, and the touch of it went like balm through my body. A light breeze cooled the air just right. Be fore long I had forgotten the raft and was dreaming of sitting beside

133

a little willow-shaded brook amid watercress and mint and forget-me-nots somewhere in New York, New Jersey, or Connecticut.

I had cooked a whole pound package of prunes in the morning and had to eat them all during the day, since they wouldn't keep in the heat. I always liked prunes. Once, in my itinerant days, I had worked in a San Jose orchard and shaken them out of the trees. Plums were lying a foot deep beneath, and all the bees in the world were buzzing around me, getting drunk on the fermented ones.

A few little dolphins had come around my feet, wondering whether they were some strange creatures of the deep they hadn't seen so far. They were about ten inches long. How they shone in the sun, like jewels that had just jumped out of nature's treasure chest. I still had the very tiny ones beneath the raft, no larger than four inches, which only came out with their mothers. And then I had two small sharks, about three feet long, following the raft. They kept together, appeared light brown in the water, and acted exactly like the grown ones.

Kiki caught a seabird last night. It was about the size of a pigeon, black with white breast and belly and a wingspread of about twenty inches. The beak was truly formidable, over three inches long and like a needle. It had come down on the kayak on top of the cabin to rest for the night when Kiki, who had stalked it while it was flying around the raft to find a spot, pounced on it from behind. She had made but one lightning move, and the bird hung slack and lifeless from her jaws. Then she jumped down to the deck with it, never relaxing her hold, and for half an hour walked up and down, her head held higher than I had ever seen it, to the intense admiration of Aussie who kept well out of her way. At last she dropped it and didn't give it another look.

I was twisting the hook out of a shark's jaws, which I had caught to get the liver for some needed vitamins, when I thought of a fisherman in Callao who had asked me to send him a shark's tooth from my voyage.

"What do you want it for, good luck?" I asked.

"For luck, yes," he replied.

"Don't you catch sharks around Callao?"

"Yes, plenty. They get into our nets and tear them."

"Can't you get a tooth from one of them?"

"I want a tooth from a shark you caught on your voyage across the Pacific."

"For hanging around your neck?" I asked. I knew that pearl and shell divers in the Pacific often wear a shark's tooth around the neck, thinking it will keep sharks away.

"Yes, I would wear it," he said and told me the story of two brothers who, some years ago, had fished for lobster and crabs among the rocks near Callao where the water was full of sharks. They were skin divers and picked them up from the bottom. One of them always wore a shark's tooth around his neck while the other didn't believe in it. They never went down together, one always remaining on top while the other was below the surface. One day the one on the bottom didn't come up when it was time, and the other went down to see what had happened. Near the bottom the water was dark with blood, and he saw sharks jerking something back and forth. It was his brother. He drew his knife and, fighting the sharks off, grabbed the body to bring it to the surface. The sharks followed him, again and again pulling his brother out of his grip, but he finally got him up on the rocks. "He himself was bitten also and walks with a limp to this day," he said. "He is captain of a fishing boat in Callao now."

"Was he the one who wore a shark's tooth around his neck?" I asked.

"Sí, señor."

I had to go overboard again to work on the port rudder which had become really useless. I always hoped to be able to do something with it. I had caught a shark earlier and, after shooting it, had slashed the body with my machete and let it trail astern to keep the other sharks busy and away from me.

The sea was quite rough, and I was submerged almost at once and had to hold my breath and wait till the stern came up again. A few more seas came over before I could begin. It was about eight o'clock, and the sun was coming up fast, burning down on my naked back. The water temperature was just right, however, and I didn't mind the continuous submersions, though they slowed me up considerably besides exposing me to the danger of being smashed against the rudder and injured, which had happened again and again. While working I kept looking back at the dead shark to see if others were still busy with it.

I was working in a strained position, with my arms deep beneath the surface and just my nose sticking out for air, trying to get a clamp around a wire cable, when another sea came over. I hung on, holding my breath, twisted into a knot and straining against the pressure of the sea, when I felt something tearing inside of me, in my left side. It was like a hook tearing me open. I cried out. At first I thought that one of the irons I was trying to lash to the rudder had pierced my abdomen. I had to let go and was washed back and forth behind the rudder, the line around my waist alone holding me. The pain eased up a bit after a while, and I managed to get up on the pontoon and to the deck, feeling certain that I had ruptured myself. I already had a hernia on the right side, which however had never seriously bothered me. The sun was hot and felt good on my chilled body lying beside the cabin. Then I examined myself. Yes, I had ruptured myself. I lay there thinking what to do about it.

After a while I remembered that my doctor in New York had put a rubberized bandage in my medicine kit, saying it might come handy if I suffered a severe sprain. I would try it. The pain sometimes was severe, and I thought morphine might help. I had asked my doctor for a few tablets, remembering what I had gone through from a perforated stomach ulcer on my first voyage. I crawled into the cabin and found them and took one, then put on the bandage. In the afternoon I was back overboard, fortified with another tablet, and finished the job.

The rupture didn't bother me unduly in the days ahead. I exposed the area to the sun, bathed it with seawater, and always wore the bandage and, before hoisting or securing the mainsail or doing other strenuous work, was especially careful.

For the last few days I had lived mostly on potato pancakes. Sometimes I ate only oatmeal. For a quick meal I had my beans and dehydrated potato strips. Beans and a scraped raw potato with plenty of lemon juice always made a meal. I think lemon juice and seawater as well as raw potatoes kept my insides in shape.

Making allowance for my wayward courses, I figured that I had now come approximately sixty-seven hundred miles. This was about the distance I covered in 1954 in the *Seven Little Sisters*, sailing from Callao to Pago Pago, American Samoa. I was way behind the time I had made then, due to my rudders.

The sea was just turning gray. I had been around the raft and checked the gear and was sitting beside the door of the cabin. I had staggered going around and hung on to everything I could reach, and my eyes didn't want to keep open. I sat there without really seeing anything. Something was wrong with me. My body felt like a deadweight, my eyelids were leaden. For a while I dozed, then pulled myself together. This wouldn't do. I should get up and begin to work...so much to do...it would soon be daylight....I slid from the box and lay down on deck. It felt good not moving. Thoughts crawled around in my head, like sluggish flames. Sometimes I dozed.

It was the water. The water was bad, and I had drunk it. It was tainted, but I hadn't thought it was really bad and could hurt me. I had opened a fresh barrel a few weeks ago. It had been cloudy and had a smell, sort of sewerlike. But I had taken a chance with it—I'd had to. I boiled it and never drank it straight. There had been some rain, not much, and I had caught what I could and used it first. But the last week or so there had been no rain, and I'd had to take my water from the barrel. Contaminated, all right. I had filtered it through cheesecloth which Teddy had packed among my things. "Always comes in handy," she had said.

I knew just what had happened. I had the best drinking water of Lima—of all Peru, I might say—which was brought down from a crystal-clear spring high up in the mountains and sold all over Lima and Callao in ten-gallon jugs. And I had the best barrels, made from Texas white oak and the insides coated with pitch and originally used for holding sacramental wine. But I had been careless. I had paid someone to fill the barrels with Callao water to keep them from shrinking while waiting for the mountain water to come down, and some of the bad local water must have remained on the bottom of the barrels below the bung hole and fouled the rest when poured in. It was all my fault, and I had no reason to complain. I thought of all the black jungle water I had drunk in French Guiana out of stagnant, foul creeks. And that had got me too in the end—yellow fever. The bush Negroes had saved my life.

I lay there and felt the sun coming up. Thoughts kept going around in my head—vague thoughts of sickness and troubles, of broken rudders and drifting helpless. I should open my eyes and see what was going on, at least look up at the sky and see what was doing up there. . . . I was far away from any land—that was one good thing. No danger unless something came up, some real storm.

My head started to hurt, and I covered it with my arm, but it didn't help. I opened my eyes with an effort. Bright morning . . . clouds in the northeast . . . clouds, clouds, my real companions . . . The raft would keep on her course—if one could call it a course. Ahead it was clear. My eyes closed again. Kiki and Aussie were forward and wrestling, for it was still cool. I could hear the thud of their bodies coming down on the bamboo slats. I had fed them early, and that was all my little shipmates asked for—a little food twice a day. What perfect creatures . . . How perfect and good everything was in life . . . I pulled out my dollar watch, which I kept on local time. Almost eight o'clock . . . I must have dozed. A cup of hot tea might help, but the thought of using the bad water almost turned my stomach. The cabin had the sewer smell also, for I kept my pail with drinking water in it. Boiling hadn't been enough or straining it through a cheesecloth. I just had to use as little as possible while waiting for rain.

I tried to get up, my head feeling big, but could only sit up. After a while I would get on my feet. Maybe it was fever. Fever from bad water. I got a little scared and pulled myself together. Yellow fever, typhoid—what else did sailors get from bad water? Sometimes rats got into the water barrels of the old square-riggers and drowned, and then they had the pest on board and threw the dead over the side one by one till no one was left. Then the ship drifted till the bottom fouled, and it sank, or it drifted on till someone mercifully put a match to it. What else could it be except the water, since I had eaten the same food all through the voyage, and my stomach had never given me any trouble? The pest—that would fix me. And Teddy—waiting, sitting in New York and waiting . . .

I got up, limb by limb, joint by joint, and dragged myself into the cabin, lifting my legs over the high step with my hands, got my thermometer out of the medicine kit, put it in my mouth, and slumped down.

When I woke up, I discovered the thermometer still in my mouth. I took it out but had trouble reading it. Finally I turned my back to the light. Just a little over 100 . . . I shook the mercury down and put it back in my mouth and four minutes later took it out. Still a little over 100. That was nothing—nothing to worry about. I took some aspirins and went back on deck, for the cabin smelled like a sewer—a real sewer. It was really terrible. That had done it all right, I felt certain. I managed to lower the awning and stretched it across the deck and lay down again.

My head was simmering, but the real mess was inside of me, in my intestines. I could feel it. But 100 fever was nothing. I really should drink a few mugs of seawater and flush myself out—a gallon even. Drive it out with the sheer weight of the water. I felt that would fix me. I should also make myself vomit—take a teaspoonful or two of mustard powder in a mug of hot seawater. That would break loose everything that didn't belong—that would bring it up all right, and rosy health would come back. I should clean myself out. How simple really—how simple . . . But the convulsions going with it, the heaving and rolling around the deck, that would tear my head off—my head, yes . . .

After a while I pulled myself together and got up and looked at the compass. I was off to the north a little, but there was plenty of slack in the sheet and tack, and I knew the raft wouldn't go into the wind—she would just swing back and forth.

I went forward, dragging my legs and holding on, and checked the gear. Everything looked all right. But the weather didn't look too good—something might be making up in those clouds. I went around to the portside. It smelled bad there, with the sun burning down on those barrels. It had burned down on them for months. I stopped and petted Kiki who was getting ready for her day's nap. Aussie came around with his tail held up stiff and high as if going on a parade. My two little characters really were tops. If man's brain were as sound as their instincts, he would perhaps know where he came from and was going.

I didn't like the clouds behind me and lowered the mainsail just to be on the safe side, in case I should become worse. I felt I might. It took a long time to secure it. I was really weak. Then I had to go out on the jibboom, clear the jib, and hoist it. The halyard then fouled on top, and I had to climb aloft.

The compass heading now was west-southwest. Both rudders were swinging as if they didn't belong to the raft. I was used to it, but it was terrible to take.

I wanted to drink, for my throat was parched, but after looking at the cloudy water in the bucket, I couldn't. And the smell . . . Perhaps I should take my temperature again. Then I remembered that Captain Hokanson of the *Santa Margarita*, the Grace Line steamer which carried the raft from New York to Callao, had given me a whole carton of pint cans of distilled water. The cans were a Coast Guard requirement for every American lifeboat, and each one was stamped with a date. I had saved them for an emergency, in case I had to go into the kayak or was wrecked on a waterless atoll.

I got one of the cans and opened it. Perhaps I should have made tea—hot, boiling tea—and poured it down my throat, but I couldn't think of starting my stove—kneeling on the floor of the cabin and coaxing it while the raft rolled from side to side and my head with it. I put lemon juice in the water and drank, then went outside and sat down on the box.

My eyes kept closing, and I stretched out on deck. When I woke up, it was a little before twelve o'clock. I looked up from under the awning at the sky. There were no clouds right above, and I should take a noon sight but knew I couldn't do it on a bet, for the sun was almost straight overhead, and my eyes would never take it. All I craved was darkness and lying still. I got the thermometer and took my temperature again. It was almost the same, just a touch more....

I lay on deck for a long time, then woke up and saw the sun ahead of me going down. She had crossed over the raft as she did every day and was about in the right place, and I knew I was pretty well on my course. I had covered some extra miles to be sure while swinging. Aussie gave a little cry forward, and I saw him playing with Kiki. She had him down and using her weight kept him pinned while holding him by the throat with her teeth. Just playing, but I thought of how she had executed that bird a few days ago—not a quiver out of him, the fastest and most painless death I had ever seen inflicted. It was about time to feed them. I took some aspirin, washing it down with a little water left from the can, then went forward. Aussie came running when he saw me and kept crying till I had opened a can and fed them. Then I went back aft and lay down. After a while I started to feel very sick and crawled to the edge of the raft in order not to mess up the deck.

I lay there till it was dark night, my head near the edge. A few times I looked up and saw stars. The awning was still up. A sea washed over and gently lifted my legs. The water was warm, and I didn't mind, but when another one slapped over a while later, I got up. I took more aspirins, then lay down beside the wheel. Kiki came around and looked at me, followed as usual by Aussie, and I picked her up and petted her. Her little body felt good to my hands and face.

I woke up, thinking someone had shaken me, and remembered with a start that I hadn't wound up my chronometers. In a moment I was in the cabin and opened the airtight box in which I kept them wrapped in plastic bags. I discovered I had wound both of them without remembering. My transistor radio, always set on WWV of the U.S. Naval Observatory in Washington, gave me the time to the second, twenty-fours a day, but something might go wrong with it and force me to depend on the chronometers alone.

The next morning I felt a lot better but still weak. I still had a little fever. In the evening, the sky being clear and the wind steady, I raised the mainsail. I had to stop three or four times before I had it up. After I had secured the jib, I lay down on my rubber poncho beside the cabin, my usual place. I slept fitfully, getting up every hour or so and looking at the sky and compass. The raft was sailing fairly fast, but there were no squalls.

Toward morning I opened another can of distilled water and, pouring it all into a saucepan and adding half a bottle of lemon juice, drank it. It was the seventh can from the carton. Then I lay down again and dozed off, and when I opened my eyes, the sun was just coming up. I felt hungry and, while getting my stove started, ate the last two biscuits I had left, which was a bit of a calamity. I cooked oatmeal and ate it with honey and butter, but was still hungry and cooked two more loads before I was satisfied. Then I brewed two cups of coffee and drank them as hot as I could. I was so happy, being all right again, I felt like singing.

The wind had been easterly while I was sick but during the latter part of the night had shifted to the northeast. The sky looked windy, and I was glad to be back on my feet. A little after nine o'clock I took a sight and worked it out. My position was longitude 158 degrees 30 minutes west and latitude 11 degrees 24 minutes south, approximately 110 miles east-southeast of Manikiki. The day was October 16. During the two days I had been sick I had made but little progress.

I knew what I needed now, what I should have—a good long sweat bath in a steam room or half an hour in a tub of hot water, salt water preferably, real hot, and followed by a big hot drink of some sort or a water tumbler full of gin. Then a ten hours' sleep under blankets in a quiet, cool room. That would bring out everything that was foul in me, through every pore of my skin. I thought of all the gyms I had been in and the workouts in double sweatshirts till the sweat rolled off in streams. And afterward the steam room . . . Whenever I felt heavy from overeating or thought a cold was coming on, I went to a gym if I could and worked out, sweating till I felt like newborn. We did the same when coming out of the woods in Washington and Oregon, the first trip always being to the sauna baths. Those brawny Swedes and Finns would lie on the shelves in the red-hot steam till the sweat poured out of their bones and marrow. They have steam rooms in the camps now, they tell me.

10

ONE afternoon a few days later, I was kneeling in the stern working on my rudder chain and the rope tackles which had done the real steering for many weeks already, when, glancing at the sea beside me, I saw within five feet of the raft a big, slow-moving brown body with white spots. Then I saw fins. It was a fish and the shape that of a huge, massive shark. I got to my feet and gazed in bewilderment, frightened a bit at the sudden appearance of such a monster so close beside me. Its tremendous blunt head terminated in a straight mouth, straight as a board almost and a full four feet across, reminding me of a steam shovel. The body was huge like that of a whale but had the large pectoral fins of sharks, each being at least six feet long. The upper part of the tail fin was about the same length. The full length of the monster was at least thirty feet, and it must have weighed tons. No doubt it was a monster shark of some sort, perhaps a whale shark of which I had heard. With its white spots covering the whole body evenly, it gave a glittering sort of appearance beneath the blue shifting waves, for the sun was full on it. It was swimming about three feet beneath the surface, not moving its head to either side in the manner of sharks, so that I couldn't see the eyes or the true shape of the mouth. It went beneath the raft on the starboard side and about in the

144

middle, almost touching the pontoon and came out under the stern close to the rudders. Then it made a circle, returning to the raft, swam slowly beside it, and again went beneath exactly as before. I got my movie camera, climbed to the top of the cabin, and began to film it. The monster was in no hurry and kept swimming at exactly the same speed, underneath the raft and up close beneath the rudders, then another twenty- or thirty-yard circle and back to the raft. I thought it might damage the rudders and got my rifle and fired at it from a distance of a few feet while it was 'longside the raft but only got a good splashing when the bullet struck the water. The monster paid not the slightest attention to it, continuing with its leisurely circling. Now and then it swam a bit higher, and the dorsal fin showed half a foot or so above the surface. Some of the little dolphins had come out from under the raft and were swimming around it, shining like bejeweled darts and seemingly as curious as I. After almost half an hour it swam away to the southeast.

Logbook entry: October 16, 1963

During the night the wind veered to the north and continued strong and steady. The raft handled good, running before it, and I let her go. I studied my charts and decided if I couldn't get west between the 10th and 12th parallel, I would continue south till the wind shifted, even if I had to make my way between the Tongas and Fijis.

Logbook entry, October 18, 1963

No sun. Wind is increasing and driving raft through a fairly high sea. She is plunging and rolling and doing everything a barrel would do but holds her course, due mainly to the centerboards. Spray and seas coming over. Steering southwest by south and will stay with it as long as possible without lowering sail. Noon sight put me at lat. 13° 30′ south. Must have strong current also to be this far south.

145

I've had thoughts of coming disaster the last few days and attribute it to my deficient diet. Perhaps I should have taken vitamins along, as Teddy and my physician advised. I am paying dearly for it, I think. Haven't caught a dolphin now for quite a while. A few of the original ones are still under the raft but know too much to go for my bait.

When I had time and my stoves felt like cooperating, I tried to cook something appetizing, but I had little to work with. Right now I would have given something for a full-grown dolphin, and Kiki and Aussie would also, I think. That would have settled the vitamin question for a few days at least.

I had hooked a shark and, after shooting it, hoisted it on board, cut out the liver, and ate quite a hunk raw and still warm, Polynesian style. I also boiled part of it. The shark was a six-footer with a large, fine liver. Some shark livers are full of vitamins, while others have little. I tried to get Kiki and Aussie to eat some, but they turned their noses away and into the wind. My stomach felt a little jumpy afterwards but settled after a few cups of hot coffee. The shark had a few fish in its stomach that I hadn't seen around the raft, probably from some reef. I was almost 14 degrees south. The course I had originally mapped out was along the 12th parallel, but I was quite resigned now to sail between the Tongas and Samoan islands should the wind hold. The Tongas are a great mass of tiny islands and atolls, many of which are uninhabited. It is an independent domain which was then ruled by a queen, and its people are supposed to be friendly.

I had caught a small shark yesterday, but just as I had it 'longside, it tore out of the hook. My mouth was already watering, thinking of its liver and a few pounds of tender meat for my frying pan. The last shark liver I had eaten had definitely given me a boost.

Last night it rained, and I caught almost nine gallons of water which should last me quite a while. When it first came down, I drank nearly a quart for I was all dried out shying away from my contaminated barrels.

The strong wind had kept up and was driving me further south, so that I wasn't too far from Tutuila where my 1954 raft was, right in front of the Government House in Pago Pago. I wondered what condition it was in. I had given it to the United States Government and the people of Samoa to take care of and put in a building to preserve for future generations. The Government, in the letter of acceptance signed by the Governor of Samoa, had solemnly pledged to do this, so no doubt everything was all right.

I was all over the fever now, and a few extra cans of beans, extra potatoes, and oatmeal had given me back the weight I had lost. First thing I had done was to take four teaspoonsful of flaxseed, let it simmer for twenty minutes in water, and, after it had cooled to a jelly, drank it. This, after a few mugs of seawater for a general tonic, took care of the intestines, the place where fever generally begins.

Logbook entry, October 22, 1963
Long: 163° 30′ west
Lat: 17° 20′ south

The northeast wind has let up after sailing almost 420 miles. When within 40 miles of Palmerston Island, it came around and started blowing strong from the southeast. Fine trade wind, and I'm sailing back north. See how far it will take me. My course is northwest by north now, the best I can do.

I just read in the U.S. Hydrographic Office Sailing Directions that the natives of the New Hebrides, toward which I may be heading, used to practice cannibalism not so long ago and are still apt to stray —when no missionaries were in the offing, I presumed. I could see myself drifting into one of the bays on my rudderless raft and the natives coming out in their canoes, looking at the raft and me and then turning around to see if some missionary was watching from the mangroves, and if not—inviting me to a feast, or rather to watch it from the inside of a pot.

A single man wrecked on a foreign shore was apt to run into trouble almost anywhere if there were no witnesses, meaning no outsiders. Teddy and I heard more than one tale from the natives in the West Indies of the days when sailing ships were wrecked on their islands and looted. On some it was the main revenue, and every sail on the horizon was hungrily watched, hoping a shift of wind or gale would put it on the rocks. They even prayed for it in the churches. The following story I heard from a preacher's son on one of the isolated Windward Islands. "One Sunday morning," he said, "my father was almost through with the sermon when the cry of *Wreck!* rang through the church. Everybody woke up and jumped for the door, almost breaking down the wall. 'Damn it!' my father roared above the tumult. 'Stay where you are, all of you. Give me just half a minute to finish this dam'd sermon, so we can all get an even start.' Within a minute he wound up bellowing: 'O Lord, have mercy on our sinful souls and let that wreck out there be a big one'!"

At the first sign of dawn, Kiki and Aussie always came aft to tell me they were hungry. Aussie used to cry, but Kiki just sat and looked at me, purring hopefully. Neither had given me any trouble at any time. Aussie knew that he was not allowed in the cabin unless Kiki was with him. I had had a box full of sand and one with sawdust for them when the voyage began, but they were long gone. They had found a place, however, where to go. Both thrived on their canned food but now missed fresh fish, especially flying fish, and each night patrolled the deck hoping that one would be washed on board. Occasionally I found a few fins in the morning, showing that they had had a feast. Sometimes shrimp or squid were washed on board. I remembered that Meekie, my black cat of 1954, refused all fish after the voyage, no matter how fresh the shopkeepers told us it was. The only thing in the line of seafood she considered was canned and imported shrimp or a bit of lobster, and even then Teddy had to kneel beside her and plead with her to take a bite.

Whom the Sea Has Taken

Logbook entry, October 27, 1963
Long: 166° 55′ west
Lat: 11° 55′ south

Wind changed to the north again, blowing very strong, and I am sailing south. The whole pattern of the weather has changed the last few weeks—it's more threatening, and the winds strike heavier. Wonder if something is making up.

They had more hurricanes further west around the New Hebrides and New Caledonia, but occasionally a severe one struck the Fijis and Samoan Islands. At the turn of the century a dozen ships were lying in Apia Harbour when a hurricane smashed down and wrecked each one. The only one to escape was a British destroyer, which had steam up at the time and could make for the open sea. Incidentally the British and Germans were just lining up for a battle to decide who should have the island when the hurricane put an end to it.

The bad weather had stayed, with heavy winds, cloudy skies, and squalls, and often the mainsail had to come down, but the wind had shifted again, and I was heading north, steering northwest by west. This was really zigzagging. I hoped it would keep up long enough to clear Samoa. What a crazy course—up and down, north and south and back up again. I was lucky I had plenty of rope for my steering tackles, which required changing sometimes every day.

I had begun to feel trapped. It was October twenty-ninth already, and I was out 117 days, two days longer than on my 1954 voyage in the *Seven Little Sisters*. Last night, when sitting by the compass wrapped in my heavy jacket which looked more suitable for Alaska, I thought of the great voyages the ancient Samoans and other Polynesians had made and what they had to go through when caught in the kind of weather I was having. Nowadays we had instruments—chronometers, time signals, sextants, charts, navigational tables, and along the shores radio beacons—so that a child could navigate, but in those faraway days any bad weather could mean death.

Thinking of the old Polynesians, I imagined seeing two large double canoes making their way through the night, each with over one hundred men, women, and children on board. They were bound for a nearby uninhabited island to gather coconuts as they did once a year. On the second day, when they were about halfway to their destination, a storm came up. They tried to keep together amid the squalls and cloud masses sweeping over the sea but lost each other from sight. Darkness set in. The gale continued during the night and in the morning showed each canoe a gray running sea, heavily clouded sky, and naked horizon. It blew for three days; then one of the canoes was becalmed for a day, after which it became squally again. The wind kept changing. The old navigator on board scanned the skies—the sun when it showed among the clouds and at night the embattled stars—to get an idea of their position, but before long every man, woman, and child in the canoe knew that they were lost. Would they find land or would they perish? It was one or the other, with the odds against them, for islands were mere dots, hardly visible from a canoe, and if passed during the night or on a cloudy day, would never be seen again. They knew many stories of canoes that had sailed away bedecked with flowers for a merrymaking on a neighboring island or to gather coconuts and had never come back. Sometimes news came years later from a canoe, perhaps shipwrecked on their shore, that they had landed on some atoll hundreds of miles away and had started a new settlement, building huts and raising families; but mostly they had disappeared—sunk without trace in the emptiness of the sea, men, women, and children.

The days went by. They lived with their eyes on the horizon, forever hoping to see the tuft of a palm, a dark smudge denoting land, or the sea breaking white on a reef. The young men among them only came down from the mast to rest their eyes from the long staring.

Sometimes they sailed fast and then again lay becalmed as if anchored in a lagoon. They cut notches into the gunwales to mark the passing days. After they had marked off twenty-three days, another storm struck them. They were then already almost out of food, and some of the children had died. They had wrapped them in tapa cloth and given them to the sea, the mother chanting in a low voice, "Shark, do not eat the little body till its soul has left." They were patient and knew that a human being must die when his time comes. They watched their bodies shrink away and the old ones succumb one after the other. After the storm they had many calms, and then the wind became steady, and they sailed before it day after day, making a notch for each one when the sun set.

They were out forty-five days, and many had died, and those who were left had no strength. The water was almost gone, for there had been little rain. The wind had continued strong and steady, and the clouds drifted high and white and were different from those they knew. They lay huddled together for warmth, for the weather had become cooler, and they looked like skeletons; only their large black eyes were bright with the fever of starvation as they raised themselves over the gunwales now and then to scan the horizon. Even the dying thought they might see the tufted head of a palm somewhere above the sea, before their heads sank back and they closed their eyes forever. Coconut palms, the sea, and a reef, and their own tribe—that had been their world since time began.

There were only fifteen left now of the many who had sailed with songs on their lips—three children, five women, and seven men. "We are far from our island and will never see it again," the old navigator whispered, opening his eyes to look at the sky once more before he died. He was aware that his time had come. A master of his craft, he had made no mistake in guiding the canoe since it left the home isle. He had been taught by his father, a renowned navigator who in turn had learned from his father. Since early boyhood he had studied the sea and signs in the sky. Then he thought of his only son, who many years ago had sailed his canoe out of the lagoon to fish and never came back. And his wife was gone now too—a few days ago they had lifted her over the gunwale, wrapped in tapa cloth and light as a feather....

A few days later the helmsman pulled himself up, stared for a moment, and cried hysterically, "Land! Land!" and pointed. Mountains had come as by magic out of the cloud-covered sea. There—there it was! Land! Faraway land lay on the horizon, a dark indistinct mass only showing here and there in blurred outlines. The skeletons came to life and, shading their eyes, stared and stared. The wind was taking them toward it, but it was still faraway.

Nobody slept that night; each one was watching the stars to check the course of the canoe, thinking that, if they missed the land, they would die the next day. Some of them thought it was not real land but only a mirage created by the evil spirit who had blown them away from their home.

In the early dawn they saw it again among the clouds, colored like the clouds only a little darker and sharper-edged. They saw mountain ridges rising and falling. The mountains of their island looked that way after returning from a voyage. When the sun rose over the sea, the mountains slowly turned green and showed deep furrows where valleys came down the slopes. They came closer and closer and then saw bays and steep headlands. There were no reefs, for their sharp eyes saw no white walls of foam, only the seas smashing house-high against the rocks girding the shore.

It was not till after dark that they touched bottom in a sheltered bay and secured the canoe to stakes driven into the sand. In the morning they found water nearby where a little stream emptied into the sea. The castaways had found a new home—New Zealand.

I had been dreaming, had been in the big double canoe with the Polynesians through whose lonely seas I was sailing now for so long already. The winds and squalls which I had been fighting for months had woven the story, and also perhaps the spirit of the invisible islands around me. I got off my perch, checked the compass, and walked around the raft to get back to myself. On the way I stuck my hand under the tarpaulin which covered my large crate forward and housed my extra sails, rope, and other gear, and stroked Aussie.

He always lay in the same place, where he could see the food bowl. Kiki lay way in the back. The rudders were moving back and forth with the sea, practically useless, but the sails and centerboard kept me on a fairly good course. I felt like eating something, but there was nothing that tempted me, and I drank some rainwater, adding lemon juice. Then I sat down again. It was a dark night, and the raft groaned and creaked as she wallowed, with water coming on deck. She was almost forty degrees off the course now. Back and forth, day and night, she swung but occasionally lay steady for hours. If the rudders hadn't broken, I might be hundreds of miles nearer to Australia. Well, Teddy wouldn't begin worrying about me yet, not till I was about 150 days out or so. By that time I would probably have met a ship crossing the West Coast–Sydney steamer route somewhere beyond the Fijis and been reported.

Logbook entry, October 29, 1963
Long: 166° 15′ west
Lat: 13° 50′ south

Wind has switched back to the northeast and am steering southwest. Hope it holds till I get past the Samoan Islands which are coming uncomfortably close.

11

I HAD been overboard three times during the last two days to fix the rudders, but they remained as good as useless. I couldn't go on like this. I looked at the sky and the sea and back at my rudders swinging in the foam, and realized that I could never reach Australia with them. I saw it clearly, saw my dream shattered. I had been defeated.

For some time already I had realized that a decision would have to be made; it had been hanging over me like a judgment. I had to try to get into a port and repair the rudders before going on. There were only three island groups I could consider—the Fijis, the Tongas, or Samoa. The Tongas were a little too far south now since I had sailed north again after another switch of wind, so it would have to be the Fijis or Samoa. Samoa was quite near, with Pago Pago in American Samoa and Apia a little further west in Western Samoa. I would have liked to sail another nine hundred or one thousand miles before giving up my dream of an unbroken voyage to Australia, but it looked almost impossible with my rudders. Samoa would be the logical place to run into, before I piled up on some reef and had the raft smashed under my feet with all my instruments, films, and notes—perhaps be smashed myself with my two little shipmates.

It was hard to give up. I had the chart of the Fiji Islands before me and studied the maze of reefs through which I would have to sail to get to Suva, the capital, the only place to make repairs. It would really be impossible without rudders. The logical thing was to try for Pago Pago or Apia. All right, then, all right . . . But it was hard to give up—I wanted that extra thousand miles or so. Then I chided myself. You fool, I said, didn't you get enough out of the voyage—seven thousand and five hundred miles alone, alone as if the whole world were entirely your own? Not a human voice ever to say yes or no to you. Could you have lived a more complete existence? Has a single day failed you? I saw all the days and nights strung out along my long trail, all the way from Callao, and had to admit that I had lived as never before. I sat by the wheel and was lost in thought till the raft went into the wind.

The eastern sky had been a lurid and peculiar sort of red with bright coppery tints this morning. In the afternoon it became hazy, and long streamers like mares' tails spanned the heavens. The wind was still from the southeast, and I was steering a course between the Samoa Islands and the Tokolaus. The day had ended with rain setting in, which kept up most of the night, then lessened toward dawn. It began heavliy again after the sun came up, so that, with the wind blowing hard and the rain smashing down, the sea looked at times like the snow-swept hills in a Wyoming blizzard.

I had learned a lot about sailing and steering from my broken rudders. Above all the voyage taught me that the sea wanted to be mastered and, with every move she made, gave you a counter move for your benefit. And so, I reasoned, it had to be with the earth and all things on it. Nature wanted to be mastered by man's will. Going on from this, a philosopher might add that it was the same with death and eternity—they too wanted to be mastered.

I had lain on a northwesterly course till November third, having reached longitude 170 degrees 15 minutes west and and 12 degrees south, approximately eighty miles southeast of Swain's Island, when the wind shifted to straight north. Again a complete shift. I kept the mainsail up and ran before it for two days; then, in the afternoon of November sixth, the wind veered to northeast. I decided to run before it again, thinking that if it stayed I might have a chance of sailing between Tutuila, American Samoa, and Upolu, Western Samoa. The condition of my rudders gave me little other choice.

About two o'clock in the afternoon the sky had begun to look bad, but I kept the mainsail up. The wind increased gradually, and when a few hours later I touched the mizzen behind me, it was as hard as a sheet of iron, and I doubted whether I could get the big sail down without having it torn. I kept racing before it until three explosions beneath me, one quickly following the other, told me that three of my centerboards had snapped off. The raft swung into the wind, and the sail went aback with a blast that stopped the raft and began beating against the mast with a fury which threatened to bring down the whole rigging. I threw the lashings over the wheel and jumped forward just as the sail was ripped from top to bottom. Expecting to have nothing left but a mass of shreds, I lowered away. The raft now swung before the wind again, and the yard was blown forward all the way to the jibboom, and I dived into the sail, thinking I had tangled with wild horses. After a long struggle, I managed to secure what was left and lashed the yard to the legs of the mast. Then I set the jib.

As soon as it was daylight, I would go forward and see just what had happened to the sail and start sewing. I had needles and thread and plenty of dacron and canvas, in case I had to patch. Lucky this happened while I still had sea room; but I wouldn't have it long if the wind kept up, with three of my centerboards gone—the two after ones and one 'midships. It could never be Suva in the Fijis now—the raft would never get there. Apia, if I was lucky. Otherwise it meant going on a reef.

I looked into the dawn, and everything appeared changed—the

raft, the sea, and most of all I. I was no longer what I had been, no longer the man sailing single-handed to Australia or even to the Fijis—I had become a man forced to give up.

Hanging on to the wheel to keep my footing in the gale, I peered into the dawn. Just what lay ahead out there in the grayness —what reef, what disaster? I didn't get a sight the day before but by dead reckoning was approximately fifty miles from Apia. Would the raft handle well enough to get over the reef? Perhaps I would sight a ship to show me the entrance into the harbor.

When it was light enough, I fixed the starboard rudder and steering gear as well as I could and then got busy with the sail. I had to take it off the yard, for it would have been impossible to sew in the wind. After dragging it aft to the lee of the cabin, I checked the damage and found two rents from top to bottom and numerous smaller ones. Sewing was tough with spray and seas coming over and the wind tearing the sail out of my hands. I used long stitches to get it up as quickly as possible, for I knew that I was drifting toward the reefs of Samoa.

After three hours I was done, bound the sail to the yard again, fastened the running gear, and hoisted it aloft. It looked all right, for the wrinkles of the hasty sewing soon straightened out in the wind. But the raft steered badly, though I had pulled up the 'midship centerboard and one of the forward ones and put them aft. During the rest of the afternoon I went up the mast a few times thinking I might see the mountains of Tutuila or Upolu. The sky had begun to look worse, and at sundown I wondered whether I would crash during the night.

About an hour after dark I saw a light aft, about half a point to starboard. At first I thought it was a ship, for it seemed to be steady; then I saw that it flashed, though the heaving sea prevented an accurate count and therefore its identification. Checking my chart, I thought that it was probably the light on the western tip of Tutuila, American Samoa. It seemed to be about five miles off. This gave me

157

a pretty good idea of my position. It also told me that I was sailing on the edge of disaster.

The wind kept increasing, and a little after nine o'clock I took the mainsail down, for the raft was becoming unmanageable. Then I sat down by the wheel, now and then getting up to stare into the darkness, always expecting to see breakers, for a shift of wind or the current might well be pushing me towards the reef. I was steering almost west, as close to the wind as I could, trying to keep away from Upolu until daylight.

At two o'clock in the morning it was blowing with near gale force, and the raft was awash fore and aft. The mast was groaning and creaking in its sockets as it snapped back and forth, and I feared the bolts holding it would shear off.

At last dawn came, and the sea began to light up. The wind was unabated and the sky full of torn clouds with one wild, wind-twisted formation dominating the southeast. Beneath it, still indistinct, lay a long, shapeless mass on the horizon—mountains. Upolu! First land my eyes had fallen on since leaving Callao 130 days before. I judged it to be about ten or fifteen miles off.

The sun came up, but the sky continued threatening with the big twisted cloud mass in the southeast refusing to break up. Slowly I approached the island, which sometimes, amid the driven clouds and squalls, showed the clear outline of summits.

At eleven thirty the wind shifted more to the north and eased up a little, and I set a course straight for the shore, figuring I would be heading toward Apia Harbour, which according to my chart was approximately twenty-five miles from Cape Tapaga, the eastern tip of the island. Then I hoisted the mainsail, but it stood less than ten minutes before the raft went into the wind. Three times I brought it back on the course, then realized it was useless and lowered the sail again. The raft just couldn't hold her course without enough centerboards. I had to get into Apia under jib and mizzen.

After climbing up the mast a few times, I saw a few white dots on the shore, almost dead ahead, which looked like houses. There was also something a little higher on the mountainside, which I took for a water tank, and this gave me a target to steer by. Then I loosened the mainsail and hoisted it for one more try, but after a few minutes the raft swung around again—the jib and mizzen had to do it. The wind was fair, however, and I was able to steer a course for what I thought was Apia Harbour.

About an hour later, when aloft again, I saw a white wall all along the foot of the mountainous shore. This was the reef—white, even, and unbroken. I had to get over it to land. The island looked majestic and beautiful with its dark green mountains rising into the savage sky, dipping down and rising again to lofty, mostly cloud-hidden peaks. The eastern end was continuously shrouded by squalls sweeping over it with trailing curtains of rain and mists.

I had hoisted the American flag upside down as a signal of distress, in order to draw attention to the raft and if possible have the pilot boat come out to show me the way through the reef into the harbor. But was there a lookout station? When I went up on the mast again, I could make out what I thought was a break in the reef and so most likely the entrance to the lagoon of Apia. The wind and current were slowly pushing me down the coast to the west, away from the town, though with my mainsail up I could have held a course for the opening.

Hours passed while I scanned the sea for a boat coming toward me, but there was no sign of life amid the whitecaps. Slowly I came nearer, the white dots that were houses becoming more distinct and visible from the deck. Where was the pilot boat? With good glasses they should have been able to see my distress flag now. I had to do something to draw their attention to me, for the reef was coming nearer and nearer; and taking off my awning, I went up the mast and tied it to the flagpole. It was about six times as large as the American flag, and anyone watching from the shore should realize that something was wrong.

159

Whom the Sea Has Taken

Kiki and Aussie are rather quiet and have not played all day. Perhaps they feel that something is going on. How they will sniff the earth and nibble at the grasses and weeds! A hundred and thirty days—poor little creatures. Deep-water sailors to the bone! And Aussie just a kitten when he came on board and now almost full-grown, with an iron-hard body, and well-behaved, for Kiki brought him up. Kiki is looking back to the open sea, and I turn her head shoreward and say to her, "Look this way, little silly, that's where you can see something. Don't you want to go a-romping on that green shore and sniff at the flowers?"

"Don't get excited," Kiki seems to say. "We'll get there when we get there."

I'm too close now to go up on the mast and leave the wheel, so I just take an occasional quick jump up on the crate to study the reef. I can plainly make out houses, warehouses, trees, and roofs. And I can see the harbor—a little lagoon with a steamer anchored in it. Everything is not too clear, however, for a haze from the driven spray lies on the water.

My eyes are glued to the reef, trying to find a spot where I can get through, but I see no opening—nothing but a solid wall of foam. In most places there seem to be two and three reefs, one behind the other—fringing reefs guarding the coast. I knew them from 1954 around Tutuila, the American island.

The wind has carried me three or four miles down the coast, and Apia is lost behind a palm-studded little headland. The reef is quite close. The time has almost come. I have to go straight in, for to my right it is breaking house-high, with reef after reef extending for miles toward Upolu's big sister island, Savai'i, with its six thousand-foot-high mountains just visible among the clouds that have piled up around them dark and heavy.

Everything is ready for the crash, and I put my little ship-mates in the cabin so that they have a chance, in case the mast comes down and the deck is raked by seas. I also have a box ready for them, with my Grace Line life ring fastened to it, so that in case of a smashup they can drift through the lagoon and to the shore. Five o'clock already and darkening fast. The sun has disappeared behind the western cloud masses lying over Savai'i.

I jump to the crate for a last look at the reef, then rush back to the wheel. Only a hundred yards now. I can plainly hear the roar of the breakers. Kiki is sitting on the high doorstep, calmly looking out. Aussie is behind her, stretched out on a pile of clothes. I push Kiki inside and close the door.

The lagoon behind the reef is dotted with large coral boulders, and the shore is about four hundred yards away, fringed with mangrove thickets above which rise the slim trunks of coconut palms.

Yard by yard I'm coming in. The reef bares its black wall of boulders, after each sea drops. A big comber picks up the raft, flings it forward, and then drops it. For a moment it lies helpless, then is lifted again and flung forward. I stare at the foul wall of the reef in front of me. Another sea picks up the raft and—I hang on to the wheel, my eyes darting up to the mast to see which way to jump should it fall.

Foam blots out everything as we strike. The shock seems to dismember the raft, and I am smashed against the spokes. We are hammered on the boulders by the seas and seem to disintegrate. Raft and cabin are engulfed in foam. All the centerboards, though only a few feet deep in the water, have broken off, and some of the deck planks have been ripped out with them. Suddenly the bow comes up and slowly drops again. A heavy sea breaks over the stern. The convulsions continue. I wonder that the mast remains standing. Then the raft begins to move from side to side. A sea lifts it and flings it ahead. It lands solid, on all three pontoons, then is lifted again and once more smashed down and lies with a list to starboard. Another sea wrenches us clear and pushes us through the foam. Again we stop, bump along a few yards, then slide forward; after another shock and lift by a sea coming over the stern, we sink almost gently down. We are over the reef and in the lagoon.

I am still at the wheel, and the sails fill with wind, and we head for the shore about four hundred yards away. We bump over boulders and hang up, but the seas coming over the reef push us clear. Twenty-five yards from the shore, which is guarded by huge coral blocks, I run forward and drop the anchor, then lower jib and mizzen. The raft swings around. After 130 days of solitude and sailing approximately seventy-five hundred miles, the raft has landed. Kiki and Aussie are on deck. "Well, little fellows, we made it," I say and lift them high up and tell them to take a look at the scenery.

Apia is hidden behind the wooded headland, and I see no sign of life in the lagoon. Dusk is setting in. After a while I notice a skiff driven by an outboard motor come out of a nearby bay with a man and woman in it. I wave and shout, and they see me and after hesitating a bit come 'longside.

"Glad to see you," I say overcome with joy at seeing human beings again. "I've just come from South America. . . ."

They stare at me, and I wonder if they speak English. "You speak English, don't you?" I ask.

"Yes, we speak English," the man says in a cultured voice, still keeping a few feet away from the side of the raft, probably not quite trusting this half-naked, sun-scorched, and white-bearded fellow on such strange-looking craft and making such a crazy statement.

I tell them who I am and ask them to notify the authorities at once—and also a radio station, should there be one, for I want the news of my arrival to get on the air as quickly as possible so that Teddy knows.

The skiff turns around and with racing motor heads back to the bay from which it came. I am alone again. The sun has set, and the mangroves cast dark shadows over the raft. Everything is quiet and so strange. The man had introduced himself as the Reverend Mr. Maddox, head of the Methodist Mission of Upolu, and the lady as his wife. I clear up the deck and feed my little shipmates, then open a can of beans and eat standing by the wheel as if that was my ordained place. I feel suddenly lonely, as if something has been taken out of my life.

162

12

ABOUT an hour later I heard voices among the mangroves and saw the dark shapes of men on the shore. Some came wading out to the raft. There was also an outrigger canoe with two men paddling. The canoe reached the raft first, and the men climbed on board and welcomed me to Samoa. One of them, wearing a white helmet, tunic, and a *lava lava*, the skirts of the natives, was a police officer who asked if I needed assistance of any kind. He said he had a car waiting and would take me to a hotel if I wanted. I told him I needed no help and would remain on board. He asked me how I had come over the reef. When I told him I had sailed over it, he shook his head. It was quite dark when he, and the others who had waded out to the raft and greeted me like a long-lost brother, returned to the shore. They told me that I had landed at Pui Paa, about five kilometers west of Apia.

For a while I was alone; then I heard voices again, and a group of young fellows came wading out to the raft and climbed on board. They all spoke English and asked many questions, and some invited me to come ashore and eat at their homes. I told them I would stay on board but would like to have some fresh fruit. One of them then went back ashore and after a while returned with a basket of ripe bananas.

"In the morning we'll bring you coconuts and mangoes," he said. "It's too dark now to pick them." They stayed till after midnight, talking and asking questions, while I ate one banana after another.

I was really sleepy then. Automatically I walked around the raft once more and checked the gear as if I were still at sea and sailing. The tide was running out now and gurgling among the pontoons and rocks and over the coral. Some of the rocks were very large, so that the lagoon around me looked as if a herd of huge animals had bedded down in it. It was strangely still to someone who had been on the roaring sea for so many months. Through the stillness came, at measured intervals, the muffled thunder of the reef as the big rollers struck. The land looked heavy and solid, and seemed to be pressing down on me; even breathing was harder. Unconsciously my mind went to the sea, yearning—as if I were uprooted here. Kiki and Aussie came around, for it was their time to be wide-awake. I lay down.

Voices awakened me. I looked up and saw a single star in the paling sky and beneath, almost touching the raft, the black wall of the mangroves. Men were wading out to the raft, stepping carefully among the boulders, for the tide was high again. An outrigger canoe with two men came 'longside, and the men climbed on board. One of them was dressed in police uniform but bareheaded. He was of tremendous size and one of the finest-looking men I had ever seen. Sticking out a big hand, he introduced himself as Leo Schmidt, Police Superintendent of Western Samoa, an independent country consisting of the islands of Upolu and Savai'i. He spoke perfect English. After congratulating me on my voyage, he invited me to go ashore with him and have my first meal in Apia at his house. He said he had his car waiting and would take me first to the residence of the Prime Minister, the Honorable Mataafa II, who was his brother-in-law. And I wouldn't have to worry about the raft, since he would put a policeman on board day and night to watch it. After showing him around the raft, I went ashore with him, first locking the cabin door but leaving a porthole open so that Kiki and Aussie could get in and out.

While I sat beside Leo Schmidt in a car driven by one of his police sergeants—a big man also and like him wearing a *lava lava*—he told me that Western Samoa was an independent country with a democratic government, having attained this status just two years before. Since the appearance of the white man in the Pacific, Western Samoa had, I learned, first belonged to the Germans, then to the British, and after the Second World War become a protectorate of New Zealand under United Nations charter until it had acquired independence. The Prime Minister, to whom we went, lived in a spacious and stately native palace, and at our approach two ancient Samoans, giants in stature, came down the steps and, speaking in Samoan, solemnly announced my arrival. The Prime Minister was a big, impressive-looking man who spoke perfect English and was the elected and astute leader of the young democracy.

In the evening when I returned, after a busy day spent meeting numerous notables of the island, I found a policeman on the raft besides many natives—men, women, and children. All day long, I was told, they had been streaming to Pui Paa from the villages to look at my raft.

I stayed up again till after midnight, talking to groups of young fellows and answering endless questions about the United States and whether I had encountered pirates, evil spirits, or any monsters of the deep. Most of them had read the British edition of my 1954 raft voyage.

The next morning at daybreak, when the tide was full, a launch of the Union Steamship Company towed the raft into Apia Harbour, where I anchored about ten yards from the shore. I now rented a bungalow at a little hotel.

The rudders were taken off and brought to the machine shop of the Public Works. They were little more than scrap iron, and the mechanics couldn't understand why such flimsy material had been used. Unfortunately they couldn't change the design of the rudders, the shop not having facilities for such work, but they made a number of sketches and showed me some quite ingenious ways of strengthening them with the welding tools they possessed, and I told them to go ahead.

Within a week I had caught up with my sleep and was anxious to be off again. In the meantime I was living in my little bungalow and nights could hear the thud of coconuts falling on the ground, while through the stillness, as if calling me, came the boom of the seas crashing on the reef. Often I turned around in my sleep and, awakening uneasily, thought I should be off again and on my way to Australia.

I feasted on fruit and vegetables and arranged for a plentiful supply to take along. My water barrels had been emptied and cleaned and then filled with seawater to keep them from shrinking while the raft lay in the lagoon. Kiki and Aussie continued to live on board, for the bungalow was no place for them, and every morning at dawn and again in the evening I went down to the raft to feed them.

One day, talking to a merchant I had become friendly with, I mentioned that I had ruptured myself on the voyage while overboard and working on the rudders.

"See our surgeon," he said, "and let him look at you. We have free medical care here, and it wouldn't cost you a penny. I'll drive you to the hospital."

I created quite a commotion among the doctors. They crowded around me with their stethoscopes, eager eyed, almost watering at the mouths to take this lean, white-bearded specimen from the sea and study him. I waved them aside, smiling. "I only ruptured myself," I said, "and want the surgeon to have a look at me before I go on."

Then I lay on the table, and Dr. Goodman's fingers probed my abdomen. "Cough," he said. Half a dozen doctors stood around watching. I coughed many times, then Dr. Goodman said that I had a hernia and there was definite danger of strangulation. He strongly advised against continuing the voyage before being operated on.

"We can do it here, or you can fly back to the States," he said. "Your hernia on the right side you don't have to worry about."

"Just what does a strangulation do?" I asked.

"It kills you if you are alone out there," he replied quietly.

I was out in the sunshine again. What should I do? I wanted to go on. I had to go on, I felt—I had to get to Australia and finish the voyage. Strangulation had sounded bad, but now, outside, it didn't scare me. I couldn't see myself undergoing an operation and perhaps being tied up for six months or so. But how about Teddy? She was the one to be really considered. What would she think if she found out that I had gone on without telling her? I couldn't do that. I had to tell her—I had to tell her and find out what she thought of it. There was no way out of it. It wouldn't be fair after what she had been through with me. This was her expedition as much as mine. She had probably had the toughest part of it. I had to tell her.

I went to the telegraph office and sent her a cable explaining the situation. The next day I had an answer:

COME BACK TO NEW YORK FOR EXAMINATION STOP
AM CABLING PLANE TICKET   TEDDY

Just like Teddy. I knew she would fly to Samoa if I didn't come to New York.

I took everything off the raft, including the repaired rudders and steering gear, stored it in a warehouse, and cabled Teddy I was coming. Kiki and Aussie would come with me, for I had found out that the Australian Government would have destroyed them had I landed there. Such was the law. All dogs and cats which did not come by steamer from the British Isles, having lived there for six months previously, were destroyed. If they did come from Britain, they were put in quarantine for six months. What would have happened, I thought, had I landed in Australia and they had tried to take my little shipmates away from me to be put in a gas chamber?

One morning when I waded out to the raft, there was no Kiki

sitting in the stern waiting for me. I unlocked the cabin, and there was Aussie—but no Kiki. "Where is your partner, Aussie?" I asked. Aussie appeared frightened. I was frantic. How could I go back to New York without Kiki? I couldn't face Teddy—she would blame me. It would spoil the whole homecoming.

News of Kiki's disappearance spread like wildfire through Apia and into the adjoining villages, for she had become the pet of the islanders. Unfortunately she was utterly unafraid of strangers, and anyone wading out to the raft to look at it—and they came day and night from all over the island—could pick her up and pet her and most likely walk away with her. Aussie, on the contrary, having known only me really in his short life, was very cautious and would have clawed his way up the iron mast should anyone come near him.

At nine o'clock when police headquarters opened for business, I told Leo Schmidt, the herculean island chief, of Kiki's disappearance, and he at once ordered a special bulletin to be beamed over the island radio, ordering Kiki to be brought back at once.

"Don't worry," he said. "If she's alive, we'll have her back. But perhaps she fell overboard."

"Kiki!" I exclaimed. "Never! A hurricane couldn't wash her off the raft. She's a sailor—both of them are."

Throughout that long day I must have been asked by at least a thousand people if Kiki had come back yet. I went to the raft a number of times, but there was no Kiki, only the still-frightened Aussie. "We can't go back to New York without Kiki," I said to him, and he seemed to understand.

The next morning, long before sunrise, I waded out to the raft to feed Aussie, and there was Kiki sitting in the stern, straight up like a furry little rabbit in a cabbage patch and waiting for me as usual, acting as if she hadn't been away a moment. "Where have you been?" I asked her, picking her up to see if she was all right, but Kiki only gave a yawn that looked bigger than her whole head and then began purring and snuggling up to me to get me busy on her breakfast. I fed her and then carried her ashore with me to stay in the bungalow till we left for New York.

I now had to decide the fate of my raft in case I didn't come back. The plane could crash, anything could happen on the long flight to New York and later on the return to Samoa or even while I was in New York. And there also was the possibility of an operation and something going wrong—anything could happen.

I decided to give the raft to the United States Government and people of American Samoa in nearby Pago Pago again, as I had in 1954. Then the two rafts would be together. I mentioned it to a merchant, a native of Apia, and opening his eyes wide, he asked, "Are you under the impression that your other raft is in Pago Pago?"

"Of course, where else?"

He cleared his throat. "It was there—it's not there now."

"Where is it then? It's supposed to be right on the lawn in front of the Government House." I was getting excited. "They sent me a photograph of it."

"Your raft isn't there anymore. It's gone—they chopped it up for firewood."

"Chopped it up for firewood! Who did?"

He shrugged his shoulders.

"It was right in front of the Government House."

"I know, I've seen it there. We've all seen it."

"Chopped up for firewood—my beautiful raft . . . My seven jungle logs . . ."

After this I could do nothing but give my raft to the Government of Western Samoa, to take care of it during my absence and, in case I didn't come back for any reason, to keep it and preserve it for future generations. The Prime Minister signed the official document of acceptance.

I was ready to fly to New York with my two little shipmates, and we boarded the local plane for the hop to nearby Pago Pago, where we had to wait a few hours for the jet coming in from Sydney which would take us to Hawaii and Los Angeles.

After we'd landed in Pago Pago and Kiki and Aussie had been taken care of, I walked over to the Government House and stood on the lawn where the *Seven Little Sisters* had been. It was empty. Sunk without trace—but not sunk flying the Stars and Stripes till the waves closed over her brave body, for she had been a fighter and had sailed to a world's record through seven thousand unbroken miles of storms and calms in 115 grueling days. That's how she would have wanted to die....

13

I WAS back in New York—back among telephones and subways, among radios and television, reporters, photographers, and editors, back in the roar and turmoil of the world's most titanic, most convulsed city. And most important, I was with Teddy again. We walked and talked and sat up until the early hours of the morning, and it was as if we had never been really parted, but that she had been on the raft with me on the whole voyage across the Pacific or that I had been with her in New York in her loneliness. She told me that she had sensed everything that had happened to me, just as I had known of her long illness.

Kiki and Aussie took the change in their strides. They walked around the hotel apartment as if they had never seen a raft, jumped over the furniture just as they had over the cabin roof, and tossed each other around on the carpet till the people below thought that a mob of kids was on the rampage above their heads. And how disdainfully they sniffed at the food, unless it was imported shrimp or lobster tidbits or something of that sort, so that Teddy worried herself frantic about what to get for them to keep them healthy and happy. "They really want flying fish, Teddy," I said one day while she was kneeling beside Kiki, begging her to at least look at the shrimp she had bought for her.

"The poor things, what they must have been through," she said. "I don't understand how they survived. And Aussie wasn't bigger than my hand. I never thought he would survive. But they look gorgeous, really, don't they?"

One day I lay on the same table again where I had been examined before beginning the voyage.

"Cough," the same doctor said, and I coughed while his fingers dug into me. He kept telling me to cough, and dutifully I coughed, and each time he probed my vitals.

When he stopped, I asked, "How is it?"

"You need an operation."

I showed him the statement of Dr. Goodman of Apia, and he said, "I fully agree with him."

"There's danger of strangulation, he told me," I said.

"There is."

"Just what is a strangulation anyway, Bernie?" I asked.

"Just what it says, Bill—the intestine that has come out can't come back in; it's pinched off by the abdominal muscles. In other words, it's strangled."

"And then?"

"Then gangrene sets in, and after a while you have a perforation, and then you are in a hell of a fix. How are you otherwise?"

"Ready to go."

"Why do you want to continue?"

"To finish the job, Bernie."

"Don't you think you did enough?"

"I cleared the raft for Australia, and that's where she's going."

"All right, Bill, but get that operation as soon as possible. Don't wait."

"I'll sure think it over, Bernie."

Teddy and I were sitting in our apartment the same evening. "Everybody's asking me why I want to go back to Apia and go on with the voyage," I had just said. "I don't understand people. Even in Samoa they asked; they even bet against my coming back."

"They think you're too old and have had enough, that's all," Teddy said, looking up from her newspaper. "I bawled out a reporter today who called up and wanted to know how you felt. 'How's the old man,' he asked. I really got sore and told him off."

"I have to hand it to you, Teddy—you never asked me why I want to go on. You asked me about everything else."

"I know you have to finish the voyage," Teddy said quietly.

I reached out and stroked Kiki, sprawling beside me on the settee. "Well, Kiki, you aren't going back, I know that—you'll stay right here with Teddy. Australia doesn't want little cats like you." As if she had heard something of importance, Kiki got up, gave a quick stretch without opening her eyes, and lay down again. "I'll be all alone this time," I said.

"I wish you would make your mind up about that operation."

"I've decided against it."

Teddy looked up from her paper.

"I thought it over from every angle—I did, really. It wouldn't be wise, not at this time. I'll tell you why. I know myself pretty well— my insides, I mean. It's not so simple, an operation. Complications can set in, for one thing. They have to cut me wide open with a hernia on each side. 'Nothing to it', they say. 'You'll be walking around in a few days as good as ever.' Oh, yes, I know that line. I don't like the idea of having been cut open and stitched up again, like a bag. Perhaps I would be the same again, but perhaps not. Who knows? Do they know? They'll tell me to take it easy for a while, give me a pat on the back, and turn me loose. If I can't jump around as I used to and feel something's gone out of me, they'll say 'What do you expect—you're past seventy, going on eighty'."

"Leave that eighty out," Teddy interrupted me angrily. "I guess you'd like to be eighty, the way you talk."

"All right, Teddy." My hand went back to Kiki and stroked her throat which she liked, whether awake or asleep. "So they'll just say, 'You're past seventy, what do you expect?' And behind my back, 'What the hell does the old guy want? In another year or two he'll be anchored in a wheel chair'."

"Of course," I went on after a while, "they have their statistics—the doctors, I mean—and seventy is aged, and that's all there is to it. Can't really blame them. Not so long ago, really, when I was loading ships in Galveston, carrying three hundred-pound sacks of cottonseed meal on my shoulders, I used to think that a man of thirty was quite old and just about through."

"You can't tell me that you had to make your living doing that kind of work," Teddy said in a severe voice.

"I was happy doing it, whether I had to or not, Teddy. I think I was just born to have a crack at it—or to be a Volga boatman towing barges, maybe. I sometimes feel sorry I missed that."

"What nonsense you get in your head," Teddy said.

"Anyway, getting back to that operation, you know what a job it is for one man to handle a raft like mine—I've told you enough about that. Well, I just can't see how I could stand up to it after an operation—not for a year or so anyway. I think everything would bust wide open again. Of course, if there was a real emergency, now, I would have it done."

Teddy flared up. "How silly you can talk! Emergency! It's an emergency in my eyes. Why wait till you're out there to get it?"

"Anyway, if I let them operate now, I wouldn't be ready for months, and by that time the pontoons will have rusted through and the raft be lying on the bottom of the lagoon. I'll get a good truss and let Bernie check it, and then get going."

"You should have two," Teddy said quickly, "in case something happens to one." Teddy was always practical.

We were trying to put Kiki in a box. A few times we had her inside, but she always managed to get out again. She didn't fight, she just struggled, and Kiki was a very strong cat. At last we got the cover over her head and fastened it down, and for extra measure

I put a few turns of stout rope around it. The box had air holes and handles and was of strong cardboard. We were going to take the train to Cape Cod to give Kiki to the same people who already had Aussie. He had been there for a number of weeks.

Teddy had intended to keep Kiki, but after Aussie was gone, we used to come back to our apartment in the evening and see her sitting by the window, sadly gazing at the bleak walls fencing us in—and wondering, so Teddy thought, whether she would ever see the blue sky again or the green grass or the open sea—so Teddy decided it would be a crime to keep her in the city.

Teddy was weeping, and Kiki gave plaintive little cries as we went down the elevator to the street. We took a taxi to Grand Central station and got on the train. When it was out of the city, we let Kiki out of the box but kept her on the leash. Kiki didn't mind the leash as long as she could sit beside us on the cushions like a regular passenger and see what was going on around her.

It was against the rules to take a cat or dog out of its cage on a train, but when the conductor came by and saw Kiki, he stopped and talked to us in a most friendly manner. After a while he was petting Kiki and said a little wistfully that she was a very beautiful cat and that he had once had one of the same tortoise coloring.

A car picked us up in Boston and drove us to Cape Cod to a beautiful estate amid gently rolling, low hills crowned with birches and pines and glimpses of the blue sea between. The man and his wife both were fond of animals, and we were happy that Kiki had found such a good home. When she and Aussie first saw each other after their five weeks' separation, Kiki ignored him utterly while Aussie acted as if afraid of her.

In the afternoon we got into the car to drive back to Boston. Aussie was in the house, already a well-established favorite, and Kiki was sitting on the doorstep, her back turned to us. It was a beautiful Cape Cod day, like something dropped down from the sky.

"I'll never have a cat again," Teddy said, wiping away a big tear. "If we only had a home, I would never give Kiki away."

The car began rolling over the gravel, and Teddy leaned far out of the window and cried, "Kiki, Kiki, why don't you look at me? Good-bye, Kiki..." Her voice began to break.

"Good-bye, Kiki—little shipmate," I cried and put my arm around Teddy.

My friends in Apia kept writing that the weather in the western Pacific was bad and unsettled. There were storms and even hurricanes and often westerly winds. This had gone on month after month, and the expected southeast trades stayed away. They sent me clippings of reports from the Fijis, the Tongas, Samoa, and New Zealand, telling of ships driven on the reefs or meeting disaster at sea with sometimes all on board lost. A Matson Line boat en route from Fiji to American Samoa had its lifeboats torn off and sustained other damage in the worst hurricane its captain, an old-timer in the South Pacific, had experienced.

My raft, I was told, was taking a beating even lying in the lagoon and twice had been blown from her anchorage and driven ashore. At last Leo Schmidt, the police superintendent, ordered twenty prisoners from the road gang into the froth-covered lagoon to tow her to a more sheltered spot. There she lay now, moored with a heavy chain a mile below Apia.

Finally I decided to wait no longer and fly back, get the raft ready, and sail. When I told Teddy, she gave me a peculiar look and said, "I've been thinking about something...."

"What?" I asked, sensing that something was up.

Teddy put her arms around me. "I want to go with you."

"To Apia?"

"To Australia."

"On the raft?"

"Yes."

I shook my head. "Impossible, Teddy."

"Why?"

176

"The reefs—the reefs, Teddy. It'll be a tough trip."

"It can't be as bad as waiting. Sitting here and waiting for news— news that never comes. Month after month. You don't know what I went through."

"I know, Teddy—I know it only too well. But it can't be done. If the raft goes on a reef, it'll be raked and battered till there's nothing left of it. We'll be washed off and cut to pieces on the coral." I shook my head again. "Do you think I could take that, seeing you go...?"

"I'm not afraid."

"I know you're not."

"And how about your hernia? If something should happen to you and you're all alone, who is going to take care of you? Don't tell me it couldn't happen."

"Teddy, this is my fight. Alone I'll get through. If the raft holds together, I'll take it to Australia."

I took one of my navigation charts of the Western Pacific and marked my projected course on it—from Apia to Sydney—then tacked it up on the wall of our apartment. "You can follow my course on it," I explained. "I figure on about fifty to fifty-five miles a day." I also showed her how to take the miles from the longitude and latitude scales on the chart's margin.

Just before leaving New York, Teddy asked, "And you will talk to me again as you did before?"

"If you want me to, Teddy."

"Of course I do. How can you ask? Don't you know that it is something very real to me?"

"I know, Teddy. It is to me too."

"Otherwise, I don't know how I could bear it. You'll be so far-away this time."

"Yes, Teddy, I'll be sailing on the other side of the world."

14

THE voice of the captain, announcing that the plane was now over Utah and flying before a tail wind at a speed of 640 miles per hour, broke into my revery. I glanced down at the snow-covered peaks of the Rockies and closed my eyes again. They were showing a movie, but I wasn't interested; my mind was on Apia. It wouldn't take long to get there at such speed. I could see the raft lying in the lagoon near Jim Currie's sawmill—waiting for me, the old girl. Yeah, I'm coming. A lot of work had to be done to get her ready. New centerboards, too, for they had all been broken in that final storm and crashing over the reef. The sails too were in bad shape and needed going over. Some of those stitches had been real "homeward bounders"—just good enough to make it to port. I had a bag full of extra sails among my baggage—used sails but overhauled and in good condition, given me by Gunnar W. Vallentine, a sailmaker on City Island, a master of his trade and well-known on the Atlantic seaboard. I had dropped in on him one afternoon scouting around for extra sails. He was an old man, tall and of powerful frame with a strong face and slow, gentle way of speaking. The walls of his office had photographs showing the different yacht rigs then in favor, but on one wall were only photographs of square-riggers. I didn't know the man's past, only that he was a Dane, and pointing to a four-masted bark said, "My first voyage was on one like that, the *Henriette*—back in 1908."

The old man's face lighted up with a soft glow, and he really sized me up. "I knew the *Henriette*," he said in his gentle way. "I was on the *Elisabeth*, her sister ship, for seven years—eleven times around the Horn. Yah, yah. We tied her up in Antofagasta when the First World War broke out, otherwise I might still be on her. When the war was over, I was in 'Frisco and trying to get back to Chile to ship on her again, but I couldn't get a ship going south and had to take one to New York. That's how I got here. Yah, yah, that's how it goes."

Then he said, "Nineteen Oh Eight, you said you was on her— do you remember her sailmaker?"

"Very well. I had the bunk beneath his. His name was Hans, and he was a Dane. The second sailmaker was a Dane too."

"Do you remember anything about Hans?"

"I had been in the same forecastle with him over two hundred days when I jumped ship in Santa Rosalia," I replied. "He was a model maker. Always busy making models of ships, even off the Horn when we were lying on our beam. He was tops, the sailors said."

"Yah, yah, that was Hans all right. I was born on the same island, and we grew up together and learned our trade in the same loft— for five years. He finished his apprenticeship just before me."

"I wonder what became of him," I said.

"Hans died last year right here in City Island. He was close to eighty. He worked for me over twenty years, right in this shop. Yah, I have some of his models in my house right now. His wife is still living over in New York. He has a daughter too. Yah, yah, what we went through in those days."

He gave me all the sails I wanted and wouldn't let me pay a cent.

Los Angeles, Hawaii, Pago Pago, and then Apia—it was only a matter of hours these days to fly half around the earth. I rented the

179

same little bungalow where I had lived before, changed clothes, and went down to the lagoon to look at my raft. It lay about three hundred yards from the shore and, the tide being low, was resting on the bottom. I waded out, keeping my shoes on on account of the coral.

There she was waiting for me, all eyes, all expectancy. I lived through everything again as I saw her lying alone and abandoned in the silent lagoon, red with rust and little better than scrap, the sun blazing down and mercilessly exposing her scars. Then I climbed on board and walked slowly around the deck. Yes, she had been battered and a lot of work was needed to make her seaworthy. I almost wondered if it could be done. The three water barrels were still in their lashings on the portside and about falling apart, for most of the hoops had rusted through and lay in pieces on the bleached deck. A good part of the split-bamboo deck covering had been torn off by the seas, and she looked as if she had been blown ashore by a hurricane.

I sat down by the wheel where I used to sit. It was very still. Not a canoe was in sight, not a human being on the palm-fringed shore. From the reef came the boom of the sea—massive, earth-shaking, tolling away, calling all men ashore to come out and head for the horizon. How clearly I heard the call.... Would she make it to Australia, would she hold together—this mass of rust beneath me? Would she become the raft of which they would say that it had conquered the Pacific—or would she leave her bones on a reef? I got up and walked around the deck again, putting my hands on everything—on masts and stays, on steering wheel and cabin and the jib-boom, touching everything, as if the mere feel of the iron would betray its strength or weakness to me. Perhaps it wasn't that; perhaps I just wanted to put my own confidence into the rust-eaten frame.

I was forward when I felt a slight lift of the deck beneath me—the incoming tide was about to float her. A feeling of exultation gripped me as she came up and was free, and I broke out in the ancient capstan chantey of the outward-bounders till it rang out over the silent lagoon.

> Westward, westward, ever westward,
> To the setting of the sun...

I had to swim most of the way to get back ashore. Jim Currie had just closed his sawmill for the night and stopped for a moment to say hello.

"I'll need new centerboards, Jim," I said after we had talked a while. "Have you any wood I can use, something that's really tough? I need two by twelve, twelve feet long, and ten or twelve of them."

"I have just what you want," he replied. "Semihard wood that wears like iron in water—grown right here on the island."

"Expensive?"

"That's on the house—and anything else you need in lumber. Just let me know when you want it."

They were all like that in Apia—all the merchants and businessmen and especially the Government.

We hauled the raft out of the water and scraped and painted the pontoons and some of the upper structure. Then all the gear had to be overhauled, new rope rove, sails checked, mended, and bound on, and blocks and turning buckles greased or replaced. I was busy from morning to night. The raft was now anchored near my bungalow, and I had rented an outrigger to paddle back and forth.

The weather continued bad, and often I got up nights, awakened by the loud rustling and thrashing of the palm fronds above the bungalow, and walking to the lagoon, watched the drift of the clouds against the moon, wondering whether the southeast wind had come at last. But there was no sign of a change, and in the morning we had rain and squalls sweeping over sea and mountains, and the lagoon was white with foam.

One day before sunrise the door of my bungalow was flung open, and a fisherman, dripping wet and almost out of breath, shouted,

"The raft is adrift!" Grabbing my shorts, I was outside in a moment and running with him along the shore. We dragged the outrigger into the water and paddled after the runaway raft, rolling and pitching out in the lagoon, hardly visible in the squall and dim light. We tied up 'longside, then jumped overboard, one grabbing the anchor rope and the other the anchor, dragging, pulling, lifting, and trying to get it into a spot among the coral where it could take solid hold. The water was up to our heads, and we had to keep coming up for air and in our desperate efforts were soon panting like exhausted whales. If we couldn't stop the raft, it would soon be in the narrow steamer channel, drift across, and pile up on the shallows beyond.

We struggled for over an hour, clawing at the bottom of the lagoon for a handhold, our hands, feet, and knees cut by the coral, but were losing ground steadily. Then they saw our plight from the shore, and two launches came out and towed us in, anchoring us in a more sheltered spot.

After new hoops for the barrels had been made by the public works, we filled them with seawater to get them tight again, but it required several weeks before all leakage stopped. When we were first filling them, cockroaches which had made their home inside came out in swarms, while many no doubt were drowned. Better cockroaches than rats or something else to foul the water, I said to myself, thinking of what had happened when the water turned bad on the way from Peru. It had been a close call then.

All preparations had been finally completed, and though the weather showed no signs of improving, I set the date for my departure. It was imperative that I get going in order not to be caught at the worst time of the year west of the Fijis, when hurricanes from the north and gales from the south churned up the sea. I decided on Saturday, June 27. All Samoa promised to be there for the send-off, and the lagoon, I knew, would be lined with multitudes, who would be bedecked with flowers and chanting farewell songs while outrigger canoes accompanied the raft out to the reef. It promised to be a holiday the island would not forget. I had everything on board except my fresh fruit and vegetables, which for the sake of keeping them fresh were in storehouses along the waterfront and would be put on the raft just before leaving. There were piles of coconuts, pineapples, papaws, and bunches of bananas and, most important, limes and lemons, to prevent scurvy. A sack of potatoes and onions I had on board already.

The raft was towed from its lagoon anchorage to the little shed-covered pier of the Union Steamship Company, where the lighters carrying bananas, copra, and cocoa beans to the steamers were loaded. Here I filled my barrels with fresh water. After I had them full, I tasted it a few times and thought it was all right but on closer inspection discovered floating matter in it. I showed it to some of the Samoans sitting on the stringer of the wharf and watching me work. "Cockroaches—legs, bellies, eggs. Full of it," they exclaimed, laughing. Perhaps they were right—the floating things looked familiar, reminding me of the soup on my first ship, the *Henriette*, which I used to carry from the galley to the forecastle. Cockroaches seemed to be an integral part of that soup, and it took quite a while before I got used to it. But time, meager rations, and the tremendous hunger of a growing boy finally caused me to close my eyes to what I had on my spoon unless it was something really too big—if I had remained squeamish and fished out every leg and feeler or egg, there would have been little soup left, and one helping was all I was entitled to.

I told Bob Dawson, the manager of the machine shop of the public works who with his crew had done a marvelous job on my hopelessly broken rudders, about the water, and he suggested I go to the hospital laboratory and have it analyzed. I did. The verdict came quickly and was emphatic: My water was loaded with germs and bacilli, besides being full of cockroach eggs, cockroach parts, and other foul matter. After a few days at sea under the tropical sun, I was told, the water would be deadly.

"Might as well have dead rats in the barrels, is that it?"

"It couldn't be much worse than it is," came the answer.

I went back to the raft, took the lashings off the barrels again, dumped the water, and went to work filling and refilling, rolling and moving them about for hours. Then I took another sample to the laboratory. It was a little better now but still bad, the chemist said and gave me some chloride to put in the water. I emptied the barrels again and, with the help of a Samoan, rolled them about the deck, upended them, and did everything I could think of without taking them apart, then filled them, put in a dose of chloride, and took a sample back to the lab. It was still not safe, but I said I would watch it and, if it started to smell, put in more chloride.

That night I was sitting on the porch of the little hotel. I had just finished dinner, and the Samoan waitress was coming with the coffee. While she was pouring it, she said quietly, "I just heard the captain of the *Aloha-Hawaii* say that he would follow your raft out to sea when you sail and cruise around you a few days and take movies. He said he would film everything you did and sell the films in the United States." The girl, a waitress at my table, was part Chinese and quite intelligent.

"Did he mean that?" I asked.

"Oh, yes—they were talking about it quite seriously. He and his men and his wife. They were not talking loudly, but I have good ears."

I thanked her and said nothing else. If that was true, the fellow would knock the skids out from under my own films, those already taken and those to come, which would be, I hoped, an important factor in paying the expenses of the voyage. He could get any shots he wanted, pick the best light, move in or out around me from morning to night, and use any kind of lens. And I could do nothing to stop him. He had a fast, big ship, and there was no law against it. I knew the fellow. He had spoken to me once or twice, asking when I would be ready to sail, but otherwise had strictly avoided me. He was a big, hulking kind of chap, heavy-jawed and tough-looking, just the sort to scheme something like that. He was not a Samoan but spoke good English. I knew little about him except that he had knocked around the South Pacific for years and had recently married a Hawaiian girl, half-Chinese and as slim as a young seal with black dagger sharp eyes who wore incredibly tight Chinese dresses. His yacht was big, seventy feet long, had two diesels and was sloop rigged. She flew some foreign flag. For crew he had three beach-combers picked up at different islands, all three bearded and seemingly slavering at the mouth for adventures.

So, my beauty, I thought, easing myself deeper into my armchair, that's your pitch. You could certainly dance rings around my raft. She'd be no more trouble for you to get around than an old water-logged drum, and you can laugh at me while shooting your film. No getting away day or night from your lenses, since I have to be on deck always.

The coffee pot had been left on the table, and I got up and poured myself another cup. I had heard of celluloid pirates, and this fellow was one if he saw a scoop; otherwise he probably smuggled or looked for wrecks. There was something unsavory about him and his gang. But, I went on thinking, perhaps the waitress was mistaken about what she had heard. She was a cool head, however. Anyone out here with Chinese blood is nobody's fool. I had to find out more. Perhaps big Nina tending the bar downstairs knew something. This captain liked to drink and spent hours at the bar at times—perhaps she had picked up something. These girls at the hotel, even though appearing dumb, knew about everything that was going on. I went downstairs to the bar and ordered a beer.

Nina was a husky masculine-looking girl with dark, coarse features and a loud strident voice, as guileless as a cow standing in a pasture. She was no longer young. I had danced twice with her, not of my own free will but because she had pulled me out of my chair from where I had been watching the weekly entertainment of hip-twistings given by the little establishment for the tourists and traveling salesmen. And once in her grip, it would have taken an all-out counterattack to get loose again. "First time I dance with a man who got a white beard hanging down to his belly," she had shrieked on that occasion.

The bar wasn't busy yet, and I had a chance to talk to her about the raft leaving and this and that, and finally mentioned the captain of the *Aloha-Hawaii* and that I had heard he intended to follow the raft to sea and take movies. Nina looked at me as if she didn't understand a word or wasn't interested, her big dark face remaining blank. Then she had to go to the other end of the bar to wait on a customer. When she came back a few minutes later, she said in her positive way: "That captain going to take pictures of you at sea—I hear it myself."

"You heard it?"

"Yes."

"When?"

"Yesterday."

"Maybe he just talked and didn't mean it."

"He mean it!" she almost shrieked, frowning that I had doubted her.

"Fine," I said quickly to pacify her. "Maybe he can take some pictures for me too and give them to me before he turns back to Apia. Don't say anything to anybody, Nina, I'm going to talk to him myself."

I walked along the lagoon to my canoe, put it in the water, and paddled out to the raft. It was the hour in the islands when the lagoon and palms seemed to be dissolved in stillness and had become mere reflections of what they had been.

I sat a long time by the wheel while the silence became ever deeper and was only broken by the tolling of the reef. I was still trying to get my bearings. What could I do? This film plot was big and brooked no delay. There was only one answer—I had to get out without anyone knowing it. I had to sneak out to sea. But how? I needed the big pilot boat to take me out through the reef and at least twenty or thirty miles seaward, and that couldn't be done without everybody on the island knowing it, including, of course, the captain of the *Aloha-Hawaii*. Any sort of secrecy was out of the question in Samoa, for such was its life, and in my case—with my departure the main topic—utterly impossible.

I had a few friends in Apia and decided to talk to them; perhaps they could figure a way out. Alone I was helpless. Even now, as I walked along the dark shore to my canoe, many eyes had seen me from the palm-hidden open huts, and many people knew that I was now on my raft. I couldn't take a step anywhere on the island, so how could I get away with my raft without everybody knowing it?

I had to talk to Captain Jones, the harbor master and pilot, and to Andy Collins. Perhaps they could come up with something. They knew Samoa and were big men in its local life. Captain Jones was a veteran of every British war since the Boer War, honest and sound as an oak and a first-class seaman. He was boss of the harbor and all shipping of Samoa. Then there was Andy Collins, American and chief engineer of the Apia Harbour Project, most ambitious engineering work ever undertaken in the South Pacific, which involved building a solid pier in the lagoon and reclaiming part of it for waterfront warehouses. He was a forceful, level-headed, and resourceful man. I would see him first, I decided.

At seven o'clock the next morning, when Mr. Collins stepped out of his car to go into his field office, I was there.

"I'm in trouble, Andy," I said.

"Come inside, and you can tell me while I make some coffee."

A Samoan was sweeping up the office, and by the time he had finished, the coffee was ready, and we sat down.

"Sugar?" Andy pushed the bowl across his desk and stirred his own cup.

I told him my story while he kept moving his spoon around and around and listened. Then he said in a matter-of-fact voice, "I have two tugboats they sent me from Canada last week, a big one and a smaller one. The big one is for outside work mostly and hasn't had a shakedown yet. You can have her any time you say."

"Is she big enough?" I asked.

"She can pull your raft apart."

"I have to get offshore at least thirty miles, Andy."

"Make it fifty, Bill; then you know you're clear." Andy knew the coast and its currents.

"Will Captain Jones be the skipper?" I asked.

"The *Savai'i* has her own skipper, but Captain Jones will arrange everything."

"The main thing is that nobody find out about it, Andy. If anything leaks out, that yacht will follow me."

"Nobody will know anything. I'll explain that to Captain Jones. I'll give him a ring as soon as he gets to the office and drop in on him later. Don't worry; just have your raft ready—we'll take it out of Apia, and nobody will know. When do you want to go?"

"Tonight."

We shook hands, and then his eyes went to his blueprints.

I had just cleared the raft for Sydney, Australia, with the customs and was in Captain Jones's office, and we were looking at some charts spread out on the table. Captain Jones's stubby forefinger pointed to the southeastern end of New Caledonia. "Once you get down there, you'll be all right," he said. "Then straight west till you hit Australia around Brisbane; from there the current will take you down to Sydney."

"With this wind we've been having," I remarked a little doubtfully, "I may have a hard time getting down to New Caledonia. I may have to go north of the New Hebrides."

"Don't, you can't make it from there." Captain Jones, in command all his life, was not one to explain things.

A bucket full of *kava*, the Polynesian drink, stood on an old filing cabinet in a corner of the room, and he picked up the ladle and took a drink. "All ready for tonight?" he asked.

"Yes."

"I'll get Creighton, the captain of the *Savai'i;* I think he's around."

Captain Jones was an old man who had seen a lot of the world from the front line and no longer got excited about anything. His office was on the second floor of the customs house, hard on the lagoon's edge, from where he had a clear view of the little pier of the Union Steamship Company, where my raft was tied up, and the whole harbor as well as the opening in the reef. He stepped out on a little porch, watched the crowd of natives loading lighters beneath, and then gave a sharp whistle. Then he came back in. "Creighton will be right up," he said.

A few minutes later we heard footsteps in the hallway, and the door opened and a heavy-set, middle-aged Samoan in khakis came in. Captain Jones went up to him. "At ten o'clock tonight," he said, "I want your tug to go 'longside of Mr. Willis' raft, make fast, and take it from the pier. After you are a few hundred yards away, you will stop, lengthen your towline, and take him through the reef and out to sea. Your course will be straight north or any other course Mr. Willis orders you to steer. Mr. Willis will let you know at what speed he wants to be towed. Watch his raft for signals throughout the night. At eight o'clock in the morning, you will cease towing, if Mr. Willis orders you to, and return to Apia. If you steered north through the night, you will then steer south. Put one of your men on the raft to help Mr. Willis; that will leave you, your engineer, and one hand on the tug. Now go back on board and tell your men to go home and get a few hours' sleep, since there may be some work tonight. Don't tell anyone that you are going to tow the raft out of Apia—not your wife nor any of the men. The trip is top secret."

Captain Jones had spoken quietly and without emphasis, like a machine, but watching Creighton's face, I knew that every word had sunk into his marrow.

On the way back to my bungalow, I stopped at the post office and picked up a bag of special mail which I had agreed to carry and which was to commemorate my voyage from Samoa to Australia. It contained over a thousand letters.

Then I hurried to my lodgings and checked out, saying I wanted to spend the last night on the raft, to get used to it. Before leaving, I sat down and wrote a letter to the Prime Minister, explaining my step and expressing my regrets as well as my gratitude for all the assistance that had been given me by the Samoan Government. I also wrote a letter to Teddy. I told her why I had to leave like this and not to be worried by anything she might read in the papers, and also that I had decided not to give my position at any time during my voyage, when making a broadcast, but would merely say, "All's well," so that neither the *Aloha-Hawaii* nor any other craft that might have similar ideas could discover my whereabouts.

The last hours I spent in a private home sheltered from a storm that had struck Samoa with thunder and lightning, gale winds, and torrents of rain.

At half past nine the little pier of the Union Steamship Company, where my raft was tied up, lay dark in the rain-swept night. A small bedraggled-looking group of Samoans stood huddled at one end. The rain rattled down on the tin roof of the shed and cascaded in streams on top of a few launches bobbing up and down 'longside and on my raft.

As I climbed down, a bolt of lightning zigzagging across the sky —slowly and hesitatingly as if feeling its way through the densely packed clouds—lighted up my way.

The *Savai'i* lay about fifty yards away, tied up and rolling in the harbor swells beside the smaller of Andy Collins' two tugs. Its engine was warming up, but the throbbing almost went unheard in the storm. I waved to the crew, and they let go at once, and the tug came toward me. When it was 'longside, one of the sailors handed me a brand new three-inch dacron hawser, and I made it fast to the raft.

"Where are you going, Willis?" one of the Samoans standing on the pier asked, stepping to the edge. He wore the *lava lava* of the natives, and his upper body was bare.

"I'm going to anchor a little way out from the pier," I replied.

The group of Samoans, who loaded and unloaded lighters by day and slept in waterfront sheds, now came to the edge to watch what was going on.

The headlights of a car turning toward the pier from the street now lighted up the shore, and a moment later I saw Andy Collins hurry through the shed, climb down to the *Savai'i*, and come to the edge of the raft.

"Everything okay, Bill?"

"Perfect, Andy—everything like clockwork."

He almost broke my hand shaking it, and I thought he might have had a drink. It was the toughest handshake I had had in Samoa, an island of strong men.

After he had climbed back on the pier, I looked up at the dark customs house and the little porch of the harbor master's office, and thought I saw a white-clad figure standing in the gloom, but I wasn't sure.

The raft moved slowly away from the pier and into the night. Halfway through the lagoon, the tug stopped, and Captain Creighton came to the edge of the raft.

"Straight north, is that the course?" he asked.

"Straight north, that's right."

"Flash your light if I go too fast."

"I will. I think about four or five miles an hour will do."

"It's rough outside," he said and, stepping back into the pilot-house, ordered his men to lengthen the towline. Ten minutes later we were through the reef and, with the sea on our beam, rolling north into the stormy darkness.

15

I WAS forward and watching how the raft took the seas. The weather seemed to be easing up a bit out here, but behind us above the mountains of Upolu the lightning still raged.

"She's going pretty good," a voice at my side said. It was William Creighton, the Samoan sailor who belonged to the same clan as the captain of the tug and who was going to stay on the raft with me till the morning. His head was bare, and his black eyes were shining in his rain-bespattered face. What a smile the Samoans have! And what teeth—strong enough to tear off the husk of a coconut, which is a job for an ax. We went back aft and stood in the door of the cabin, for a rain squall was just sweeping over the raft.

Hour after hour went by, while Creighton told me of his voyages among the islands. He had been sailing since he was a boy. Occasionally I looked at the compass and checked the heading, but she always lay right on it—due north. Obviously the tug had a good helmsman.

Finally it began to dawn, and we rolled on through the gray seas till almost eight o'clock, when I waved to the tug to stop. We had come about thirty-five miles. I let go the towline, and then Creighton and I set the jib and mizzen and put in the six centerboards. Three of them were too wide for the slots, and I had to narrow them down with an ax. I lowered them all to about five feet below the pontoons, and when everything was done, the tug came 'longside, and Creighton, timing his jump well, leaped on board. I think he was a handy seaman. As soon as he was off, the tug swung around, her crew waving, and giving three toots with her whistle, opened up her engine. She had a low deckhouse and stack, and disappeared within a few minutes between the waves on her way back to Apia. It was exactly nine o'clock on June 27, 1964.

The wind eased up more, and at ten o'clock I hoisted the mainsail. I was steering northwest to clear Savai'i, the big sister island of Upolu lying a little northeast of it. The rest of the day I was busy putting out two twelve-foot-long iron booms from each side of the raft. They were part of a design I had worked out while in New York which should enable me to carry two extra sails. The design consisted of a twenty-foot-long yard bolted across the top of the mast, well above the yard that held the mainsail and extending four feet beyond it on each side, and the two booms just mentioned jutting out from each side of the deck at right angles. The peaks of the two extra sails would be hoisted to the end of the long yard and the two lower ends made fast to the booms running out from the side of the raft. Both sails were staysails and about thirty feet long and ten feet on the lower leech. Since the extra yard was high up on the mast and extended well beyond my regular mainsail yard, the two wing sails, (as I called them) could not interfere with the mainsail. If the wind was straight aft, I could carry both "wings" at once, since they stood far out on each side, catching the wind not used by my two mizzen sails and not taking away any from the mainsail. If the wind was from the quarter, I could use one. The upper yard and the two booms were of heavy three-inch iron pipe and strong enough for any wind. Bob Dawson of the Public Works Machine Shop had cut and welded the pipes as well as bolted the extra yard across the top of the mast, with his public-works mechanics. The two booms, however, I had to put on myself now, since they would have prevented me coming alongside the little pier where I had to get my water.

It was late in the afternoon before I had the booms out and all the running gear measured, cut, and rigged. At sundown I hoisted one sail. The peak went up to the block with a dozen pulls, and the halyard was made fast to an extra rail I had lashed to my deck stanchions. Then I pulled one corner of the sail out to the end of the boom and the other to the side of the raft. The sail stood perfect and could be set at any angle.

The wind dropped during the night, my first night back at sea, and then died altogether. All morning I was becalmed, and about noon the mountains of Savai'i appeared out of the haze in the south. I was drifting back. The calm continued all day and during the night, and in the morning I could see Savai'i again, much closer now. I remembered that a Japanese trawler fishing out of Pago Pago, after being disabled at sea by a fire, had drifted 350 miles from its position northwest of Upolu on its reef and been totally wrecked.

The calm continued, and as the day advanced, I could see Savai'i's high wooded mountains take shape. In the afternoon I decided to send an SOS. I hoped it would be picked up by the Apia radio station and the pilot boat be sent out to tow me clear of Savai'i, a matter of only about twenty miles.

I set my little Marconi lifeboat transmitter on the automatic SOS signal and wave length and, kneeling before it, turned the handles. The transmitter was bolted to the side of the cabin behind the wheel. After sending a few calls, I felt a severe pain in my left side which increased to such an extent that I had to stop. I tried again after resting a while, and again the pain forced me to quit. What could it be? I wondered. The mountains looked terribly near, and I took hold of the handles again. When the pain became unbearable, I put my left hand over the bad spot and cranked with the other. No doubt it was the hernia acting up, but having had pains there before,

I didn't think it could be anything serious. But I had to stop sending.

I lay down beside the wheel for a while and massaged my abdomen, then got up and tried the transmitter once more. I had to do something, or I would drift on the rocks during the night. A few times I turned the handles, then had to stop again and knew that it was really serious, whatever it was.

Lying down again, I examined myself as well as I could and thought it looked like a strangulation. It seemed to be exactly what the doctors had warned me against. There it was, looking me in the face—strangulation, gangrene, perforation, the works. Maybe death on the raft, within sight of Samoa. Strangulation—gangrene—perforation . . . Now get out of that! I said to myself. I saw the whole thing clearly. I had strained myself ever since leaving Apia, raising the mainsail and handling the centerboards, according to the wind and seas, and especially when putting out the two iron booms, which was really a three-man job. I remembered I had been feeling bad all day, that my mind hadn't been too clear, and at times a sort of dizziness had come over me.

I tried to get the hernia back in, meaning the pinched-off part of the intestine, while lying on my back with my legs up to relax the abdomen. I tried every form of manipulation, at first gently, then, as I became desperate, more forcefully until I realized it might aggravate matters. My whole abdomen had become distended. Now and then I looked at the mountains of Savai'i lying in the glassy sea beside me, but they had lost their terror, since I had a greater danger to contend with.

I thought I knew what was happening. Everything in the intestines was blocked up and couldn't move down, while, in the heat of the body, gases were forming and couldn't escape. And all the while the pinched-off piece of intestine was putrefying and sooner or later would burst open. Just how soon could that happen? And what would happen after it had burst open? If I had been within reach of a doctor, he would have opened up the split in the muscles more, put the intestines back in, and sewed everything up again. So at least I thought. Easy enough if a man was on an operating table under an anaesthetic.

I tried everything I could think of. I even had the crazy idea of performing an operation on myself, thinking that a small cut in the right place might do the trick—perhaps no more than an inch or so would do it. But, I realized, if I made a mistake and cut too deep or wide of the mark, not being able to see among the blood and inflammation—where would I be then? All that was nonsense, of course. I had some morphine left from the first part of my voyage, a few tablets, but decided not to use any and deaden myself—I needed a clear head now if ever in my life.

I was swelling up more all the time, and there was dizziness, and I was feverish; sometimes I felt like vomiting. I could barely touch the spot now. Finally I started my two kerosene stoves, filled two saucepans with seawater and, when it was hot, put packs on my abdomen. I did it for hours; then, finding no relief, thought I might be doing the wrong thing applying heat and stopped. The problem seemed to be to relax the muscles. If they were relaxed, the piece of protruding intestine could slip back inside. Good thing, I thought, that my food had been of the very plainest the last few days—ship's biscuit, beans, and sauerkraut, which always agreed with me and created no gases besides leaving very little waste matter. In Apia also I had eaten very little the last days. All this no doubt helped me now, I reasoned; otherwise I might already be out of my head and staring over the side for a way out.

The sun was almost down. I saw the mountains looking down at me. They appeared almost human, as if they knew my thoughts but had decided to remain immovable and not to help. "He broke the law," they seemed to say. I had to do something, for time was running out. Was there anything I had not tried? I went over everything I had done—everything. Then I had an idea.

I took a line of half-inch rope and reeved it through a block hanging from a davit welded to the base of the cabin near the door, fastened one end around my ankles, and grabbling the other, began pulling myself up. I pulled gradually, twisting and moving my body while feeling its reaction, until only my shoulders remained on deck. Then I made fast. It seemed to ease me a little. Here I'll hang till something happen, one way or the other, I decided. I had done everything else and this was the last. I had vomited a few times and was quite dizzy. My whole abdomen was in bad shape, hot and distended.

I swung back and forth to the rolling of the raft, while trying every movement and twist and manipulation with the full weight of my intestines now on my heart and lungs. Sometimes I hoisted myself higher until I stood almost on my head; sometimes I lowered myself. I also hung by one leg, the left or the right, always watching which position relaxed the abdomen most.

It was about eight o'clock at night when I became aware of a feeling of relief. I had been dozing a bit while hanging, I think, or perhaps I'd just been out of my mind. Everything was still sore to the touch, but the pinched-off piece seemed to be back inside. I remained with my legs up until I was certain, then very gradually lowered myself to the deck. There I lay still, not quite able to believe that I was all right.

How beautiful the night looked to me suddenly, how like a divine fluid the silent sea in which I lay. Mother! I cried, utterly overcome. Your guardian angels ... How often had she spoken of my guardian angels. And I thought of Teddy with such intensity that I felt certain she became aware of me faraway in New York.

Still lying, I put on my truss. It was a good truss but really could not be expected to stay in place during my strenuous labors, when I changed position continuously, and finally it had slipped and, exerting pressure in the wrong place, had forced a piece of intestine out of the opening in the abdominal muscles.

The night was over, and it became gray, and then the grayness of sea and sky separated, and gradually Savai'i rose before me in all her pearly robes, trailing down in majestic folds from her summits into the sea. It had changed its position—it was not nearer and lay a little more ahead. I realized I had drifted to the east, the set now being more from the west. There was still no wind, and the raft lay as helpless in the sea as before.

In the afternoon I saw behind me, almost unnoticeably faint, the outline of a mountain ridge of Upolu and knew I was still drifting eastward, like the Japanese trawler that had been wrecked. An hour before sundown, a wind came up, and my mainsail filled, and I was on my way again. Soon it was blowing strong and steady, and I set my port wing sail. During the night the wind went more easterly, and squaring the yard, I ran before it with both wing sails set. It was the first time I was under all sails—the two new wing sails, my two mizzens and mainsail, and directly in front of it the extra sail to catch the wind in the empty arch below, hanging from the jib halyard and stretched hard down across the deck. The raft was now a mass of white sails spreading out from the high topmost yard to a distance of ten feet to each side. This gave the raft a full forty-foot spread altogether, and she must have looked like a snow-white swan with half-lifted wings making its way over the sea. In case of a sudden change of wind, however, it meant working fast to keep the sails from being torn to shreds.

I drank my first seawater today, about half a mugful solely for medicinal reasons. Incidentally I had no salt whatever on board.

The raft rolled considerably more now with the long yard high up on the mast, but the extra speed gained from the two wing sails and the greater ability to maneuver would make it easier to keep away from the reefs which lay ahead and were more important than the inconvenience of rolling. The reefs were the big factor I had to contend with on this voyage, and from the moment of leaving Apia I had lived with my eyes on the charts. It was quite different when

I had left Callao in South America, for then I had four thousand miles of open sea before me.

It was cloudy and blowing with near gale force, and I should have taken the mainsail down, but the clouds were thinning, and not having had a sight for a few days, I hoped the sun would come out. Afterward I would take care of the mainsail. I was standing in the cabin door, holding my sextant behind me to protect it from the spray, ready to jump on deck the moment the sun broke through the haze and fuzz of drifting clouds. It was still a few minutes before my computed noon.

Suddenly the raft went into the wind, and the mainsail began beating against the mast with such force it threatened to reduce it to rags. The whole raft was shaking. I put down the sextant, jumped on deck, and lowered away. The raft rolled before the wind again, and the sail ballooned out, forcing the yard all the way to the jibboom. I crawled underneath as usual and tackled it from the bow, trying to get one of the gaskets around it, but again and again the sail got away, no doubt making me look like a pigmy struggling with a giant. Then I heard the ominous sound of the sail tearing. I redoubled my efforts and was making some headway when with a demonic blast my hands were torn loose, and I was hurled backward and overboard. There was no rail forward to hold me—not even a line stretched across the open gap between the jibboom and last deck stanchion.

I was in the sea, upside down and struggling to get to the surface and grab hold of something while the raft was plunging over me. There was the chain connecting the two rudders! I hooked it with my leg and then had my hands on it and climbed back on board. It took over half an hour before I had the sail lashed to the yard and secured to the mast.

The first thing I did afterward was to fasten a line to the foot of the aftermast and let it trail fifty feet behind the raft—a lifeline in

199

case I should fall overboard again. I also wondered whether I had become soft while in New York to be knocked overboard like that.

Logbook entry, July 3, 1964
Long: 173° 50′ west
Lat: 12° 48′ south

Weather continues bad. Wind still south-southeast. Still under double mizzen and jib. Put chlorine in my three barrels to prevent fouling of water. Took about 30 sights at noon standing on top of my big crate and hanging on to cabin top with my belly, but the raft was rolling and wallowing too much to get an accurate one. For supper I had potato pancakes which finished the day just right.

Time was beginning to lose its importance. My course, my sights three times a day when the sun was out, and the wind became the main things in my life again. I also recorded my thoughts in my logbook as I had done since leaving South America, unless the raft's shaking and laboring made it impossible to write, which it did often enough. Samoa had already become dim. Its smiling faces had sunk back into the intense green of leafy walls, the soft glow of fires before open huts had disappeared, and no longer could I hear the low voices singing to the reef and the sea and to the fallen gods.

What sort of a voyage would this be with such an ominous start? I thought of the mean-faced planter in Apia who, half-drunk or in some sort of trance, had walked up to me sitting in a chair and declared vindictively, "You will land in New Guinea—not in Australia," and walked away again. New Guinea was certainly the last place I would have picked for landing, having heard from men who had lived there of the New Guineans' weakness for "long pig," meaning the white man's flesh. Their own flesh went into the pot simply as "black fella"—either into the pot or on hot stones wrapped in leaves to bring out all the flavor. My prophetic planter, a surly, unpredictable sort of fellow, was supposed to be gifted with second sight.

I discovered that a stave in one of the water barrels had broken, and all the water down to the break had run out. Two barrels were left, however, besides the rainwater I was catching, and there was little likelihood of running short. My potatoes were spoiling fast, and most of them had to be thrown overboard. I think they had been dug months before and been kept in storage. My onions, on the other hand, were firm and sound and like the potatoes also came from New Zealand.

After a silence of four days due to bad weather, I cranked up my transmitter and sent my usual message: SALVITA III ALL'S WELL WILLIS to the New Zealand air-force station in the Fijis. Originally I had promised to give my longitude and latitude also, but the celluloid pirates had decided me to sail on a blacked-out course. My broadcast time was 22 hrs. GMT on 8364 kc.

The wind was consistently south by east and even south, and had me worried about getting south to New Caledonia after rounding the Fijis. I had already been pushed north to the 12th parallel, way out of my course, and was finding it hard to get back south.

A few birds were tumbling among the distant waves, but so far I hadn't caught a fish though I generally had a line out, baited with a lure or spoon. Not even a friendly shark came around to donate his liver and replenish my vitamin deficiency, and I bemoaned the heaps of coconuts, bananas, avocados, and papaws and especially all the limes and oranges I had to leave behind in Apia in my nocturnal flight.

Kiki and Aussie were still part of the raft, and often when at the wheel and looking forward, I imagined them coming around the corner of the cabin to visit me. I missed them very much and thought that, if I met a British ship coming directly from England with a cat on board, I would ask for it, since according to Australian law it would be allowed to land.

I had a most unexpected feast. Checking up on my provisions a few days ago, I came across a large and impressive-looking tin.

Memories of Lima arose. More than a year ago it was, while getting the raft ready, that an Australian lady living in Lima presented me with a tin containing a plum pudding with instructions not to open it until Christmas day. Intending to live up to the order, I had put it on the bottom of a box and entirely forgotten it. During all the 130 days of the first voyage and while in New York later, it had lain amid my other tins patiently waiting for Christmas. It was a beautiful tin, promising all sorts of delights to a half-starved man. But I had to wait until Christmas, for that had been the agreement. But was it really an agreement? This was only July, and I certainly wanted to be in Australia before Christmas—if I wasn't, I would never get there. I decided to open it on my seventy-first birthday which was coming up soon, August 19. That would really be celebrating it. And so I left the tin out where I could see it and wouldn't forget it again. For two days my eyes were caught by it and made my mouth water; then I decided to open it right then and there. I reasoned that I might be on a reef somewhere on August 19 and the raft broken up, or I might have fallen overboard again, as I had before, and terminated the voyage by going down to Davy Jones or the Deep Six, as American seamen call it. Then this doubtlessly exquisite plum pudding would be lost. It would be foolish and weak to expose it to such a fate after having waited so long. After all, what was a certain day out here, especially a birthday? The only day that really counted was a sunny day with a fair wind. I opened the can. Before I had it fully open, I could smell that it contained a masterpiece of a pudding. I wasn't disappointed and finished it the same day.

The bad weather showed no signs of letting up, and I doubled up on the lower ends of all my stays, where they were exposed to the seas and spray, with chains and cables to keep them from breaking. I also lowered the mainsail and sewed a large piece of real canvas across the whole top and six feet down to protect it from chafing against the forestay. Almost every seam of the big sail had now been gone over but it still had its shape with the name *Age Unlimited* showing proudly above the sea. Most of the original letters sewn on in City Island had long been blown to tatters and had to be patched. Some that had disappeared altogether had been painted on.

Logbook entry, July 9, 1964
Long: 176° 48′ west
Lat: 12° 35′ south

Sailed across Waterwitch Bank from one end to the other. Found a heavy ground swell but no breakers. Saw some birds fishing, and occasionally a small fish jumped. Also saw some flying fish. I dropped a weighted line and struck bottom. Sailed with jib, squaresail, two mizzen, and port wing sail.

At night the Big Dipper stood abeam and quite high, handle up and lower end pointing to the invisible North Star. The friendly constellation made me think of the hills of southern California where my raft dream began. "Just keep going," it seemed to say. "It's a small world, after all, that you live in down there."

I was hanging by my feet and swinging back and forth like a side of beef, for the sea was rough and the raft rolling. I was suffering from another strangulation. For a few weeks I had been having trouble with my hernia; in fact since my first attack off Savai'i I had rarely been free from pain. Perhaps I had to expect it with the endless straining day and night, the lack of fresh food, and insufficient sleep. Another factor was the already mentioned impossibility of keeping the truss properly adjusted.

I hung until the ropes cut into my flesh, then lowered myself, put a padding around my feet, and hoisted myself up again. Since I didn't weigh much, I had no trouble getting as high as I wanted. I did everything I had done while off Savai'i, and after almost two hours the pinched-off part went back inside. This time my cure weakened me considerably, and for quite a while I had to remain lying on deck before I could get up.

Logbook entry, July 11, 1964
Long: 178° 23' west
Lat: 13° 13' south

The sun rose behind a wall of titanic-looking clouds shaped like the entrails of a gutted firmament, which were spilling slowly out upon the sea. They seemed to be moving in on me with startling nearness. I think it was the most fantastic spectacle my eyes had ever seen in the sky.

My frying pan had developed two holes and was summarily dropped over the side. Luckily I had a small one left. Had it quit also, I would have bent a piece of tin into shape and cooked "jungle" style as in my Kansas harvester days of long ago—around 1915.

My waist line was twenty-six inches, I discovered, the lowest I could remember having had. Lowering and raising the big sail took away ounce after ounce of my weight. I kept my little hand winch well greased and oiled, but sail and yard seemed to weigh tons, after I'd gone up and down a few times and battled to keep them from tearing to pieces.

It had been a busy day from dawn to dusk repairing gear. The night had set in clear. I had had a new moon for three or four days already and was heading down past the Fijis and hoped to be around them within four or five days. This would put me on the Great Circle route of the Sydney-to-San Francisco run. I wondered if I would see any steamers. Every time the new moon came around, I wanted to ask, "Where have you been? I sure missed you."

Why am I out here? Why? I had been asked this often. I look at my questioner and sometimes say, "For the glory of God and the faith of man."

"What do you mean by faith?"

"Faith in what's above you and what's in you, man."

204

Whom the Sea Has Taken

Logbook entry, July 14, 1964
Crossed the international
date line, and my position
is:
Long: 179° 40′ east
Lat: 13° 30′ south

When news spread in Western Samoa that I had just come from South America and crashed over the reef, the authorities sent an ambulance to Pui Paa where I had landed, thinking I was badly in need of medical assistance. I guess news of my white beard panicked them. I was thinking today that, if my rupture kept acting up, I might need that ambulance when landing in Australia.

Logbook entry, July 18, 1964
Long: 177° 15′ east
Lat: 15° 23′ south

I had just got through working out my sights at three thirty P.M. when I saw a coconut floating past, just a few feet out of reach, and drift astern, bouncing up and down like a bubble. It was a brown old nut, and two lively crabs less than three inches long were riding on it, doing a ceaseless balancing act that was a wonder to see. They seemed to feel very much at home. Was it a honeymoon trip? Perhaps they could have shed some light on the migration of crabs in the South Pacific. I could imagine Jack the crab saying to Jill the crab on the sands of some faraway atoll, "Come on, Jill, let's take a ride."

The wind had been almost straight south for days and was slowly but relentlessly pushing me toward the New Hebrides. I was worried. Should I change course and go north around the islands, while I still had sea room, and later try a breakthrough to Australia from the Coral Sea? Or should I stay on my course a little longer, hoping for a more easterly wind? The latter was a gamble. I spent hours over my charts wondering what to do. I also had to consider that if the wind continued south by east in the Coral Sea I would finally have to tackle the Great Barrier Reef or, as an alternative, sail all the way north around it and through Torres Strait. That meant I might not even get to Australia but land in New Guinea somewhere.

I sang a bit last night, mostly old sailing-ship songs and chanteys. There were some Cape Horn beauties for which we sang the chorus to some brass-lunged old-timer, while the wind drove solid spray into our throats and we stood waist deep in the water, wondering whether the comber coming over the rail would lift the whole line of us pulling on the rope—ten or twelve men—and send us into the scuppers or over the bulwarks into the sea.

About drinking seawater, another angle is perhaps to be considered, namely the instinctive craving for something vital, for some vital element lacking in all our preserved food. This had been very noticeable with my two cats, Kiki and especially with Aussie, who came on board a kitten used only to drinking milk.

Logbook entry, July 25, 1964
Long: 174° 43′ east
Lat: 17° 45′ south

I had tried to get south and clear the southeastern tip of New Caledonia for a straight run to Sydney, but bad weather and head winds again and again forced me back north and to the west. Finally the wind assumed gale force, blowing straight from the south. I had poured over my charts in the wildest night since leaving Apia, while the raft seemed to be coming apart, and realized that there was no chance to continue on my course. I had to run north, in the opposite direction, to keep from being blown on the rocks of the New Hebrides. That had been two days ago.

My sheets and tacks, doubled up with one-inch rope, stood like iron bars, and the mainsail seemed on the point of being blown away. But the sail had to stay aloft, and if it blew out, I had to set others.

I was in the cabin, trying to boil some water for a cup of tea, when a sea struck it with such force that I thought it would be torn off. It shook frighteningly while streams of water came like jets through the boards. I think that only my three water barrels, lashed to the foundation of the raft and taking the brunt of the onslaught, kept it from going over the side.

How close was I to the shore, that was the question? I had not had a sight for some days and was navigating by dead reckoning. According to my last not-too-accurate observation, I was dangerously close to the coast of one of the eastern islands of the New Hebrides—either Pentecost or Maewo, the two most northern. Twice in the morning I thought I had seen the outlines of hills on the horizon, but each time they quickly disappeared amid the squalls sweeping over the rain-smudged sea. My dead reckoning put me somewhere near the southern end of Maewo, but I realized that I could be miles out in my figures. Now another night was coming. What would it bring? I wondered, staring into the dusk. I knew I wouldn't be able to hear or see breakers until I was among them. My eyes went to the rigging. Would everything hold? The ropes and stays would, for I had doubled up on everything—sheets, tacks, halyards, and braces—and all the stays had preventers; only the mainsail had me worried. It stood like a big white wall seemingly hugging all the wind in the sky to its broad bosom. In front of it the partly torn-off letters of *Age Unlimited* were snapping in the gale like frightened little pennants.

Would I pile up on Maewo? The Sailing Directions of the U.S. Hydrographic Office said that its entire coast was almost uninhabited, steep-to with no bay or anchorage, and that a mission station was located somewhere. If I cleared Maewo, I would head west again and try to get through the Banks Islands, clear Cape Cumberland, the northern tip of Espiritu Santo, largest of the New Hebrides islands and to the west of the eastern group I now had to contend with. And then would come my real struggle—in the Coral Sea, a sea full of reefs, and finally the Great Barrier Reef, the rampart of eastern Australia which I had been told could not be crossed.

Perhaps this would be my last night on the raft, for if I struck the coast, it would disappear in the breakers. I decided to send a message, an SOS, hoping it would be picked up somewhere, perhaps by a trading vessel among the islands; then they would know at least where I had been. There was no radio station nearer than Nouméa, New Caledonia, hundreds of miles away, but I would try.

I took the cover off the transmitter and began turning the handles to warm it up. I could hardly move it and, after struggling a while, checked the indicator light. There was no glow. I tried a few times more, but the light remained dead. It had given me trouble for weeks and now seemed definitely finished.

I put the cover back on, got up, and stared into the darkness, feeling for a moment with benumbing force my utter isolation on this savage coast. Then I climbed up on the mast but could see nothing except the darkening sea. An hour later it was night. It passed slowly, as the others had, in stormy darkness in which the wind was howling its torn anthems and the floods of the sea were smashing and roaring into each other, rising and falling and rushing on in white-capped fury.

The dawn came gray, but about sunrise it began to clear a little, and I had hopes for a sight. Blue patches appeared during the morning, and about half an hour before noon the sun came out. I began taking sights at once, continuing until I was certain the sun had passed her zenith and was on the way down. Then I went into the cabin, sat down, and took the average of my ten highest readings and from this worked out my latitude. I was clear—clear of Maewo, clear of the New Hebrides. I felt like shouting. I stared at my figures—15 degrees 48 minutes south latitude—and checked with the chart again. I was clear—north of Maewo. I went over everything a few times. The strain of that long fight to get north was over, but I had still to be careful, for on my chart, No. 2866 of the U.S. Hydrographic Office, it said beside Maewo:

Caution.
The north coast of Maewo
is rep. to lie 6 miles N.W.
of its charted position (1947)

I decided to stay on my course for four or five more hours before turning west and sailing through the Banks Islands into the Coral Sea. In the afternoon I would try to get my longitude.

It was not until eight o'clock in the evening that I swung around until my bow pointed west. The weather had moderated considerably during the afternoon, but the sun hadn't come out, and I didn't get the longitude to fix my position. I was sitting on a narrow plank I had fixed between the cabin and the frame of the steering gear, from where I could see the compass and also reach the wheel, and was looking into the darkness, still not fully believing that I was out of danger. Gradually I became drowsy and, spreading out my rubber blanket beside the cabin, lay down. I was pretty well fagged out but didn't dare to fall asleep not knowing that was ahead.

I had dozed off and, startled, woke up again and listened intently to what the wind and seas were saying as if I had never heard it before. Then my head sank back like a lump of lead, and everything ebbed out of me, and the raft made its way alone.

It was after midnight when I jumped up as if someone had shaken me and looked at the compass. West by north—on my course. I had been asleep but for how long? The sea had gone down, and it was strangely still, which startled me. The night was very dark, and the waves slapped softly against the pontoons. I went around the compass stand to the wheel and almost turned to stone. A high, black mountain lay close behind me—close enough seemingly to be touched. Had I just passed it or was the raft just being drawn into it? It struck me like a crouching, immense monster that had subdued the very sea. The raft seemed to be helpless, completely under the spell of that black, hypnotizing mass.

Then my head cleared. It was an island I had passed—passed while

I lay asleep. My brave little raft had cleared it by itself. Who had been at the wheel—what angels? I looked up at the sky and then back at the frightening mass that seemed to dominate the sea and sky and still draw me back into its darkness.

Very slowly, as the raft sailed on, it became smaller, and I knew I was safe. According to my chart it was Mera Lava, the most southern and easterly of the Banks Islands. I had therefore made a considerable northerly drift after changing course.

Just before daybreak I saw a small island in the sea ahead of me. The wind had then gone down more, and when the sun came up, I was nearly becalmed. The island ahead was then about five miles away and a little to starboard.

After the morning haze had disappeared, I went up the mast and saw land in different places, but rain squalls, sweeping over the sea, obscured it again and again. A few squalls came over the raft also, dropping light showers of rain. Mera Lava, the black dome-shaped island which had so startled me, though still quite near, disappeared for long periods amid the clouds and squalls pushed against it by a distant wind.

As the morning advanced, the sea continued calm with a light swell running, ruffled here and there by cat's-paws. A set was slowly taking me to the southwest, past the tiny island ahead which, according to my chart, had to be Merig. The Sailing Directions gave this information:

Merig Islet (St. Claire) position 14° 17′ S. longitude 167° 48′ E., height 200 ft., no anchorage, landing difficult; in 1934 it had 27 natives.

Mera Lava (Star Peak) island, the Sailing Directions said, lay sixteen miles southeast of Merig and was the southeastern end of the Banks Group. It was twenty-nine hundred feet high and steep-to all around.

All day long I drifted back and forth, watching the islands come out of the squalls and disappear again. In the afternoon I had drifted to within a mile or less of Merig. I kept my glasses on its shore, wondering whether I would see a canoe paddle out to me. It looked abandoned, with not a sign of life among the coconut palms with which the island was covered. And I was dying for fresh food, suffering from lack of it perhaps more seriously than I realized. And there were tons of fresh coconuts almost within reach. "Be sensible," I said to myself, "and don't hunger for those nuts. Can't you see the seas breaking on those rocks? Be sensible." But I couldn't take my eyes off the island. There might be an opening among the rocks somewhere, I thought. I needed fresh food—hadn't caught one fish since leaving Apia. Those coconuts would give me new life. I scanned the sea and clouds, wondering about the weather. There seemed to be no impending change. My drift had shown me another island, heretofore hidden behind Merig, which I took for Santa Maria, a large island also belonging to the Banks Group. It appeared to be about twenty miles away.

Another hour had passed, and I was standing beside the cabin, and my eyes were on the little green island, now almost on my beam —green to the very top with loaded coconut trees. I could plainly see the nuts with my glasses. I had to get some—I needed fresh food to keep going. My onions were getting bad, and all my potatoes were gone. I needed fresh food, or I would be in trouble. It was still a long way to Australia, and the hardest part no doubt was yet to come.

I took my little ten-foot-long Samoan canoe from the roof of the cabin where it had been lashed beside the kayak, checked the outrigger, and put it in the water. Then I got in myself. Besides two paddles, I had a machete, a hatchet, an ax, some rope, a fishing line, a can for bailing, and some sacks to hold the coconuts, also some matches.

I was fully aware of what I was doing, paddling away from the raft and leaving it in the open sea, and felt guilty of an almost unpardonable offense. But I wanted coconuts, fresh food—my very soul cried for them.

I began skirting the rockbound shore on which the sea was breaking. No opening, no ledge, was visible to which I could jump and drag my canoe. I could see the palms clearly, saw the big clusters of nuts hanging down. There was no sign of a hut under the trees or a canoe pulled up on the shore. Slowly I paddled past, my eyes as much on the raft, which stood motionless and as if anchored in the sea, as on the palms. At last I swung around the island and could see the raft no longer. To live here, I was thinking, in this green cage, this green paradise full of fruit and fish, lobsters and clams—but how long before I would be consumed with longing for the open sea and the freedom to which man is born?

Then I noticed that the sea had become a bit ruffled, and the sky darkened a little. With one stab of the paddle, I swung the canoe around, almost turning it over, and then dug in fast and deep, the water foaming to my wrist, swinging from side to side as I shifted the paddle. Within a minute I could see the raft. Her sails were down, of course, but she was drifting. I went after her. Suddenly the lashing of the outrigger broke, and the whole framework of wood came apart. I had put too much strain on it turning the canoe around, and the native lashing of coconut fiber, probably rotted from lying on top of the cabin in the sun and rain, had parted.

The canoe was short, squat, and cranky, and would have turned over had I tried to fix it from the inside. I went overboard most carefully and over the stern, and began to repair the damage, using my knife and the fishing line. While I was working, the forward lashing also came apart. It developed into a job of swimming and holding on in the now quite lively sea, and before I was through, I had been beneath the surface more than above and used my teeth as much as my hands. My left forefinger was useless for, while slackening away on the mainsail tack in a gale about a week before, I had almost torn it off. It took over an hour before I had finished, could climb back into the canoe, and follow the raft—now quite a distance away on the darkening sea. I paddled with extreme care, for there were other parts on an outrigger besides the lashings which could come loose and which it would have been almost impossible to repair in the water. This slowed me down to a creeping pace, and it was a full hour after dark before I was 'longside of the *Age Unlimited* again.

Why had I done it? Standing safely on deck later and steering into the night, I could hardly believe that I had been guilty of such stupidity—leaving the raft adrift in the open sea and paddling off to an island to get coconuts. That's what I had done. Perhaps, I thought now, more even than the hunger for fresh food, for something vital to put into my body, had been the pull of that lonely and beautiful bit of earth. It had cast a spell on me, the earth-born, sea-weary wanderer, and I had succumbed. But I had failed and had to get along on my scanty food again. Perhaps I would catch fish.

16

THE New Hebrides lay behind me. I had sailed between Cape Cumberland, its northwestern headland, and Santa Maria and was making my way south into the Coral Sea. The wind continued as it had been, south by east, and only occasionally became more easterly. I was gradually getting south but also west toward the Great Barrier Reef. I knew something about it from a mate I had sailed with years before on a tanker. He had been captain of a small coastal steamer, carrying supplies from Port Darwin to the missions scattered over the desolate shores of northwestern Australia, and later had owned a lugger fishing for pearl shell and trepang on the Great Reef with a crew of Malayans and Australian aborigines to do the diving. From him I knew that the Great Barrier Reef extended from just north of Brisbane for almost thirteen hundred miles all the way to Cape York, the northern end of Australia in the east, and beyond, across Torres Strait, to the coast of New Guinea. Its width varied from twenty to thirty miles. Between the inner or western edge of this vast mass of reefs, containing more coral than all the rest of the earth, and the mainland of Australia lay the Great Barrier Reef Channel, from thirty to twenty miles wide and slowly narrowing toward the north. This channel had deep water but was studded with rocky islands and was used by vessels plying along the Australian coast and those bound north through Torres Strait to Indonesia, Japan, and China. Navigation in this channel was dangerous, and most ships carried extra pilots. The Great Reef itself was considered almost impassable.

If I couldn't get south through the maze of isolated reefs blocking the southern end of the Coral Sea, I could do two things—attempt to sail through the Great Reef into the inner channel; or sail all the way north along the whole Barrier and land somewhere in New Guinea, or try sailing westward through Torres Strait into the Arafura Sea, then try for a landing somewhere on the northern coast of Australia which was practically uninhabited.

The wind had gone a little more easterly in the afternoon, and I could steer almost south, which was ideal, and I hoped it would keep up. There was a new moon, and I wondered whether I would see the coastal hills of Australia by its light. During the day I had made a few sketches, first time on the voyage. My forefinger was still bad, but I hoped the damage wouldn't be permanent.

The night of August 8 was stormy, and the mainsail was down. The wind was south by east and coming in heavy gusts, and about ten o'clock I went forward to pull the jib over to port, thinking the raft would make a better course. The sail stood like a slab of marble in the wind, and I was pulling with all my strength to get it over, standing with my back to the jibboom. The sheet on which I pulled ran through a block fast to the side of the raft. I was pulling with one hand while holding a turn around the forward stanchion with the other. In spite of all my efforts, I couldn't get the jib over, and finally took the turn off and hauled away with both hands. I tried a number of times but didn't have enough power, and after resting a few moments tried again. This time I gave everything I had. Suddenly something parted, and I flew backward, struck the iron jibboom and crumpled up. While I was falling, it flashed through my mind that I would break my back if I struck the iron.

For a few moments I lay benumbed by the shock but sensing that something terrible had happened to me. I saw the block with

215

the jib sheet lying on deck before me. The strop holding it to the edge of the raft had given way, rotted from long exposure to sea-water. Was my back broken? I was unable to get on my feet and had to drag myself aft like a dog that has been run over on a road.

For some time I lay beside the cabin, wondering just how badly I was hurt; then I tried again to get up but couldn't. My legs were limp and felt like not belonging to me. I lay there, and the night wore on, while the raft rolled and the sea pounded it and now and then a wave came on deck. By the stars I knew that she was holding her course fairly well, running with the jib and double mizzen. And all the time I wondered just how much I was injured. My back was smashed, I knew, but just where and what would it do to me? Was a vertebra broken, and would my legs be paralyzed? Sailing a raft alone through space, through every kind of weather, one learns to face facts. Would I get up again or remain lying on deck?

I lay there thinking. Everything that had happened since leaving Apia in that stormy night ebbed away as unimportant, ebbed away into nothing—all the near disasters, all the blood, sweat, and tears left behind on my long trail westward. And so the night wore on. The raft labored and wallowed while I lay motionless, but my mind was always on my legs which were without life.

The sails were standing full, though the jib was hard to see from where I lay, the jibboom going up at such a steep angle. I looked up at the mast and my Samoan flag, a little black patch in the dark night. I had raised it in Apia when going 'longside of the little Union Steamship pier and had never taken it down. It was a large flag originally, but most of it had been blown off, for it had been in some hard gales when clawing off the coast of the New Hebrides. I had decided to keep it up till I reached Australia; then I would take it down—what was left of it—and keep it, though ordinarily I didn't go in for mementoes. It was like a compass, always showing me the direction of the wind, by day and in the blackest night, and had become invaluable, considering how close I had to steer to the wind to get south. Then I thought that perhaps I should have kept the turn around the stanchion and only pulled with one hand, then nothing would have happened. But no man could have pulled the jib over that way, with one hand.

Would my condition last? That was the question. I knew a bit about broken backs and how it left a man, for I had loaded ships for over ten years in Galveston, Texas City, and Houston, handling every kind of heavy cargo—timber, steel billets, cotton bales, and coal—and had seen men smashed up. On the frontiers I had also seen them—on bridges, in shipyards, in oil fields, and in the big woods of Washington and Oregon, in the old days when the work was really murderous among the falling giants. A few lines I had written one evening after picking up a smashed logger came to my mind:

> For thousand years like kings they stood,
> For thousand years alone;
> We struck them with our ax and saws
> And hurled them from their throne.
>
> We brought them down amid the stumps,
> The thunder and the cries,
> But many a logger on the slopes
> Amid the bramble lies.

I had pulled some clothes down from the bulkhead to lie on and fallen asleep, and then I had a real nightmare: I was lying on a beach and couldn't move, for I had just been washed up from a reef, over which I had clawed my way with bloody fingers while the breakers smashed down on me and kept flinging me about. Barely alive, I had heard the roar of the seas coming over the reef behind me to pull me back out again. That's when I awoke.

Finally the night was over. I had slept and awakened and stared into the night and imagined things, and then daylight came as always. I felt no real pain, but everything was benumbed from the smash, and I still couldn't move my legs. And so it was all that day, my raft jogging along by itself through our little universe as if it didn't need me. I knew that I was drifting north toward the Solomons, and, if I couldn't get up, would land sooner or later in some mangrove-hidden little bay. The Solomons were the ancient hunting grounds of black-birders "recruiting" natives for plantation labor. How I had devoured those stories as a boy—of Bully Hayes and other dynamite-tossing captains. Many schooners had sailed in that bloody trade but not all came back; looted and burned, they sank in some bay, while the crew went into the pot or was staked out at low water for the sharks after a sandpapering with a shark's hide had taken off their skin. But perhaps I would drift more to the west and land in New Guinea somewhere; it all depended on the wind and currents.

Two days and nights had passed, and still I couldn't use my legs. My arms were as strong as ever and could drag me about, and when hungry I opened a can of beans and ate a biscuit. Fortunately my food was easy to get at, since everything was in wooden boxes on the floor of the cabin. My flesh, where I had struck, had swollen so enormously that it felt as if a pillow were attached to me, and within that smashed flesh, if I touched it right, the pain was extreme. I knew definitely that something was broken. The spot was a little to the right side of the end of the spine. The paralysis, I thought, was caused by the shock on the spinal cord somewhere, or a vertebra had been damaged—perhaps fractured or just thrown out of alignment.

One night, the third after the accident, I wrote a little song. I had been feeling better at the time, more hopeful. Perhaps my energies, geared for months to ceaseless activity and so suddenly bludgeoned by the blow that felled me, were awakening. I wrote it to the tune of an old-time favorite, a song of the convicts transported to Australia in the early days of the nineteenth century, known in America simply as the "Prisoner's Song."

> I lay on my raft on the ocean,
> The night was black on the sea;
> My body was weary and broken,
> And I slept and a dream came to me.

I saw my mother come walking
Through the waste, through the foam and the spray;
I heard her gentle voice talking
As I did in the days faraway.

She stood my side in the tempest,
She kneeled by my side on the sea,
Her hand touched my brow like a blessing;
Then I was all alone on the sea.

I lay on the planks in the tempest,
And the stars stood in glory above;
And I slept like a child in its cradle—
Like a child that has only known love.

After I had composed the lines, humming the tune all the while, a peace and happiness almost beyond comprehension descended on me. This state of mind continued throughout the night. It was as if my voice, vibrating within me, had set a thousand chords in motion.

Three days later I was standing. Holding on with both hands, I stood beside the compass and looked at the heading. I had to hang on to keep from falling, but I was standing. I had just got up on my feet after being paralyzed for six days.

My legs were like putty and threatened to give as the raft rolled and stamped, but I hung on and remained on my feet. Every moment however my strength was coming back. I looked up at the sky and the sea and the whole universe, and could have shouted with joy, but the moment was too big—one could only pray. I lowered myself down to rest a little and then got up again. Strength flooded into my legs as from a mysterious source. I had made it!

A few hours later I could make my way around the raft. It was like a reunion. Every rope was there, everything—all the rigging and the masts and the wet deck and, high above in front, like a white plowshare pulling a rusty plow, the big jib, the sail I couldn't pull over in the gale. It was August twelfth and my position latitude 13 degrees 47 minutes south longitude 163 degrees 15 minutes east.

My flesh was still hanging like a pillow from my buttocks, and even when coming near any object, I howled or held my breath in terror, knowing the pain it would cause if I touched anything. When I lay down, it had to be on the left side or on my stomach. I had taken a mirror and held it behind me, wondering what this hanging pillow of flesh looked like, and saw my whole buttocks a black and purple mass such as I had never seen on a human being. When I could get around a little better, I took pictures of it, movies and stills, feeling that I had to make a record of it.

After I had taken the August twelfth sight, I knew that I would have little chance of getting through the Coral Sea to the south and that Sydney was almost out of question. I had drifted too far north, to within 180 miles from San Cristóbal in the Solomons. But I was still bound for Australia and would go on struggling, through the reefs of the Coral Sea, and, if I had to, I'd tackle the Great Reef itself or sail north around it. A lot depended on my back, for I was still moving around like a cripple, and occasionally my legs went numb, which frightened me. Otherwise I was improving quickly.

Two days after my recovery, while I was standing by the compass in the morning and looking at the gray sea, a big shark shot out of the water not far from the raft to at least a third of its length, while pursuing a dolphin. It was of monstrous size to judge by the head and thickness of the body, almost looking like a whale. But I could make no mistake about the sickle-shaped mouth lined with teeth across its underside. The body, as much as I could see of it, was a vivid light blue and, together with the snowy whiteness of the belly, quite startling against the dismal gray of sea and sky. The dolphin had escaped, streaking away with the speed of thought just as the jaws of the monster snapped together. It was the biggest shark I had ever seen, and for a little while I was actually afraid walking on my wave-washed, open deck, as I realized that such monsters lived unseen but every ready beside me. I would have liked a piece of his liver to fill in my fresh-food deficiency, but even if I had managed to hook him, he would have pulled the raft around like a child's toy, splashed tons of water over it, and finally broken chain, swivel, and line.

Two flying fish had fallen on deck early in the morning, first one and about an hour later another. Both dropped almost at my feet. The first one I ate raw to lose none of its food value, and the other I fried for breakfast with beans, sauerkraut, and a cup of hot coffee.

The sea in the early morning was always beautiful. A flying fish leaped like a dazzling spearhead out of the waves and soared in a long, graceful curve before the wind, against the background of a rainbow painted on the silvery curtain of a thinning squall. Two small white birds began their tumbling among the seas, fluttering like handkerchiefs.

I woke up and stared into the night, gripped by sudden apprehension, for I had dozed off knowing that my course was directly on the track of the Hong Kong–Sydney steamers. Almost dead astern and coming up, I saw the light of a ship. It was as if someone had warned me. The night was dark and cloudy, and visibility low, and I judged it to be about two or three miles away. The sea was rough.

Since I carried no running light, I flashed a light on the sails to let the ship know of my presence and, a few minutes later, decided to get it 'longside by flashing an SOS. A lot had happened since I left Apia, and a lot might happen yet among the reefs, and I realized I should let the world, and especially Teddy, know where I was. I doubted whether any of my broadcasts had been picked up by the New Zealand air force in Suva, since my transmitter had worked badly from the beginning, and besides, I had never given my position. I was out almost two months now, and many, I felt certain, already considered me lost.

After I'd flashed an SOS about half a dozen times, the steamer, less than a mile away now, answered by blinking from the bridge. The message was much too fast for me to pick up, and I answered with another SOS. The ship blinked again, and again I could do nothing but flash my distress signal upon the dark sea. When I received no answer, I went into the cabin, wrote down R—A—F—T in Morse and flashed it a number of times. This brought more blinking, fast as the rattle of a machine gun, and could have been in some Himalayan dialect for all the good it did. I flashed RAFT once more, but the ship seemed to move away, and I went into the cabin to make myself a cup of coffee, disappointed and ready to forget the whole incident.

It was just a few minutes after midnight of August 19, my seventy-first birthday, and I had been thinking what a pleasant surprise it would have been for Teddy to get the news on that very day that I was still alive and sailing.

While I was kneeling beside my stove, the cabin became suddenly filled with light streaming through the after porthole. The steamer was coming up astern, its big searchlight full on the raft and flooding it with its glare. By the time I had hoisted the American flag, it was ranging 'longside with such speed and so close that I was afraid of being run down.

"Who are you?" a voice hailed me from the bridge.

"Captain Willis on the raft *Age Unlimited*," I answered.

"What do you want?"

"Just report me, that's all."

He had drifted almost on top of me and taken the wind out of my sails; I had everything set and hollered at him to get away. As he turned, he swung his stern almost into the raft, missing it by a mere ten or fifteen feet. Then it was gone back into the night. Its stern light remained visible for a while, then only showed between the rise and fall of the seas. The ship was on a course to clear the Chesterfields, the same course I had been fighting for since passing Cape Cumberland, the northwest corner of the New Hebrides. She would clear the Chesterfields and all the other reefs in the southern end of the Coral Sea most likely by daylight, having timed herself for it, and once in the open would run down to Brisbane or Sydney.

I was happy, for Teddy would probably know within a day that I was alive. But would she? I remembered the S.S. *Whakatane*, the New Zealand freighter I had spoken between the Galapagos and Marquesas on August 16, 1963, just about a year ago—three days before turning seventy—and that Teddy didn't get the report till over two months later. All those long days, weeks, and months she was sitting in her apartment in New York, wondering whether I was still alive, for nothing had been heard of me while the report lay forgotten in some pigeonhole in Hawaii.

I was still crippled, still had that pillow of flesh hanging from my buttocks, and to touch the broken part was still almost as painful as pulling out my eye, and while looking up to the bridge of the steamer, I had wondered if it was wise for me to continue my voyage. Here was a way out. . . . It was a mere thought and at once discarded.

The same day Teddy received the following telegram from the Australian Consulate General in New York:

MRS. WILLIAM WILLIS

AUSTRALIAN AUTHORITIES ADVISE MASTER OF BARON JEDBURGH REPORTS HAVING SIGHTED RAFT AGE UNLIMITED 12.15 AM AUG 19TH POSITION 15° 44′ SOUTH 159° 45′ EAST

Two days after speaking the steamer, there was little wind in the morning, and the raft barely moved. By noon I was becalmed, and in the afternoon the sea became glassy with not a single cat's-paw ruffling her levels. There was no swell. As the hours went by, I seemed to lie on a mirror. The sky was clear except for a spread of smudge in the north. It grew slowly larger but didn't look threatening as two arms began reaching out from it like wings. Finally the sky darkened, and the wind came but so gradually that I didn't take down the mainsail. The wind kept increasing as the hours passed, and a little after nightfall I realized it was dangerous to continue and went forward to lower the sail. Sheet and tack stood like bars and the sail like a sheet of iron, and I knew I couldn't handle it. It had to stay.

It was a wild ride through the night, and touch and go at the wheel to keep the raft before the wind. Toward sunrise the weather moderated, and an hour later I lowered the mainsail to repair the night's damage.

For the next two days I sailed without seeing the sun and, when it came out on the third day, found that I was almost forty miles south of my dead-reckoning position. This was the first time I had been in such southerly set, but unfortunately it didn't keep up.

On August 26 a ship coming up behind me from the north passed to port about three miles away. It was cloudy at the time and visibility low, and I didn't see her till she was already past my beam. I set off three red flares, but she continued, doubtlessly not seeing me. My idea was to stop her and have her report me in case the other ship had not. She was a big, dilapidated-looking ship of outmoded design with the engine aft.

A dark, long-winged bird streaked low over the gray waste. Raindrops fell heavily on the sea. The raft rolled and pitched, and a patch of foam, large as an acre, lay just abeam of the raft where a big sea had broken. Most of the bamboo slats had now been washed or torn off the deck by the seas, and the water spurted up between the planks as high as my head. From beneath me came the continuous knocking, slapping, and pounding of the waves.

It had been a gloomy day, but the night sky presented me with a breathtaking sight. It was as if somewhere in the firmament a mass of diamonds had been exploded, had scattered, and become fixed. A thousand geometric designs were staked out on the black chart of the heavens—crosses, triangles, and squares of all sizes—and blazing away. One could, by gazing into this splendor, easily imagine seeing everything ever beheld by human eyes on earth.

The weather had been bad, and most of my navigation had to be done by dead reckoning; then the sky cleared for a fix and showed me Marion Reef right in my path. After passing it to the north, I steered west and began leveling off for the Great Barrier Reef, about 120 miles away, for the final showdown. I had sighted Marion from the masthead, seen the seas break on it, and doubted whether the raft could have survived such battering if caught. In some places it was breaking with tremendous force, and though miles away, I seemed to hear the thunder and feel the seas strike. My back was still bad, but the big swelling was going down. I still limped.

My chart of this part of the South Pacific, No. 825 of the U.S. Hydrographic Office, reached only to the 147th meridian (east) and showed the Australian coast only to latitude nineteen south, which meant that I would be sailing blind when tackling the Great Barrier.

Everything had been made ready for the assault. My binoculars were hanging from a nail beside the door where I could grab them easily, and all the gear had been checked and ropes strengthened and extra lashings put on. Coils of rope were kept handy around the deck for a quick grab if something gave way, and my homemade anchor was ready to go overboard. I had made it from an old ammunition box given me by the commander of a submarine in Callao just before leaving. "Can you use this iron box," he had called down from the pier. "I can," I replied, and the sailor carrying it lowered it down. It had been lashed to the top of my water barrels during the voyage and used to store shackles, bolts, clamps, chains, and turning buckles. After my regular anchor had been washed overboard while I was paralyzed, I decided to make it do the work of one, filled it with broken chains and all the odds and ends of iron I had on board, and lashed it so it wouldn't come apart.

I had passed the reach of my chart and was sailing into unknown waters but knew that I was approaching the Great Reef. I had been steering west but changed course to northwest in the afternoon and at six, when it grew dark, lowered the mainsail to slow up the raft during the night, hoping to see the Reef in the morning. Before sundown I had been up on the mast and scanned the horizon, feeling a bit like the early explorers when in unknown and possibly dangerous waters. They, when near a coast, had to make their way by taking soundings from the bow or from boats sent ahead.

In my case I realized that tides and currents and the timing when hitting the reef might have the final say whether I would get through. But was it possible to get through? I didn't know anything except that I was heading for a coral wall extending for almost one thousand three hundred miles along the coast of Australia which as far as I knew was impassable, though no doubt certain channels existed; that it was from twenty to thirty miles wide and consisted of hundreds of reefs linked together in the earth's most formidable sea barrier. I had decided to tackle it rather than sail north hundreds of miles along its edge, risking being blown up on it at any time.

Breakers ahead! My first sight of the Barrier Reef. Standing high up on the mast, I could see a white line on the horizon, not too long. I could see nothing to either side. What lay behind it? Was it an isolated shoal or a spur running out from a larger mass? Was it a trap that would close on me if I continued? I was heading straight for it. The sun was well on the way down, and not daring to come closer in the dark, I climbed down and lowered the mainsail. Then I went on the other tack. I would try coming in again in the morning, by daylight, when I could see what I was doing.

In the morning I could see no sign of the reef and after raising the mainsail steered west again. The wind was steady, and I hoped to make contact with the reef sometime around noon, not knowing its direction or what sort of drift I had made during the night. If the raft struck the reef and remained fast, I had decided to build a catamaran by lashing my kayak and canoe together, put my instruments and valuables in one and, sitting in the other, try to paddle

226

through the reefs to the Inner Passage and so eventually reach Australia.

I steered west all day but didn't sight the reef and at nightfall lowered the mainsail again and changed course to northwest to avoid smashing up in the dark. The following day in the afternoon, when up on the mast, I sighted several lines of breakers and, picking what I thought was the best opening among them, made a course for it. Climbing up later to check, I saw reefs closing in on me from either side. I was already trapped.

An hour later I was close to the reef, and the muffled roar of the breakers crashing at different angles around me engulfed the raft. Peering over the spokes of the wheel, I picked the best spot. The raft was obeying the rudders perfectly. As I sailed her in, I said aloud: "Steady as she goes now—that's the spot. A little left—left more—hard left! Hard over and hold her!"

The sun was shining on the blue water and glittering on the white crashing walls. Everything was thundering as the cataracts rose and tumbled before me. I looked over the side while skirting the edge of the reef and saw the foul ground beneath, dirty green and yellowish black, like lumps of rags. The roar of the seas had become a soothing melody, for there was little wind, and the tide, I thought, was ebbing.

I was in a channel about fifty yards wide and sailing over coral heads and foul patches. My mainsail was still up to give me steerage way, but the centerboards I had raised clear of the pontoons. I continued about a quarter of a mile, then touched bottom, bumped over it, and went on about twenty yards more when I struck again. But again the raft wrenched itself free and, with the mainsail still standing full and driving, ground and scraped its way over the bottom for another twenty or thirty yards till she struck solid and was fast. I lowered the mainsail, secured it, and then went up the mast to have a look around. The tide was running out and the reef becoming bare. I was near the outer edge where the sea was still breaking high. The inner part, into which I had entered through a now-quite-narrow channel, was covered with great patches of coral, but most of it was still under water. The reef looked irregular in shape and seemed to extend for miles. The tide wasn't out enough to give me an accurate idea of my position, but I thought my best bet to escape was to the west.

After coming down from the mast, I took a bucket and went over the side to look for clams, crabs, and shrimp. Among the pools were dry spots where I could walk. The pools were fairylands of coral of all shapes and colors and of almost unimaginable delicacy. Each bush or cluster of coral seemed different from the other and more beautiful. The colors were purple, red, yellow, and green, but of tints never seen on earth. Some of the pools were becoming bare in the receding tide. I had seen coral in different parts of the world but such beauty of designs and colors I had never imagined. And all this lacework, this fantastic creation, fragile as the breath of a little child seemingly, had grown beneath the very tread of hurricanes and in the daily smash of roaring breakers. There were foul patches, too, of slimy moss, broken coral, and ugly sand.

Now and then I stopped gazing and picked up a crab for my bucket, a clam, or a darting shrimp. There were wondrous shells too and especially cowries, glossy white or speckled, and many kinds of sea urchins, some with long spines with red dots on the ends and a lot of trepang or *bêche-de-mer,* creatures shaped like sausages, dark and ugly but a great delicacy in China. The trepang and pearling luggers, I had been told, had first opened the coral shores of northern Australia.

I also came across two giant clams with shells half an inch thick and so deeply buried in sand and debris that I couldn't move them and went back to the raft for a scoop. They were of tremendous size when exposed, and one must have weighed almost three hundred pounds and the other about two hundred. A human foot caught between those halves when they closed would have been broken like a match.

Finally I returned to the raft and feasted on my crabs, shrimp, and clams, my first fresh food since leaving Apia, devouring a good part of them raw just to get my teeth into something vital. Then I spread out my poncho, listened a while to the whispers of the night-shrouded reef and the thud of the collapsing seas farther out, and then dozed off.

The incoming tide awakened me. It came with countless little babbling tongues, making its way unseen in the darkness among the labyrinths of coral covering the antlered heads, the delicate twigs, and snow-white candelabra of the wonderland. The tongues became louder and louder, and gradually the night became filled with clamor as the rush increased. On the outer edge of the reef the heavy assaults of the sea had begun shaking the very darkness, and soon the water was halfway up on the pontoons. The reef was being covered—the fairyland went back to its solitude and dreams and silent labor. And now the raft, standing like a breakwater in the way of the floods, was attacked with all ferocity. Sea after sea struck it, reared up and smashed on deck and against and over the cabin. Soon it was flooded. I stayed on deck as long as I could, then climbed into the rigging, wondering whether the tide would float us off before the cabin went over the side. After I had been almost an hour in my perch, the raft began swinging from side to side, the jib which I had set standing full and keeping her before the wind. Then she gave a jerk and, I thought, moved ahead a little, and climbing down I went aft to the wheel and tried the spokes. The rudder was clear. I flashed my light overboard and saw that the chain connecting the two rudders also was clear. She was rolling a little now, and I thought was ready to go. Should I set the mainsail to help her? I wondered. I decided to wait, for the tide was still coming up, was still young, and didn't have its full lifting power. I was on my way back into the rigging when the raft gave a lurch and moved ahead. I jumped back to the wheel. We were sailing! Bumping and hanging up, and now and then striking solid but always in the end getting free again, we sailed. My eyes were on the darkness, steering through the broken surface of the reef, avoiding as best as I could the patches where it broke white. Finally I sailed through a stretch of open water for almost a mile, which made me think I had cleared the reef, and I was on the point of taking a sounding when I saw breakers close ahead and, trying to get through, struck again. The raft got loose, moved ahead a little, and then sat fast and at once was pounded by seas. I climbed into the rigging but could see little except broken water and thought I had sailed into a patch of boulders and coral heads. While I was on the way down to the deck, she began moving and laboring so that I had to hang on. Suddenly a big sea coming up behind lifted her, and she was free.

It was getting toward morning, and before long I should be able to see what lay ahead. I took a sounding with a shackle tied to a fishing line and struck bottom at fourteen fathoms. Was I in the Inner Passage? I wondered. I continued taking soundings, and the depth remained almost the same, between twelve and fifteen fathoms which made me think that the reef was well behind me, and I would be safe in setting the mainsail.

I lashed the wheel and went forward to loosen it when I saw breakers almost in front of the bow and had just time to hang on when we struck. It felt as if we had rammed head-on into a boulder.

The tide was falling now, but I took a chance and raised the mainsail, thinking she might get loose. She did feel the pull of the big sail and moved a little as if she knew that I wanted her to get off, but the coral on which she sat kept her fast. I waited a while and then lowered the sail again.

An hour later it was daylight. The sky looked dark with slanting clouds racing past from the southeast. A little after eight o'clock, the tide was low. I had secured the sails, cleared up the deck, and done what I could in the cabin. It was a sad-looking mess, with all the soaked blankets and torn sails I had nailed up inside, all around the bulkheads to keep the water that came in through the boards from damaging my instruments, charts, and other valuables. Then I sat down and ate, and afterwards went up the mast with my glasses and made a careful survey of the reef and what lay ahead. I even drew a sketch. The reef was much smaller than the one I had been fast on before. It had some very large boulders toward the open sea and was oblong in shape. Toward the northwest and west, all the way to the horizon which would be my course, I saw open water. This filled me with joy, for I felt certain that I would get off at full tide. I would hoist every sail I had to accomplish this. Perhaps I would make it this time—clear the reef and reach the Inner Passage. Then to Australia . . .

After coming down from the mast, I lay down, for it had been a hard night, full of labor and of facing the possibility of seeing the raft smashed beneath my feet and being washed off myself. After an hour or so, unable to sleep, I got up and taking my bucket walked out on the reef to get more clams and shrimp. The reef was almost barren, consisting mainly of foul patches and broken masses of coral besides numerous coral heads. Trepang was plentiful and so were clams, and in one patch hundreds of beautiful sea stars were lying almost on top of each other. On the seaward side was a strip of what appeared to be solid land, meaning it was above high water at all times. No vegetation was visible on it. I didn't walk out to it, since it would have meant swimming through a stretch of foul-looking and deep water which was in part open to the sea and I thought might have sharks in it.

It was a gray, slow-moving day, and the wind moaned over the barren reef to the low-drifting clouds, but at last the tide began coming in. Higher and higher it came and more violent became the assaults along the edges of the reef, until it was flooded and became a roaring mass of breakers and only the large boulders remained visible and, on the seaward side, the strip of solid land. Against the latter, the sea seemed to exert all its fury. I was in the rigging, for breathing in the flying spray had become almost impossible on deck, and was waiting for the tide to come up more. It was almost an hour before the raft began to stir a little, and I climbed down, set the jib and mizzen and then the mainsail. Expectantly I waited, but nothing happened; the raft remained fast. I was standing forward where it was more sheltered, wondering whether to go up the mast again, when suddenly she moved violently under the impact of seas crashing into her stern, and plunging down in the bow, she freed herself and was sailing.

We struck bottom now and then but kept going, for the wind was quite strong, and the sails exerted a tremendous pressure on the hull. Sometimes, however, it seemed almost miraculous how she kept going, bumping and slugging her way over the wave-swept coral. At last, having cleared what looked like a last barrier of breakers, I was in deeper water. For a while I could still see foul patches beneath me; then they disappeared.

I was steering northwest through a gray sea, and behind me the white walls of the reef were becoming smaller. My soundings showed fourteen fathoms beneath the raft. Was I in the Inner Passage now? I wondered. I had no way of knowing, since I had no chart to give me the depths. It was after three o'clock, and the weather looked stormy, and in the south something seemed to be making up. Should I steer west and try for the mainland now, assuming that I was in the Inner Passage, or steer more northerly and hold off for the night? It would soon be dark, and by steering west I took a chance of smashing into one of the rocky islands strewn along the Australian coast. I had better go north, I decided, carry just enough sail for steering and turn west by daylight. Either way I had to take chances sailing into unknown waters.

I lowered the mainsail and made everything clear for the night, then cooked a meal of two packages of dehydrated vegetable soup thickened to a stew with my crab and shrimp meat and spiced up with a liberal dose of mustard powder, which unfortunately had become mouldy some weeks ago.

By the time I had eaten, night had fallen. I felt a little depressed standing by the wheel and steering into the darkness, and to bring up my spirits started to sing. But I wasn't successful. What lay ahead now? I asked. Would I make it at last? With any luck I should be in Australia in a day or two. But would I be? It seemed so far away yet, so impossibly far that I was almost afraid to think of it. So much had happened—all my plans had really gone wrong from the very moment of leaving Samoa. I had survived and was here; somehow I had got this far, but that was about all. And now, sailing into the stormy night, straight into unknown waters with reefs on one side of me and rocky islands on the other.

I went to the rail and took a sounding, found fifteen fathoms again, and went back to the wheel. I was getting sleepy. Darkness, wind, and seas were benumbing my senses. Visibility was low, hardly more than a few hundred yards—a thick, stormy night. Was there any shipping in these waters? I had my flashlight handy and would stop anything I saw with an SOS to get information. I was almost worn-out and after a while lashed the wheel and sat down on my narrow board with my back against the cabin, hoping I wouldn't fall off, and soon began to doze.

The roar of breakers awakened me, and I jumped to my feet. A white wall was just ahead, thundering and smashing up high. I jerked the lashings from the wheel but knew it was useless—too late. I took the shock at the wheel and almost had my arm broken. On a reef again . . . Seas were coming over on the portside—one after another, quick like sledgehammer blows. The raft listed to starboard under the onslaught. I grabbed a line I had fastened to the canoe, to have something to hang on to in case I should be washed overboard or the raft break up—though I knew I wouldn't have much chance to survive in those breakers—and then climbed up the mast. After a while I came down again and put on my life vest, a gift from Andy Collins in Apia. Where did this reef come from? I wondered. Then I realized that wind and current had thrown me back on the Great Barrier Reef.

For over an hour I hung in the rigging, watching the breakers come out of the darkness and smash into the raft; then it swung around and was free. The tide had lifted it, and I was sailing again. The sea had gone down considerably, and before long it was daylight. It looked like another cloudy day. My soundings showed seven fathoms.

I had been on the mast several times and seen no breakers, but at eleven o'clock saw a white line to my right about two miles away. Ahead it looked clear, and I continued on my course. Later I saw a similar long white line, denoting breakers, to my left but still open water ahead. I thought I was sailing between two reefs but, after about an hour, saw that they came together ahead of me. By this time there was no way out, and I had to continue. I kept as much as possible to the right, the sea on this side not breaking so high, and finally, picking the best spot, struck the reef. The raft bumped and scraped over the bottom for a short distance and then moved ahead smoothly, the coral being about two or three feet beneath the bottom. There were a lot of foul patches and occasional boulders, which I had to keep away from, and numerous short lines of breakers, but the raft handled fairly well in spite of the centerboards being up.

I sailed on and on, hour after hour, always only a few feet above the coral, seeing the same beautiful colors and exquisite shapes lying beneath me as I had seen before, though they were not quite as vivid since the day was cloudy. Now and then I bumped into coral heads but was always lucky getting off. I saw no breakers except two lines stretching away on each side about a mile away and sometimes barely visible, which I took for the outer edges of the reef. The sun was beginning to go down at last, and I wondered whether I would get clear before dark and escape another pounding when the flood came in again. I thought the raft could hardly take another beating. Three of my centerboards had been broken off on the reefs, and the heavy iron slots holding them ripped out with part of the deck planks.

How different, I thought while sailing over the lagoon, had this part of the voyage been from the first one. This time there had been no long periods of calms when I had gazed into the emptiness around me and heard the whispering of madness. During this voyage the strain had been mainly on the physical man. Again and again I had spoken to my heart and lungs and faltering muscles, saying, "Get going, old-timers! Sure, you will land somewhere—you are bound to!" And each time new strength surged into my rope-worn fingers, while my eyes, wan with anxiety, scanned the horizon for reefs.

Two hours later I sailed over the edge of the reef into deep water and, to judge by the heavy swell, was in the Inner Passage. The sun was just about setting, and the sky looked stormy as it had the night before. The wind was still south by east. I decided to steer a little more westerly this time to avoid being blown on the reef again.

17

MY mind was benumbed—all enthusiasm, all zest and eagerness for living had gone out of it. Perhaps I had been through too much on the voyage, and the last days on the reef had finished me. I was just a sailor now, staring into the darkness with little left but the aim to bring his ship and himself to a safe landing. This change had come about during the previous night after I had cleared the first two reefs and was in the Inner Passage. Standing by the wheel then, I had thought that I would reach Australia some time in the morning, and the voyage would be over. I had envisaged this with great distinctness. I had seen Australians come on board and greet me, quiet, friendly men and full of understanding. So strongly and deeply had this vision of my landing and being safe become implanted on my mind that it became a reality—not permanently of course but implanted so deeply in my subconscious that it came back again and again in moments of danger. The first time I became aware of this was when I awoke to see the raft almost in the breakers of the last reef. Then I saw the Australians, just as they had come on board to greet me, on the raft crowding around me, and I became angry that they didn't jump in and help but left me to struggle alone. The next moment, of course, my head cleared. In my subconscious however the Australians remained,

appearing again and again and always under similar circumstances—
when the work seemed almost more than I could handle.

I remembered I had had similar experiences, extending over several
months during the first part of my voyage, from Callao to Samoa,
when my mother and Teddy appeared to me.

I was at the wheel and steering through the night. The wind had
increased and was blowing with near gale force. I had hoisted the
American flag upside down to bring any ship I might sight 'longside,
so I could get information about the Inner Passage. I had also hoisted
a large square of canvas with a ball, fashioned out of sacks, directly
beneath, which was an international signal of distress.

Gradually, as the hours went by, I became sleepy and began to
doze. Now and then I looked up, went to the compass, and checked
the heading, then sat down again. It was hard to keep awake, and
when I finally almost fell off my seat, I spread out my poncho and
lay down. I just wanted to lie still—lie without moving a muscle.

Suddenly I jumped up, for I had seen a light. I had been asleep
and seen it in my sleep but didn't realize it in the suddenness of my
awakening. I felt so certain that I had actually seen it that it took
quite a while to convince me I had been dreaming. I just couldn't
get my thoughts together. The night was black, and the sea high,
and standing beside the compass my eyes bored into the darkness,
still convinced I would see a light. A few minutes later, still standing
by the compass, I saw a tiny light about a point to starboard right
in my line of vision. It appeared and was gone. Then it came again.
Sometimes I didn't see it for a few minutes, but it always came back.
Was it a ship perhaps or a fishing boat bobbing up and down in the
seas? The night was like a cave, but the tiny light came through as
clear as a star. I lashed the wheel and climbed into the rigging and
finally made out that it was a lighthouse. There were four flashes and
then a stop for eight seconds before the flashes returned. If I had had
a chart, I would have been able to identify it and know my position,

but now I only knew that there was danger ahead. But where was the danger—to the right or to the left?

Four flashes, then eight seconds of darkness—I could see it now from the deck. I swung the raft over to the right, merely on a hunch, but after sailing for about twenty minutes brought it back till I had the light about two points off the starboard bow.

As I came nearer, I realized that the light was on a prominence, most likely on an island lying in the Inner Passage, for I couldn't be near the actual coast yet, according to the course I had steered after clearing the reef. A while later I saw a reflection of the light directly beneath the tower, either on rocks or the leaves of trees. How close was I? In the tumultuous night and lying so low in the sea, it was difficult to form an accurate judgment. I now had the sensation of being swept rapidly forward.

Suddenly during the eight seconds of darkness, I saw the island, sprawling black in the sea beside me—sinister, terrible, and strangely close—before the light began swinging around again. I pulled the wheel hard over and stood as if transfixed, staring into the night, feeling helpless in the grip of powers beyond my control. Something that would destroy the raft and me was taking shape in that terrible darkness before my very eyes, and I was helpless. Suddenly the light went out. I held my breath almost paralyzed by terror. The light didn't come back, and then I realized that I had sailed into the obscure sector, the ultimate warning that rocks were ahead.

The raft struck with shattering force, reeled, and went into what I can only call convulsions, bounding up and down like something demented. It had been hurled high up on rocks and was pounded by the seas. It was a life-and-death struggle among rocks and cataracts and the hurricane fury of the wind. I flashed my light over the side and saw a large, bulging rock on which the raft lay in its throes. Beyond, on the starboard side, were masses of jagged, high rocks standing like tombstones, while ahead was a solid wall of still larger rocks; to the left I could see only breakers.

But I hardly knew what I saw, for my mind was benumbed from

238

the shock of striking and the titanic conflict of the elements in the center of which I so suddenly found myself. The raft, being of iron and rigid, couldn't break to pieces as quickly as a wooden boat and did a sort of death dance before it slowly but inevitably came apart on the bulging back of the boulder. Pounded by the seas, lifted high and dropped, sliding from side to side, it was unable to move ahead or get free again.

I was hanging on, waiting for the raft to become a heap of smashed iron. It was, at times, like hanging on to the inner edge of an exploding crater. Again and again my hands were torn loose from the ropes, which I hung on to with such force that it threatened to break my fingers, my elbows, or tear my arms out of their sockets. Never had I experienced such helplessness, such inadequacy of human strength against the aroused elements.

Time went on unrecorded. I had become one with the tortured raft—one with the pounding, the rocks, and the breakers. Had half an hour passed? Or a whole hour? Or perhaps two? I was a being apart from time—a being flung into the eternity before the end.

Suddenly, as if unable to exist longer in such agony, the raft started to list to starboard. Higher and higher she rose till she stood almost on edge. She had slid off as far as she could, and was up against the jagged rocks and threatening to turn completely over. I knew I was trapped where I was, hanging on to a rope, with one foot on the edge of the deck and leaning out as far as I could. But there was nothing else I could do, for it would have been impossible to get up the almost vertical deck to the other side, while to escape over the stern, even if I could have moved, was impossible on account of the breakers, and ahead was the wall of rocks. I would have to jump if she turned over, but knew I couldn't jump twenty feet, the width of the raft, and so would be pinned and crushed beneath.

Then the raft came down again—at first gradually, for the wind was holding her, then with a shock that threatened to dismember her. Within what seemed to be but a few minutes, she then began to list to port, to the other side, just when I thought I would be safe there. It struck me in my own fear as the final effort of the raft to escape the horrible pounding. I was now hanging on to a rope with one foot on the edge of the raft and as trapped as I had been on the other side. But again she dropped back, and the deck lay level. Then, perhaps a minute or two later, I saw the water streaming past and, staring at it for a few moments unbelieving, realized that she had slid off the rock on the portside and that we were sailing. The jib, standing full in the gale, had pushed her back on an even keel, and the seas had washed her off the rock.

I sailed close to the wind to get away from the island (I later found it was one of the Brook Islands) and after a while noticed that the raft didn't obey the wheel. My flashlight lighting up my wake told the story—the chain connecting the two rudders had parted. I had to steer, or I would go back on the rocks, so, tying a line around my waist, I went overboard and connected the loose ends of the chain again, using a rope to bring them together and swallowing more water than I had on the whole voyage. While in the water, I noticed that the lower part of both rudders had been rolled up like scrolls of tissue paper. Only a titanic force could have exerted the pressure of such twisting of thick iron.

It now became a nightmare, steering to keep the raft from going on the rocks again, for one rocky little island after another arose around me. Being in a daze, I lost all track of time, just as I had when hammered on the rocks.

At last I noticed a grayness over the water. Could that be the dawn? I couldn't believe it—the night had been too long, too full of terrors ever to leave again. I looked at the illuminated dial of my clock and saw that it was almost five. Yes, night would soon be over. But I thought that something terrible would still have to happen before it became light.

The maze of small islands and rock masses, amid which I had been trapped, lay finally behind me, and I could see a larger island to my left (Gould Island) and a smaller one (Combe Island) to the right farther away. I sailed between them. Dawn was really on the way now. It looked like a cloudy day. After a while I cleared the island to my left and in the distance saw a long mountainous ridge, either another large island (Hitchinbrook Island) or part of the mainland. Then more islands appeared to my right, in line with the first one and strung out evenly toward the west. I thought they might be reaching all the way to the coast, forming a barrier, and therefore steered to the left to keep away. This group of islands, I found out later was the Family Group, named so by Captain Cook in 1770, the first white man to see them.

At nine o'clock I saw, spanning the opening between the large mountainous island to the left and the chain of smaller ones to the right, a long, low line. That had to be Australia—it could be nothing else. I went up the mast for a better look and, when I came down, felt certain that I was heading straight for the coast of the mainland of Australia. It was a level wooded shore, a gray dismal-looking stretch, for visibility was bad, and now and then it rained.

Slowly I came nearer, steering for what appeared to be a flat bay, wooded along its entire length. A few times I went aloft to find out what kind of a coast it was, whether rocky or with a fringing reef, and discovered that it was a sandy beach with the surf breaking evenly and only moderately high. I saw no houses or signs of human beings, and in the drizzling rain the shore remained gray and desolate looking. I could make out the trees now which appeared to be eucalyptus and looked wild and ragged with whitish, gaunt trunks and stiff limbs making me think of dry bones. Some were uprooted and lay on the beach.

I had taken soundings all along and was now sailing over two fathoms. I had come quite near. Only a few more minutes now ... It seemed impossible to come to an end like this, just jogging along— after that nightmarish voyage from Apia, that terrible last night which still had me benumbed, all that long, long strain. . . . And now the end, my goal, this low, silent shore—Australia ... I set off two red flares, in case someone was on the beach, and a few minutes later, shortly after eleven o'clock, swung the raft into the wind, let it drift in, and dropped my anchor. I paid out on the line until she touched the sand, then made fast, secured the sails, and cleared up the deck. The raft was then wallowing broadside to. I put my clearance papers from Apia, my passport, and other documents that might be helpful for identification in a small canvas bag, also a few distress flares, a knife, and small machete, matches and a compass in case I had to go through the woods. Then I jumped into the surf. The water was up to my waist, and I had to struggle against the backwash to get ashore. At last I stood on the beach. Australia—after 204 days in all, and eleven thousand miles! In that moment all Australia contracted into the tiny spot upon which I stood. I wanted to kneel down and embrace the wet sand. Yes, I had made it—the world's largest ocean lay behind me. The date was September 9, 1964. My exact geographical position was: 18 degrees 0.25 minutes South 146 degrees 01.5 minutes East.

I turned left toward the point I had steered for, hoping to find people, and began walking along the narrow beach. Occasionally I looked back at my raft rolling in the surf, the distress flag fluttering big in the wind. It was still raining and the clouds drifting low and gray.

Now and then I had to jump up on the bank, when a larger sea came roaring up or a fallen giant blocked my way with roots or limbs. After walking about a mile, I came to the point and saw, beyond, a lagoon or bay fringed with dense mangrove thickets. At its farther end a creek (Murray River) came into it. Could I walk around it? It didn't look promising, but I went into the woods a little way till I struck mangroves and saw the creek running back into the country, then knew that it was useless to go on and turned back to try the northern point of the beach.

When I came to my ceaselessly rolling raft, I climbed on board, checked the anchor rope, and then went back ashore. The woods looked the same here but the trees were somewhat higher. The big eucalypti looked weird and beautiful and as if belonging to a world

I had not known, with their twisted smooth calico trunks from which the red or silvery bark hung down in long mournful tatters. A few times I left the beach and went into the woods, thinking I might find a road or trail, but each time was stopped by swamps and a thick green vine that made walking almost impossible. Once I heard what I thought was the whistle or call of a man but, after answering it a few times, discovered that it came from a bird.

I had walked about a mile when I came upon a large gray steer feeding in the bushes. He didn't see me but, after I had passed, got my wind and, tossing up his head while giving me a quick look, ambled away. A little later I saw what looked like a small kangaroo sitting like a statue in an open patch and watching me. When I came nearer, it hopped into the thicket.

I was now close to the point I was aiming for, which ran out from the beach in a little spur of sand. A low dune lay in front of it, and walking on I saw above it the roofs of a few houses. Now I'll find people, I thought but, when I stood on top of the dune, discovered that a little bay separated me from the houses. The bay, like the one on the other point, was solidly lined with mangrove thickets. Seeing no people on the other side whom I might signal to, I decided to walk around the bay and went into the woods, which consisted here mostly of high bushes and open patches of sand. Among the bushes were the tracks of what I thought were large dogs and the sharp hoof marks of wild pigs. After I had covered about a quarter of a mile, I struggled through the mangroves to the bay, to check where I was going, and saw that it was hopeless to continue, for a little further up a creek (Tully River) barred my way. I then turned back to the point on the beach from where I had seen the houses, having decided to swim across the mouth of the bay. The sun was within an hour of going down, and I wanted to get to people so that the news of my landing would reach Teddy as quickly as possible.

I stood on the beach and was about to take off my clothes when I saw a man and woman walking on the sand on the other side, their backs turned to me. I shouted, but they seemed not to hear and, opening my bag, I took out a distress flare and sent it up. The couple now stopped and saw me, and I shouted that I wanted someone to come over with a boat. "I'll come right over," the man answered, and the two walked quickly away and disappeared in a stand of trees, and shortly afterwards the roar of an engine shattered the stillness as a speedboat came racing across the bay to me. The man and woman were in it. They drove the boat up on the sand, and we met. They were somewhat taken aback when they saw a gaunt, old and sea-stained man with a beard down to his chest and rolled-up dungarees. "I'm Willis from New York," I said and stuck out my hand. The man was Hank Penning from the nearby little town of Tully. The lady was his wife.

They took me across the bay, and after an hour's ride in their car, I was sitting in the little office of the local police station, and they were checking my passport, clearance papers, and everything I had. No one up here, it seemed, had ever heard of me. After everything had been checked and copied, and I had tied up my papers again, another man came in and, looking suspiciously at me, asked me to show my papers again. He scrutinized everything most carefully and took notes, then went out on the porch, where he remained standing in the shadows and watching me.

After a while someone came in from the porch and told me the other man didn't believe a word of what I had said but was certain I was an escaped convict from faraway Norfolk Island.

"Norfolk Island," I said. "That used to be a convict settlement if I remember right, isn't it?"

"Yes," the other smiled. "It was closed down around 1850."

"Holy smoke!" I exclaimed. "Over a century ago ... Do I look that old? I've been through hell and back all right but didn't know it took that much out of me. Say, that would make me the oldest man in Australia."

We both laughed, but I thought I would take a look at myself as soon as I got to a mirror.

A few minutes later the telephone rang. It was Sydney—someone had notified the wire services, and they wanted to talk to me. Now I knew it was merely a matter of seconds before Teddy would find out that I had landed.

Soon the big heart of Australia opened wide in welcome. From every house in its cities, from every hut in the backbush, rang out the cheers. The land of the brave Down Under loved the sea and the men who went out to face it. Teddy flew out to meet me, and we spent wonderful hours walking and driving through forests and hills, through all the colored magic of a different world. Of course I had not forgotten to deliver the bag of special mail which I had carried from Apia.

The Australian Government—through the good will of Harry Holt, Minister of Finance, now Prime Minister of Australia, a lover of the sea and its dangers with whom I became acquainted over the telephone—ordered the raft brought from the desolate Queensland beach where I had landed to Sydney on board the M.S. *Boonaroo*. For carrying the raft back to New York on the S.S. *Pioneer Gem* I am indebted to Joseph Curran, President of the National Maritime Union of America and to the United States Lines, and to the Farrell Lines for taking it to Newport News, Virginia, where it will remain in the Mariners' Museum.

ENVOI

Why did I make this voyage? Dig deep enough, and you will find that it has been your dream also—even if you have never been to sea or your fathers before you. Sometime, perhaps long ages ago, they had this same dream, and it is still in your flesh and will always be—be you seventy or a hundred or a boy of twelve, for dreams never die.

But perhaps this explanation sounds too distant and too mystical to describe my urge for the solitude of the sea and unbroken horizons, and I will try to come a little closer to the subject: Ever since I was a child at my mother's knee, I heard her speak of the beauty of open fields and woods and the wide and endless sea. Truly a dreamer and seer she was, for then she had only known the sea from pictures. And so I am just walking her way.